Key Topics in Study

Social Science Lexicons

Key Topics of Study
Key Thinkers, Past and Present
Political Science and Political Theory
Methods, Ethics and Models
Social Problems and Mental Health

Key Topics of Study

Edited by Jessica Kuper

ROUTLEDGE & KEGAN PAUL
LONDON AND NEW YORK

First published in 1987 by
Routledge & Kegan Paul Limited
11 New Fetter Lane, London EC4P 4EE

Published in the USA by
Routledge & Kegan Paul Inc.
in association with Methuen Inc.
29 West 35th Street, New York, NY 10001

Set in Linotron Baskerville
by Input Typesetting Ltd., London SW19 8DR
and printed in Great Britain
by Cox & Wyman Ltd., Reading, Berks

Library of Congress Cataloging in Publication Data

Social science encyclopedia. Selections.
  Key topics of study.

  (Social science lexicons)
  Selections, arranged by topic, from: The
Social science encyclopedia. 1985.
  Includes bibliographies and index.
  1. Social sciences—Dictionaries.   I. Kuper,
Jessica.   II. Title.   III. Series.
H41.S6325   1987   300'.3'21   86–33861

British Library CIP Data also available
ISBN 0–7102–1169–4

Contents

Key Topics of Study: the entries

anthropology
archaeology
business studies
cliometrics
criminology
demography
development studies
economics
education
epidemiology
ethology
evolution
geography
history
international relations
labour relations
law

linguistics
mass media
mental health
penology
policy sciences
political science
political theory
psychiatry
psychoanalysis
psychology
race
social problems
social work.
sociobiology
sociology
women's studies

Contributor List

General Editor: Jessica Kuper

Bird, James H	Dept of Geography, University of Southampton
Bliss, Christopher	Nuffield College and Dept of Economics, Oxford
Blondel, Jean	Pro-Vice-Chancellor, and Dept of Government, University of Essex
Brown, R J	Social Psychology Research Unit, University of Kent
Brunner, Ronald D	Colorado Center for Public Policy Research, University of Colorado
Chamberlain, Mariam	Russell Sage Foundation, New York
Cohen, Stanley	Institute of Criminology, The Hebrew University of Jerusalem
Dahrendorf, Ralf	Former Director, The London School of Economics and Political Science
Engerman, Stanley	Dept of Economics, University of Rochester
Feinberg, Walter	Dept of Education, University of Illinois at Champaign-Urbana
Floud, Roderick	Dept of History, Birkbeck College, University of London
Fox, J Robin	Dept of Anthropology, Rutgers, The State University of New York
Friedman, Gary D, MD	Dept of Medical Methods Research, The Permanente Medical Group Inc., Oakland, California
Grammar, Karl	Institute for Human Ethology, Max Planck Institute for Physiology, Seewiesen, West Germany
Greenberg, Joseph	Dept of Anthropology and Dept of Linguistics, Stanford University

Hodder, Ian	Dept of Archaeology, University of Cambridge
Hudson, Liam	Dept of Psychology, Brunel University, Uxbridge, Middlesex
Ingleby, David	Dept of Development Psychology, University of Utrecht
Keyfitz, Nathan	Center for Population Studies, Harvard University
Kuper, Adam	Dept of Human Sciences, Brunel University, Uxbridge, Middlesex
Lazare, Aaron, MD	Massachusetts General Hospital, Boston
Long, Norman	Dept of Rural Sociology, University of Wageningen, The Netherlands
McHenry, Henry M	Dept of Anthropology, University of California, Davis
McQuail, Denis	Dept of Mass Communications, University of Amsterdam
Miller, David	Nuffield College, University of Oxford
Moore, Sally Falk	Dept of Anthropology, Harvard University
Poole, Michael	Dept of Business Administration and Accountancy, University of Wales Institute of Science and Technology, Cardiff
Reynolds, P A	Vice-Chancellor, University of Lancaster
Shils, Edward	Committee on Social Thought, University of Chicago, and Peterhouse College, University of Cambridge
Spector, Malcolm	Dept of Sociology, McGill University, Montreal
Timms, Noel	Dept of Social Work, University of Leicester
Tobias, Phillip, MD	Dept of Anatomy, University of the Witwatersrand, Johannesburg

Van den Berghe, Pierre	Dept of Sociology, University of Washington, Seattle
Walker, Nigel	Institute of Criminology, University of Cambridge
Zaleznik, Abraham	Harvard University School of Business Administration

Introduction

The social sciences are too often pursued in isolation. It is still possible to take a degree in psychology, for example, without learning anything about anthropology or linguistics; or in economics without a grounding in political science, demography, or law. Specialization has its advantages, but the elegant closure of an esoteric analysis may be very misleading if it does not do justice to the complexity of relevant social and political institutions, economic forces and personal motivations.

The present volume introduces you to a wide range of social science disciplines. They are not all full-blown intellectual traditions, to which, for example, a university department would normally be consecrated. Some take as their subject-matter specific areas of human activity – like linguistics. Others focus rather on particular problems, like criminology, penology and epidemiology. Some major social sciences are concerned with activities which pervade all social action, like economics or political science, though they may be thought of as the study of particular institutions, 'the economy' or 'the state'. Others, again, attempt to document and explain man's behaviour almost in its entirety, but from a particular perspective – like history, psychology or sociology. None, however, can afford to ignore the others.

At times specialists in one discipline regard their neighbours as competitors, but the inherited disciplinary boundaries are often clearly inappropriate. Social problems are no respecters of hoary academic territorial settlements. Further, some of the brightest social scientists are convinced that the best new ideas in any discipline will almost inevitably come from across the disciplinary boundaries. In short, anybody operating within the social sciences, at whatever level, and however narrow his or her concerns, needs an up-to-date map of the whole terrain.

This first volume in the series of *Social Science Lexicons* offers a sketch-map of a vast territory, a map which later volumes will help you to fill in. The authors, all leading authorities in their particular fields, define the subject matter of their disciplines, introduce the main theories and current preoccupations, and suggest further readings. The first entry, by Ralf Dahrendorf, discusses the notion of 'social science' itself.

Social Science

Social science is the ambitious concept to define the set of disciplines of scholarship which deal with aspects of human society. The singular implies a community of method and approach which is now claimed by few; thus the plural, social sciences, seems more appropriate. As commonly understood, the social sciences include, centrally, economics, sociology (and anthropology) and political science. At their boundaries, the social sciences reach into the study of the individual (social psychology) and of nature (social biology, social geography). Methodologically, they straddle normative (law, social philosophy, political theory) and historical approaches (social history, economic history). In terms of university departments, the social sciences have split up into numerous areas of teaching and research, including not only the central disciplines, but also such subjects as industrial relations, international relations, business studies, social (public) administration.

The term, social science(s), does not sit easily in the universe of scholarship, especially not in English. *Sciences sociales* and *Sozialwissenschaften* are somewhat happier expressions, though they too have suffered from being interpreted either too widely or too narrowly. Frequently, social science is meant to define either sociology, or synthetic social theory only. Everywhere, the implied analogy to the natural sciences has been contested. In 1982, the British government challenged the name of the publicly financed Social Science Research Council, arguing *inter alia* that 'social studies' would be a more appropriate description for disciplines of scholarship which cannot justly claim to be scientific. (The Council is now called Economic and Social Research Council.)

The history of the concept does not help much in trying to make sense of it. Today's social sciences have grown out of moral philosophy (as the natural sciences have emerged from natural philosophy). It has often been observed that their separate identity owes much to the great revolutions of the eighteenth century, the Industrial (English) and the bourgeois (French) Revolutions. Among the Scottish moral philosophers of that time, the study of political economy was always coupled with that of wider social issues (though not called social science). With the ascendency of positivism in the early nine-teenth century, especially in France, positive philosophy, or social science, took the place of moral philosophy. Positivism, according to Auguste Comte (1830–42; 1844), emphasizes the factual as against the speculative, the useful as against the idle, the certain as against the indecisive, the precise as against the vague, the positive as against the negative or critical. It is thus both science in the sense of nineteenth-century materialism and prescription. Comte borrowed the term, *science social*, from Charles Fourier (1808) to describe the supreme synthetic disci-pline of the edifice of science. At the same time, he had no doubt that the method of social science (which he also called social physics) was in no way different from that of the natural sciences.

Five developments, either stemming from Comte or encour-aged by different traditions, have helped confuse the methodo-logical picture of the social sciences:

(1) Many of those who took the analogy to the natural sciences seriously, engaged in social research. The great factual surveys of Charles Booth in Britain, and of the Chicago School in the United States, bear witness to this trend. Frederic Le Play had started a similar tradition in France. In Germany, the *Verein für Socialpolitik* adopted the same research techniques. Such often large-scale descriptive enterprises are the precursors of modern ('Empirical') social research and analysis.

(2) Science, of course, is more than fact-finding. Thus a natu-ral-science notion of theoretical social science has informed at least two of the heroes of sociology, Emile Durkheim (1895) and Vilfredo Pareto (1916). Durkheim in particular was im-pressed by the need to study 'social facts', whereas Pareto stimulated both metatheoretical insights and specific theories. They have had few followers.

(3) Instead, by the turn of the century, a methodological dichotomy was born which gave rise to a third aspect, or notion, of social science. Against the ambitions of those who tried to emulate the natural sciences in the study of social phenomena,

the German school of thought gained ground, according to which social phenomena do not lend themselves to such rigid analysis, but require a different approach, one of *Verstehen*, of empathy and understanding. Max Weber (1921) straddles different approaches, but introduced into social science what were later called 'hermeneutic' or 'phenomenological' perspectives.

(4) It will readily be seen that all three approaches mentioned so far are most closely associated with the subject of sociology and its history. Indeed, economics soon began to go its own way. Ever since the decline of the German historical ('romantic') school of economists, it developed as the discipline which of all the social sciences most nearly deserves the name, science. Economic knowledge is to a considerable extent cumulative; theories are developed and tested, if not always against reality, then at least against models and their assumptions. *Verstehende* economics, even descriptive economics, have become the exception.

(5) Max Weber also insisted on another distinction which defines the fifth aspect of social science, that between knowledge, however gained, and values. Prescription and description (or theory) belong to different universes of discourse. The distinction was explosive at the time (*Werturteilsstreit*), and continues to be that, although political theory, moral philosophy, jurisprudence have gone their own ways, and the study of social policy has shifted from the prescriptive to the analytical.

These then are the disparate methodological elements of social science today: empirical social science, descriptive in character if not in intention, increasingly sophisticated in its techniques which are themselves manifold; rare attempts at developing theories in the strict sense, attempts which are neither universally recognized nor cumulative; *verstehende Sozialwissenschaft*, perhaps best described as the historical analysis of the present, often full of empirical data as well as attempts at explanation, the bulk of today's social science; economics; and explicitly prescriptive social theory, often political in substance and intent.

Looking at the social sciences as a whole, this is quite a pell-mell, and is perceived as such. However, all attempts to produce a new synthesis have failed. The most ambitious recent examples are those by Karl Popper (1945; 1959) and Talcott Parsons (1937; 1951; 1956). Popper insists that there is one logic of scientific inquiry. It is the logic of progress by falsification: we advance hypotheses (theories), and progress by refuting accepted hypotheses through research, that is, by trial and error. Popper did not primarily have the social sciences in mind, but it is here that his language has created havoc. Everybody now 'hypothesizes', though few such projects are even capable of falsification. More importantly, Popper's logic, if misinterpreted as practical advice to scholars, leads to an arid notion of scholarly activity, especially in the social sciences. If hypothetico-deductive progress is all there is, then 99 per cent of all social science is useless. Popper's logic of scientific inquiry provides but one measure of advancement; it is not a litmus test for distinguishing between what is and what is not social science. Indeed, Popper himself has written important works of social, or at any rate social-philosophical, analysis.

Talcott Parsons's attempted synthesis is even more ambitious in that it is addressed to the theoretical substance of social science. Throughout his numerous abstract analyses, Parsons has argued that the substance of social science is one, social action, and that even the incarnations of social action stem from the same general model, the social system. The social system has four subsystems: the economy, the polity, the cultural system, and the 'integrative' systems. Economics, political science, the study of culture and that of social integration (sociology) are thus related, and interdependent, disciplines. Descending from the social system, all subsystems require similar analysis. Parsons's claims have had little effect on social sciences other than sociology. Economists in particular have largely ignored them. Their central weakness may be that while society can be looked at in this way, it need not be. In any case, different social sciences have continued to go their own way. Have they progressed? It would be vain to deny this, though concepts of progress differ with different methods. At the same time, the social sciences have probably given us *multa non multum*. Perhaps a more modest approach is indicated today. In the absence of a synthesis, it is desirable to let a hundred flowers bloom. Each of the social sciences will continue to contribute to knowledge. It is not unlikely that important developments will occur at the boundaries of different disciplines. It is also probable that most social sciences will incorporate several of the approaches which have split the subjects. Though the search for synthesis will never cease, in fact the social sciences will for some time remain a variegated and somewhat disparate group of intellectual endeavours.

Ralf Dahrendorf
Former Director, London School of Economics and Political
Science

References

Comte, A. (1830–42 [1896]), *Cours de philosophie positive*, Paris. (English translation, *The Positive Philosophy of Auguste Comte*, London.)

Comte, A. (1844), *Discours sur l'ésprit positif*, Paris. (English translation, *Discourse on the Positive Spirit*, London.)

Durkheim, E. (1895 [1938]), *Les Règles de la méthode scientifique*, Paris. (English translation, *The Rules of Sociological Method*, Chicago.)

Fourier, C. (1808), *Théorie des quatre mouvements et des destinées générales*, Lyon.

Pareto, V. (1916 [1935]), *Trattato die sociologia generale*, Rome. (English translation, *The Mind and Society: Treatise on General Sociology*, 4 Vols, London.)

Parsons, T. (1937), *The Structure of Social Action*, New York.

Parsons, T. (1951), *The Social System*, Glencoe.

Parsons, T. and Smelser, N. (1956), *Economy and Society*, New York.

Popper, K. (1945), *The Open Society and Its Enemies*, London.

Popper, K. (1959 [1934]), *The Logic of Scientific Discovery*, New York. (Original German edn, *Logik der Forschung*, Vienna.)

Weber, M. (1921 [1968]), *Wirtschaft und Gesellschaft*, Tübingen. (English translation, *Economy and Society*, New York.)

Anthropology

I am dealing here with 'anthropology' understood as the holistic 'science of man'. There is confusion in the use of the term since in Europe it usually means simply 'physical anthropology'. However, it is fairly well understood now, especially in the Americas, that 'anthropology' describes a discipline comprising the study of primate and human evolution, prehistoric archaeology, linguistics and social/cultural anthropology, the latter understood as the comparative study of preliterate peoples. This is a minimum definition and the cavils and exclusions would constitute a whole article. This also raises the first question: what is this disparate collection of disciplines doing under one heading, itself claiming to be a discipline? After all, what is *not* the 'science of man'? Earlier versions of 'anthropology' in fact excluded linguistics (the province of comparative philology) while having something to say about language, but they *included* 'technology' or 'material culture', now neglected almost entirely. These inclusions and exclusions are part of the history of the discipline. Since it grew up around museums in large part, 'artifacts' loomed large, and for long stretches of the discipline's history ethnographers 'collected' customs and culture traits much as their museological colleagues 'collected' artifacts. As anthropology eventually developed in many universities independently of museums, artifacts declined in importance. But, for example, in the US, where much work was done for the Bureau of American Ethnology, the 'recording of native languages' became central, and the science of 'descriptive linguistics' was developed almost entirely *within* anthropology. In Britain, again, where the Colonial Office sponsored much research, native languages were learned, but the 'science' was already owned by philology.

Roughly, however, wherever it is found, when anthropology is treated as a holistic science (largely in the US), it recognizes the two major divisions of 'physical anthropology' and 'cultural anthropology', and even if scholars may specialize wholly in one or the other for research purposes, in the education of an anthropologist these are both 'required' (as are some linguistics and archaeology). 'Survivals' of this remain in the undergraduate curricula of some British universities, but by the postgraduate stage they are totally separated. How did they come to be related, and why are they now only so tenuously linked, and what is the future of this relationship?

As a discipline, anthropology took shape in the 1860s, and was established in the universities by the turn of the century. It developed originally outside the universities: Tylor in England was a Quaker businessman, and Morgan in the US, a lawyer. Indeed, Tylor's nonconformity excluded him from an education at Oxford or Cambridge, but the liberalization of these universities allowed him, later, to teach there and to establish anthropology as 'Mr Tylor's science'. His text, *Anthropology*, of 1881 marks the establishment of the discipline in England, as does Morgan's *Ancient Society* (1877) for the US. Many commentators have taken pains to point out that both writers inherited a tradition of social evolutionism from the French and Scottish Enlightenment thinkers and from Spencer, that owed nothing to Darwin – even vice versa. This has perhaps been exaggerated, and there is no question that the *physical* evolution of man would not have loomed so large in the development of anthropology had it not been for the Darwinian revolution and the need to come to terms with it. For anthropology was born of what Owen Lovejoy (1936) called the 'temporalization' of the idea of the 'great chain of being' in the eighteenth century. The secularized version showed a debatable gap between the 'highest animals' and the 'lowest savages' and a progression upwards to the highest civilizations. Side debates between 'progressivists' (usually secular and anti-clerical) and 'degenerationists' (usually clerical and orthodox) consumed much energy, but the strength of the 'progressive' paradigm was more in tune with the tenor of the times, and Morgan and Tylor embraced it. Anthropology's special brief among the intellectual disciplines emerging in the second half of the nineteenth century, then, concerned the 'lower races' and the variety of explanations for the emergence of the highest civilizations. At this stage the distinction between it and 'sociology' was not all that clear, but as sociology in England took on a more Fabian tinge and in America a concern with the immigrant, the differentiation became clearer: anthropology was primarily to deal with the material and spiritual culture of the 'lower races', with peasant folklore, with the distribution and origin of physical types and, later, when evidence became available, with human evolution, because this bore precisely on that origin.

'Physical anthropology' as such was a slow starter because, despite the impact of Darwin, evidence was scanty, there was at first no genetic theory and then dispute among the geneticists and, also, within the 'liberal progressive' tradition of anthropology, there was a growing opposition to racial thinking led primarily by Boas in America. In England as well the subject was split over race since the early disputes on slavery in the amateur anthropological societies. On both sides of the Atlantic (including the continent) there were those who seized enthusiastically on 'eugenics' – and considered themselves the true progressives – and those who followed Tylor and Boas on 'the psychic unity of mankind' and refused to trace cultural differences to racial sources. The disputation was bitter, and its residue continues to plague anthropology, which was forced to become the science that dealt with racial variation and yet was at the same time concerned to deny its cultural significance.

In Europe this 'split mind' was perhaps somewhat less in evidence, since from the start physical anthropology was never that well integrated with cultural anthropology. It was mostly taught in medical schools in departments of anatomy, and 'ethnology' or 'ethnography' was taught separately – often attached to museums. The concerns of the latter disciplines – such as 'diffusion versus independent invention' and the like – while sometimes invoking racial arguments, were largely unconcerned with what the anatomists were doing; and the latter were very little in touch with the geneticists. Archaeology was still largely 'classical' or 'Egyptological', and so there was no concerted 'physical anthropology'. Where there was, it largely concerned the descriptive typology of races. Meanwhile, 'ethnology' – the concern with 'primitive peoples' – took a decidedly 'sociological' turn in France under Durkheim and his school and in England under Rivers at Cambridge. Thus a 'holistic' anthropology never really got off the ground in Europe.

In the US, however, the nutcracker continued to squeeze. 'Physical anthropology' was firmly established in anthropology proper: Boas (1911) did important work on the head-shapes of immigrants, and Kroeber wrote extensively of fossil man and primate intelligence in his *Anthropology* (1923). But at the same time, Boas was elaborating the theoretical basis of cultural relativism (and training students like Mead and Benedict to produce the 'proof'), while Kroeber took an extreme culturalist position in his doctrine of the 'super-organic' nature of culture. The net result was a firm ideological position in which culture became a prime mover, a reality *sui generis* as was 'society' for Durkheim. In the work, for example, of Leslie White (1949), this was taken to its extreme: culture operated entirely according to its own laws. This was of course the logical extrapolation from Tylor's position, but Tylor would have wanted to lodge this, ultimately, in the natural process. It was symptomatic of the later developments that when White brought out a revised edition of Tylor's *Anthropology* in 1960, he omitted the 'Darwinian' chapter on 'Man and other animals' as 'not consonant with modern knowledge'.

This general thrust, although plainly ideological in origin, was also sustained 'scientifically' by both positive and negative developments. On the negative side, fossil evidence was thin, disputed (in the case of Dart's *Australopithecus*) or fraudulent (in the case of Piltdown). Genetics was divided, and until the remarkable burst of talent in the 1930s (Huxley, Haldane, Fisher, Sewall Wright), serious evolutionary genetics was retarded – and we must not forget that it was not until the 1950s that the genetic code was broken. Ethological work was being done, but it was not well known. Even if it had been known its significance would have been missed, since the

general triumph of behaviourism – the main 'positive' development – would have excluded it. Instinct theory was thought to
be thoroughly discredited, and behaviourism, established with
equal firmness in the US and USSR, dominated psychology,
linguistics, philosophy and anthropology. It was, of course,
totally compatible with, and generally welcomed by, the
proponents of cultural determinism.

The other major intellectual force that hit anthropology was
psychoanalysis. Kroeber was analysed and was a practising lay
analyst for a while, but the major impetus came from Linton
and Kardiner. Psychoanalysis was married to cultural relativism and produced the 'culture and personality' school which
was prominent in the 1930s and 1940s. Even here, however,
there was an attempt to translate Freudianism into a behaviour-
istic system. The epitome of this was probably Murdock's *Social
Structure* (1949) in which behaviourism, Freudianism and the
'cross-cultural method' were combined in an attempt to answer
traditional questions of kinship theory. 'Culture and personality', as a subfield of anthropology, was comfortably in line
with the assumptions of cultural relativism: each culture produced its 'basic personality' which was unique and a result
of cultural conditioning. A few 'holistic' anthropologists like
Hallowell (1959) tried to keep 'culture and personality' in an
evolutionary framework, but theirs were lonely voices.

After the initial Freudian-Behaviourist stage, this movement
fragmented into a general 'psychological anthropology'. Fragmentation became characteristic of anthropology from the late
1950s, as we shall see, and 'psychological' anthropology tended
to take off after the latest fads in psychology generally. Perhaps
the strongest development, and in the long run the most lasting,
was the alliance with cybernetics, topology, systems theory,
computers and 'cognitive psychology'. This proved prophetic,
since there is no question that 'cognitive science' is one of the
more durable, coherent and exciting areas of development in the
behavioural sciences generally. It moves naturally into strong
association with neuroscience, the most obvious growth area
in the physiology of behaviour. Already 'neuropsychology' is
established, and a field of 'neurosociology' cannot be far behind.

In picking out the trends with durability, as opposed to the fads, it is important to note ecology. This was in danger of being a fad during the 1960s and 1970s, but it had fairly deep roots in anthropology and has survived and flourished. Early on, it was a province of zoology, and attempts to look at ecological systems were confused with 'environmental determinism' and Marxism. Often, as with White (1949), they were grandiose and unsophisticated, but Julian Steward (1955), for example, kept a high standard of ecological thinking to the forefront of the anthropological imagination. The impact of the 'ecological crisis' sent many young anthropologists into this area, and some of the best. The connection again with systems theory was quickly established, and this was excellent in ridding the discipline of antiquated 'cause and effect' thinking. It was also very important that anthropological ecology arose, essentially, out of the 'archaeological' wing of the subject. This revolutionized archaeology which, for example, under Binford (1972) at New Mexico, found a new sophistication and much closer links with 'cultural' anthropology proper.

As is often the case with these internal developments, however, fanatics take them up as causes, attach them to ideologies, and try to claim 'total' explanation of social facts for them. For the cognitive anthropologists this meant a curious version of solipsism – in the case of 'structuralism' a kind of collectivist solipsism, with almost a revival of the idea of a 'group mind'. With the ecologists, on the contrary, it became what early critics had feared – a crude materialistic determinism advanced in the name of 'cultural materialism' and claiming, strangely, to be 'Marxist' in some cases. This fad seems to be passing, and if ecologists can (a) stick to their cybernetic models and (b) expand their models of feedback systems to include other variables – such as cognition and communication – then there is much promise here. The work of people like Rappoport, for example, continues to impress in this area.

The mention of communication points to another strong trend in 'holistic' anthropology. The influence of linguistics, as we have seen, has always been strong in American anthropology, and various linguistic models have been tried as paradigms for examining other areas of culture – by Pike, Kluckhohn, and others. It was this influence that led to the whole 'language and culture' movement that for a while rivalled 'culture and personality' for centre stage. At first this was largely concerned with arguing the 'Sapir-Whorf' hypothesis about – again – the *deterministic* role of language; but this developed into the basis of 'formal analysis' of cultures through set theory and componential analysis. While this ran into difficulties (to do with its solipsistic problems) it did mean that there was a useful pre-adaptation for the assimilation of French structuralism under Lévi-Strauss, itself a product of de Saussure, Jakobson and European linguistics. The idea that all culture was like language in being an arbitrary 'code' which could be broken, thus 'solving' the messages contained in everything from myths through kinship systems to art, was certainly attractive. It corresponded to a revolution in American linguistics from outside anthropology, but one that had a tremendous impact, namely the Chomskian transformational grammar, which rested on similar premises about universal, rational mental processes. (In structuralism the issue of 'innateness' is skirted; for Chomsky it is central.) This was all rightly opposed by the ecologists, who insisted that cultures were not *just* systems of communication but existed in real adaptational situations. But, as we have seen, the ecologists themselves need to take more note of communication, and ultimately, as Richard Alexander (1979) has said, they have to include the genes, 'since so far no one has found any other way to make a human being'.

This brings us back to what was happening in physical anthropology. We have established the 'split', which was partly ideological but also partly based on the paucity of usable material and theory in biology itself. Even students of animal behaviour, themselves biologists, had little help from genetics, for example. This help existed potentially in the work of Fisher in the 1930s, but it was missed until the 1960s. The growing body of work of the ethologists which studied, after all, the social interactive behaviour of animals, was little known until its popularization in the 1960s. But during those same remarkable and effervescent 1960s there was a positive renaissance of physical anthropology, which dropped its obsession with racial typologies and suddenly turned into a powerful science. Several things contributed. The first was an upsurge in fossil finds. This was not solely due to the Leakeys and Olduvai Gorge, although no one can underestimate their importance. All over the old world crucial finds were made that rapidly filled in the 'gaps' in the fossil record and revolutionized our notions of the age of the hominid line – pushing it back into the pliocene (to 3.5 million years). At the same time, under Washburn at Berkeley and his student DeVore at Harvard, and under Hall at Bristol, there began a fantastic development of primate studies. Although this has now spread to embrace zoologists, psychologists, ethologists, neuroscientists and others, its early inspiration in America (and in Japan where studies got under way after the end of World War II) was anthropological. It wanted to help understand human evolution by looking at the social behaviour of our closest relatives; but at the same time, its methods were borrowed from social anthropology: long-term studies in the field, living in daily contact, and even some kind of 'participant observation', with the animals.

Again cross-referencing began. It was soon obvious that this was close to what ethologists were doing, and thus a new interest in their work was engendered. The ethologists had been concentrating almost entirely on animal *communication*, and the primatologists were able to introduce a healthy measure of ecology. As usual this became a polarized argument on the futile 'nature versus nurture' issue, but there are signs that at long last this tedious debate (which after all was settled by Kant and resettled by William James) is being seen for what it is, and an 'interactionist'•set of hypotheses are taking over. Like all these developments, primatology became largely an end in itself for its practitioners, but this over-specialization is perhaps necessary. Most people are not good at synthesis: to use one analogy, there are a million good bricklayers for every good architect. But too much bricklaying can slow down development in a discipline, and can kill it altogether by inducing total fragmentation. Primatology became so popular that most departments have at least a 'token' primatologist. Since they tend to be obsessive about 'data' and basically non-theoretical, they do not threaten, unlike their more theoretically aggressive 'ethological' colleagues. As 'symbolic' anthropologists attest, people are happier with limited categories and firm boundaries. Disruption of these produces reactions of witchcraft, pollution and taboo. (There are of course neural mechanisms which explain why this happens – but 'symbolic' anthropologists would reject such an intrusion of 'other' data as 'reductionism'!)

Other developments were largely technical. Improved methods of dating grew apace. These were again shared with the archaeologists, so cross-boundary ties were possible. Also, primatologists were pushed into being more 'zoological', hence forcing the connection with biology. Studies of chimpanzees in the wild had to be measured against the studies of chimpanzee communication in the laboratory (largely undertaken by psychologists). All this made for a ferment and the rapid development of primatology, but the result was not at all a closing of the physical-cultural gap. If anything, the cultural anthropologists began to close ranks and became even more stridently ideological, denying more forcefully than ever the relevance of these data the more forceful the data became. Attempts like those of Tiger and Fox (1970), for example, to call attention to this relevance, not only for anthropology, but for human survival, were largely sidestepped or attacked as 'reductionist' or 'revivals of Social Darwinism' or reactionary or whatever. Some commentators realized that they were a genuine attempt to be 'true to the broadest mandate' of anthropology (Seigel), but these were few. Of course these attempts did have their problems. They were overly impressed by the ethologists and hence concentrated largely on communication which, as we have seen, needed the corrective of ecology. The development of primatology made this more possible since much more complex creatures with higher levels of social learning were involved than those popular with the ethologists. There was response, but it was limited. 'Cultural' anthropology, in the 1960s and 1970s, was not moving in that direction.

A lot of this had to do with two factors in the sociology of anthropology itself: the post-Sputnik explosion of the number of departments and professionals, and the turmoil in society itself over civil rights and Vietnam.

The proliferation of academic anthropologists took place, for obvious reasons, largely within 'cultural' anthropology – new departments usually did not have the infrastructure necessary for ambitious physical anthropology programmes – and so largely within its assumptions. This coincided with the upsurge of physical anthropology, as well as exciting developments in neuroscience, endocrinology and genetics, but the fast-developing cultural anthropology departments tended to proliferate in unrelated directions. 'Area' studies were big for a time, since money was available; this was true also of 'medical' and 'urban' anthropology. 'Symbolic' anthropology was popular – it needed little investment of either money or brains, and could pick up on what was happening in structuralism and linguistics ('semiotics' as it soon became). Bold souls like Sebeok tried to initiate 'zoo-semiotics' – recognizing the connection to ethology – but this went nowhere. An almost frantic fragmentation was taking place. This was *not* healthy specialization: that can only take place in a science that already has a central theory within which to specialize. The too-rigid expansion of anthropology in America, combined with the demands of the promotion system and the entrepreneurial nature of academic life, simply led to a proliferation of mini-specialisms and a chasing after every fad to come out of Paris or Frankfurt. Among these the oddest was the revival of 'Marxism'. It was not a Marxism that many of those truly familiar with Marx could easily recognize. Partly, it was highly fashionable to be 'radical' during this period in academic circles, and fashionably daring to be 'Marxist' – in some version or another, usually acquired second hand. Marx was pinned to the social radical mast-head much as Darwin had been to that of the social Darwinists, usually with about the same lack of relevance. The most interesting area of this development was essentially a revival within anthropology of the tradition of the 'sociology of knowledge' – or the 'social construction of reality', as Berger and Luckmann (1966) chose to call it. The 'Marxist' anthropologists behaved as though this was a remarkable discovery and quoted Althusser and 'hermeneutics' a great deal. But, curiously, it sat well with the 'symbolic' and 'cognitive' developments and so got its hearing. As Berger recognized, though, there is a circularity in the argument: the mind is a social construct, but the mind 'constructs' society. The only way out of this is to examine the mind as an evolutionary product (Donald Campbell's 'evolutionary epistemology'); but this, naturally, does not sit well with the current ideology. The other 'radical' impetus came from feminism, but since this was essentially an anti-intellectual movement (at least in America) its relevance was limited to its ability, which was considerable, to harass those it considered opponents. (In Europe there are genuinely interesting developments in this area, but these have not penetrated to North America.) 'Urgent' anthropology spawned a good deal of interesting work on rapidly disappearing hunting and gathering societies, a development further encouraged by the renewed interest in human evolution: many of those engaged in the 'Man the Hunter' movement were also primatologists.

The overall impression of this period is one of chaos. The pressures to 'radicalism', 'urbanism', 'relevance' and so on, together with the sudden affluence of what had always been a small and exclusive discipline, produced not progress but simply a proliferation of fads. It may take many years for the ill effects of this period to work themselves out. Meanwhile, we might ask what has been happening to the classic areas of social anthropology? Where, for example, is kinship? This had always been the central topic – the key to anthropological thinking and theory, responsible for more than 50 per cent of publications. Well, it continued to receive 'structural' attention from Lévi-Strauss and a few of his students, and it provided subject matter for the 'componential analysts' – but otherwise it all but disappeared. This is one of the stranger modern developments. It is as though philosophy decided to abandon logic. No history of the period is possible yet, but when one is written this will have to be dealt with. Partly, kinship was simply submerged by the 'urgent' and 'relevant' concerns, which, demanding little intellect and much passion, were more in tune with the times. Partly also, it got bogged down with intricate 'in-house' disputes that simply began to bore people – the 'prescriptive marriage' debate was one. To get out of this impasse, Schneider (1968), for example, led kinship studies into the 'symbolic' camp in America. This was at exactly the time when a combination of 'biosocial' movements were putting kinship back into nature with a vengeance!

This must surely rank as one of the great ironies of intellectual history. For all those years, social anthropologists had been insisting that kinship *was* the heart of social structure, and the study of it was the great strength of anthropology. In the 1960s, Hamilton, picking up on the work of Fisher in the 1930s, re-established the importance of kinship in evolution with his theory of 'inclusive fitness'. One would have thought that social anthropologists would have been ecstatic, and felt that they were totally vindicated. Some were – a few – and immediately saw that the 'gap' could here be bridged at the more crucial point of theory. But the majority were uninterested or simply hostile. The lack of interest of course stems from the drifting of anthropology into the morass of 'soft' specialisms we have noted – and the concomitant decline of interest in kinship. The hostility is more interesting. Some of it came from the deep-rooted antipathy to evolutionary biology that we have noted, and there were several half thought-out 'rushes to judgement' – Sahlins producing the most notable. Other hostility was more overtly political and was sparked off by the media hype surrounding E. O. Wilson's *Sociobiology* (1975). We live in a social, political and media-dominated world, and ideas do not exist in a vacuum. But it was obvious that Wilson, who combined all the available entomological, ethological, and primatological evidence with the evolutionary theory derived from Hamilton and Trivers, was making a grab for a *total* explanation of *all* social behaviour from insect to man. As early as 1971 Tiger and Fox had recognized that Hamilton's work was important in understanding altruism. But Wilson's ambitions put the social sciences on the defensive. This, combined with a highly touted 'radical' attack, muddled the debate – which simply seemed parochial and confusing to the Europeans. At the same time, the grab by the evolutionary biologists for a *total* explanation was offensive to those physical anthropologists who, through studies of primate behaviour, anatomy, the brain and the endocrine systems, had been labouring to produce *proximate* explanations of behaviour. There is in fact no real conflict. *Proximate* mechanisms must always be referable back to *ultimate* mechanisms, that is, those of natural selection which produced them. But certainly, and again, ironically, the physical anthropologists felt as threatened as the cultural! The media hype (in a nation where being a 'celebrity' is the equivalent of being knighted) hid from intellectual view, for example, the fact that a small group of anthropologists and others were already co-operating to produce a combined ultimate/proximate approach. In the same year as *Sociobiology* (1975), Fox edited *Biosocial Anthropology*, which proposed exactly such a programme and included work from primatology, ethology (Bischof, Blurton Jones, Chance), and endocrinology. It was politely received, but lacking the hype, did not get centre stage, and no one noticed the real alternative it offered.

This recital of the recent history of kinship shows that, within this next decade, it is doubtful that the gap will be closed. But eventually the sheer weight of evidence from the physical sciences is bound to tell. This may mean that, as Wilson has predicted, a new 'biosociology' will emerge that will simply bypass the social sciences. It may be, however, that after the smoke of controversy has cleared, anthropologists in sufficient numbers may realize that for intellectual survival if nothing else, they had better re-tool their skills and accept their natural alliance with the natural sciences in the framework of natural selection (that is, evolutionary biology). At present this is hard to see. The subject is shrinking, not expanding, and once exciting areas, like British social structural analysis, seem to have run into a dead end. French anthropology seems exhausted after the heady popularity of structuralism. If the future is anywhere it is in America, but whether anything viable will emerge from the current chaos and ideological muddle is hard to see. What is more likely – and this is evident from the near collapse and 'reorganization' of the professional association – is that a series of relatively autonomous specialisms will diverge from one another and gravitate towards their nearest relatives in other fields. Thus the 'cognitive' anthropologists, for example, are already part of a 'cognitive science' movement starting its own newsletter and so on, and incorporating psychologists, neuroscientists, linguists, and artificial intelligence experts. Many of the 'physical' specialists already prefer to gravitate to close neighbours like genetics or anatomy. The 'ecologists' likewise are breaking away. This leaves the 'cultural' anthropologists moving if anything closer to the humanities in the pursuit of 'meaning' through 'symbols'. It would appear that 'Mr Tylor's science' is in total disarray.

This does not mean that excellent things are not being done in the various subfields. They are. But I have been concerned here with the ideal of an integrated, holistic field of anthropology proper, and this seems, at the moment, unrealizable. There are glimpses of hope within the field which suggest that some integration is possible. A number of young people do take up research in the 'biology of social behaviour' – but it is not well supported. Some of those, like Laughlin and d'Aquili (1974) who helped to pioneer such an integrative approach (their 'biogenetic structuralism') continue to press the analysis into areas like ritual, which had been the preserve of the social/cultural wing. More significantly, an outstanding practitioner of the 'symbolic' approach, Victor Turner (1983) was affected by the new information, and studied brain mechanisms. If there is any hope for the holistic science it lies in these directions, and the work of Chagnon and Irons (1979), Konner (1982) and Chisholm (1983) combines the best of training in physical and cultural anthropology with a refreshing, integrative approach. The possibilities are there, but it is hard to see their making much headway against the ideological inertia of this sadly fragmented discipline.

Robin Fox
Rutgers University

References

Alexander, R. (1979), *Darwinism in Relation to Social Affairs*, Seattle.

Berger, P. and Luckmann, T. (1966), *The Social Construction of Reality*, Garden City, N.Y.

Binford, L. R. (1972), *An Archaeological Perspective*, New York.

Boas, F. (1911), *The Mind of Primitive Man*, New York.

Campbell, D. (1974), 'Evolutionary epistemology', in *The Philosophy of Karl Popper*, La Salle, Ill.

Chagnon, N. and Irons, W. (1979), *Evolutionary Biology and*

Human Social Behavior: An Anthropological Perspective, North Scituate, Mass.

Chisholm, J. (1983), *Navaho Childhood: An Ethnological Study of Child Development*, Chicago.

Chomsky, N. (1957), *Syntactic Structures*, The Hague.

DeVore, I. (ed.) (1965), *Primate Behavior: Field Studies of Monkeys and Apes*, New York.

Fisher, H. A. L. (1930), *The Genetical Theory of Natural Selection*, Oxford. (2nd edn revised and enlarged, New York, 1958.)

Fox, R. (ed.) (1975), *Biosocial Anthropology*, New York.

Hallowell, A. I. (1959), 'Behavioral evolution and the emergence of the self', in B. Hegers (ed.), *Evolution and Anthropology: A Centennial Appraisal*, Washington.

Huxley, J. (1942), *Evolution: The Modern Synthesis*, London.

Kardiner, A., Linton, R. and West, J. *et al.* (1945), *The Psychological Frontiers of Society*, New York.

Konner, M. R. (1982), *The Tangled Wing: Biological Constraints on the Human Spirit*, New York.

Kroeber, A. L. (1923), *Anthropology*, New York.

Laughlin, C. D. and d'Aquili, E. G. (1974), *Biogenetic Structuralism*, New York.

Lévi-Strauss, C. (1958), *Anthropologie Structurale*, Paris.

Lévi-Strauss, C. (1973), *Anthropologie Structurale Deux*, Paris.

Linton, R. (1945), *The Cultural Background of Personality*, New York.

Lovejoy, Arthur O. (1936), *The Great Chain of Being*, Cambridge.

Morgan, L. H. (1877), *Ancient Society*, New York.

Murdock, G. P. (1949), *Social Structure*, New York.

Pike, K. L. (1954), *Language in Relation to a Unified Theory of the Structure of Human Behavior*, Glendale.

Rappoport, R. (1968), *Pigs for the Ancestors*, New Haven.

Sahlins, M. (1976), *The Use and Abuse of Biology*, Ann Arbor.

Schneider, D. (1968), *American Kinship: A Cultural Account*, Englewood Cliffs, N.J.

Steward, J. (1955), *Theory of Culture Change*, Urbana, Ill.

Tiger, L. and Fox, R. (1970), *The Imperial Animal*, New York.

Turner, V. (1983), 'Body, brain and culture', *Zygon*, 18.

Tylor, E. B. (1934 [1881]), *Anthropology*, 2 vols, London.

White, L. (1949), *The Stience of Culture*, New York.
Wilson, E. O. (1975), *Sociobiology: The New Synthesis*, Cambridge, Mass.
See also: *archaeology; linguistics.*

Archaeology

Archaeology often appears to mean different things, from the particular to the general, in different contexts. At one extreme it can refer to the recovery of ancient remains by excavation, 'digging up pots and bones'. But even field archaeology now includes a wide range of activities, from survey, the cleaning and recording of industrial machines (industrial archaeology), underwater archaeology to air photography. Excavation itself involves both archaeological concepts such as context, association and assemblage, and external techniques such as methods of probing below the surface soil with magnetometers, pollen analysis to reconstruct past environments and data processing with computers. More generally, archaeology is often used to refer to what archaeologists do, including what is more properly termed prehistory or history. All reconstruction of the past which is based on material remains other than written records might be termed archaeology. Yet within historical archaeology use is often made of written records as part of the interpretive process. The boundary between archaeology and history (including prehistory) is blurred, because the interpretation of layers on a site is closely dependent on accumulated knowledge about what went on at any particular place and time in the past. Since there are few Pompeiis, and archaeological remains are typically fragmentary and ambiguous, the burden on theory is great. Theories and paradigms often change with little contradiction from the data. There is much scope for historical imagination.

Views differ as to the degree of rigour and certainty that can be obtained in reconstructing the past from archaeological remains, at least partly in relation to whether one thinks archaeology is really an historical or an anthropological science. Unfortunately, the two approaches have normally been opposed. Those who claim that the purpose of archaeology is historical emphasize the particularity of past cultures, the unpredictability of human action, and the role of individuals. They state that each past culture has its own value system which it is difficult for archaeologists to reconstruct with any confidence. Prehistory and archaeology are interpretive by nature. For those who claim that 'archaeology is anthropology or it is nothing', and who believe in the cross-cultural method, allied with positivism and with laws of evolution and systematic relationships, rigorous explanation of events in past societies is feasible. The concern with scientific explanation has been particularly strong in America, but the two views of archaeology, as history or science, have a long tradition in the discipline.

The History of Archaeology

Speculation about the human past began in classical antiquity, but investigation of monuments and artefacts dates back to the Renaissance and increased markedly in the eighteenth and nineteenth centuries as part of national interests, pride and identity. This early archaeology had its origin in (1) the study of oriental and classical antiquities such as Pompeii, (2) the recording of European monuments such as Stonehenge and Carnac, and (3) the interest in human origins as an outcome of developments in geology and biology.

The initial concern was to establish a chronological sequence, and in the early nineteenth century in Denmark C. J. Thomsen grouped antiquities into stone, bronze and iron and gave them chronological significance, while J. J. A. Worsaae provided stratigraphical evidence for the sequence. The scheme was argued on ethnographic grounds to relate to a development from savagery to civilization. This idea of Sven Nilsson was, in the second half of the nineteenth century, developed by Sir Edward Tylor and Lewis H. Morgan, and it influenced Marx and Engels. An evolutionary emphasis in archaeology was, in the debates about the origins of man, also closely linked to Charles Darwin.

In this early period of archaeology, an evolutionary approach was closely allied to a cross-cultural emphasis, scientific optimism, and notions of progress from barbarism to industrial societies. Yet in the early twentieth century, and particularly after the First World War, the main concern in archaeology became the building up of local historical sequences, the identification of cultural differences and the description of the diffusion and origin of styles and types, V. Gordon Childe crystallized earlier German and English uses of the term culture and defined it as a recurring association of traits in a limited geographical area. These spatial and temporal units became the building blocks for the definition of local historical sequences and the diffusion of traits. Childe described the prehistory of Europe as at least partly the result of diffusion from the Near East, 'ex Oriente lux'.

But Childe was already responsible for reintroducing an evolutionary emphasis in European archaeology by taking up Morgan's scheme, while in America Julian Steward and Leslie White embraced similar ideas. Rather than describing sites, processes were to be examined. In particular, attention focused on the economic relationships between a site and its environment. The work of Clark in Europe and Willey and Braidwood in America pioneered this new, functional, integrative approach which owed much to developments in anthropology. The discovery of physical dating methods such as radiocarbon (C^{14}) measurement freed the archaeologist from a reliance on typology, types, cultures and associations in establishing chronologies.

A full mixture of evolutionary theory, anthropology, and science in archaeology was attempted in the 'New Archaeology', a development of the 1960s and 1970s, spearheaded by Lewis Binford in America and David Clarke in Britain. Although there were many differences between these and other New Archaeologists, the overall concern was to introduce scientific, rigorous methods of explanation into archaeology. Rather than describing what happened in the past (the perceived view of earlier, historical approaches in archaeology), they tried to explain why events occurred. Ethnography and anthropology provided the theories for the explanation of past events, and a sub-discipline, 'ethnoarchaeology', developed in order to study more closely the relationship between material culture residues and processes in the living world. From such studies they hoped to build laws of cultural process from which particular archaeological occurrences could be deduced. They frequently referred to positivism and Hempel's hypothetico-deductive method.

The Current Scene

Much archaeology today, particularly in America, remains within the grip of ecological functionalism, evolutionary theory and positivism, in the aftermath of the New Archaeology. The enduring concerns have been with process, the application of systems theory, positivism and scientific methods, including the widespread use of computers for the storing and sorting of field data, statistical manipulations, taxonomy and simulation. Cemeteries are examined in order to identify age, sex and status groupings as part of 'social archaeology', and settlement data are searched for organizational clues. Evolutionary theory is referred to in the definition of bands, tribes, chiefdoms and states and in discussions of the transformation of these categories through time. There are both Neo-Darwinian and Neo-Marxist schools.

Yet for many archaeologists, particularly in Europe, archaeology remains an historical discipline. Many field archaeologists, funded by central or local government or by development contractors, find that the academic rhetoric of their university colleagues has little relevance to their problems and interests. The split between theory and application is widening. Similarly, museum curators are aware that popular interest centres on local and regional historical continuity, and on the material achievements of foreign cultures, rather than on cross-cultural laws of social process. In addition, many academic archaeologists cling to the historical tradition in which they had been taught and reject the claims of the New Archaeology.

An emerging feeling in archaeology is that the old battle between historical and scientific-anthropological views of the past is inadequate. The concern is to allow the particularity of historical sequences, and the individuality of culture, while at the same time focusing on social process and cultural change.

Ian Hodder
University of Cambridge

Further Reading
Binford, L. (1972), *An Archaeological Perspective*, New York.
Childe, V. G. (1936), *Man Makes Himself*, London.
Willey, G. and Sabloff, J. (1974), *A History of American Archaeology*, London.
Wheeler, M. (1954), *Archaeology From The Earth*, Harmondsworth.
See also: *anthropology; history*.

Business Studies

The term business studies is a loose generic title for several related aspects of enterprises and their environments, foremost amongst these being administration and management, accounting, finance and banking, international relations, marketing, and personnel and industrial relations. There is considerable disagreement, however, on the extent to which scholastic, managerial or professional values should predominate in the framing of the curriculum and in research and teaching objectives.

It is usual to trace modern ideas on business studies to formative developments in the United States, where the Wharton School of Finance and Commerce was the first of twenty schools of business administration and commerce to be founded between 1881 and 1910. But it was particularly in the next two decades, when a further 180 schools were established, that the distinctive American style of business education, with a high degree of abstraction and a quantitative approach to the solution of problems, became firmly rooted (Rose, 1970). Management education developed much later in Europe, originally under the tutelage of practitioners from the United States. Indeed, in Great Britain, it was not until 1947 that the first major centre, the Administrative Staff College at Henley, was inaugurated. There are now several leading European institutes for business and management studies. In recent years, too, in both Europe and Japan, there have been active attempts to develop programmes which are distinctive from the original North American model, a change which has been facilitated by the considerable interest in business studies in Third World nations and by the rigorous analytical techniques which have latterly evolved in the United States.

The precise causes of the expansion of business education are open to some doubt, although processes of rationalization in modern societies and the rapid growth in numbers of managerial personnel have been signal influences. Further favourable trends have been increased international competition and investment, major technical changes, a larger scale and greater complexity of modern enterprises and a facilitative role of governments (Poole, Mansfield, Blyton and Frost, 1981).

However, opinion differs on whether business studies should become an empirical social science or whether, to the contrary, it should be founded on a series of prescriptive values (what should be accomplished) and ideas (what can be achieved) in actual employing organizations. A particular problem of internal coherence in business education also stems from the varied subject backgrounds of research workers and teachers, a situation which has militated against an adequate interdisciplinary synthesis.

In principle, the theoretical linkages between the main areas of business studies are examined in business policy, although this has in practice become a highly specialized area dealing primarily with the intertemporal concept of strategy. In substantive terms, organizational behaviour is the most obvious branch of study that connects the disparate approaches within the business field. Nevertheless, its excessive reliance on contingency theory (which implies that whether a particular organizational form is effective depends on the nature of the environmental context) has proved to be an encumbrance, since challenges to this approach have ensured that there is no longer a generally accepted model for conceptualizing business behaviour.

A further critical issue in business studies is the extent to which, regardless of cultural, socioeconomic or political conditions, common administrative practices are appropriate on a world-wide scale. The earliest perspectives tended to assume a considerable uniformity, the various strands being combined in the 'industrial society' thesis in which a basic 'logic of industrialism' was seen to impel all modern economies towards similar organizational structures and modes of administration (Kerr, Dunlop, Harbison and Myers, 1960). This complemented the earlier work on classical organization theory, which postulated universal traits of business management, and on studies of bureaucracy, which arrived at similar conclusions. In this approach, too, a key assumption was that there had been a divorce of ownership from control in the business enterprise that, in turn, had ensured the convergence of decision-making processes between societies with ostensibly irreconcilable political ideologies and economic systems.

More recently, however, the 'culturalist' thesis has emerged as a check-weight to these universalist approaches. This assumes great diversity in business behaviour and ideology occasioned either by variations in the 'task' environment (community, government, consumer, employee, supplier, distributor, shareholder) or, more especially, in the 'social' environment (cultural, legal, political, social). Above all, it emphasizes that each new generation internalizes an enduring strain of culture through its process of socialization, with people in different countries learning their own language, concepts and systems of values. Moreover, such deep-rooted cultural forces are continually reasserted in the way people relate to one another and ensure that organizational structures which are not consonant with culturally derived expectations will remain purely formal (Child and Kieser, 1979).

Divergence in business organization and practice can also stem from temporal as well as spatial differences between societies. Indeed, 'late development' would appear to enhance a mode of industrialization quite distinct from the earliest Western models, with the state being more predominant at the expense of a *laissez-faire* ideology, educational institutions preceding manufacturing, more substantial technical and organizational 'leaps', human relations and personnel management techniques being more advanced, and large-scale enterprises being deliberately constructed as a spearhead for economic advancement (Dore, 1973). In this respect, too, the choices of strategic élites are as important as the constraints of environment and organizational structure in determining which types of business conduct become ascendant in any given society.

Since the Second World War, business studies have also been particularly influenced by notions of 'human resourcing'. This relates to the central issue of whether business managers have wider moral obligations above those of seeking to enhance profitability and efficiency. External social responsibility refers to the interests of the community and wider society, and to various groups and individuals located outside the organization (Ackerman and Bauer, 1976; Davis, Frederick and Blomstrom, 1980). It is particularly examined in the context of marketing policy, where various ethical questions are raised by the strategies and techniques for promoting different types of goods and services. Internal social responsibility concerns employee welfare and satisfaction and interpersonal and intergroup relations in the actual enterprise.

Interest in this latter group of questions has helped to occasion a major expansion in research and teaching in the areas of personnel management and industrial relations. The personnel function relates to the objectives, policies, plans and practices affecting people within work environments and, although the relevant body of knowledge is not settled, the main areas covered are 'employee resourcing', 'employee development' and 'employee relations' (Strauss and Sayles 1980; Thomson, 1981). In industrial relations, too, trade unions have been seen as increasingly influential and legitimate in decision making, while a variety of schemes for employee participation and industrial democracy have been viewed as appropriate for the future organization of internal relationships within the enterprise.

In the curriculum objectives of business studies, however, a principal problem is engendered by differences between professional and managerial approaches. Classical models of professionalism have always emphasized the role of the professional body as a means of social control and as an accrediting agency. This contrasts sharply with the rationale of the modern corporation as a management-directed organization that involves an attempt to ensure control over the specialists carrying out a variety of work functions. Such a tension is manifest particularly in the areas of accounting and law where, traditionally, a professional orientation has been paramount.

More recently, though, the former subject in particular has become significantly more 'behavioural' in focus, and its current techniques and information are increasingly allied to conceptions of management control.

In the future, there are thus likely to remain far-reaching differences of view on the appropriate aims of business studies, reflecting professional versus managerial objectives, the extent to which an empirical social science should be developed (if necessary at the expense of consultancy-style links with ongoing enterprises), the diverse disciplinary backgrounds of the practitioners, and the degree of commitment to external and internal social responsibilities. Nevertheless, the expansion of interest in business education is likely to continue and a wide range of new ideas on principles and practices of administration to be formulated. Moreover, the resolution of the various specialist debates is likely to be closely in accord with wider movements in advanced industrial societies, and to reinforce the thesis that there is a wide degree of choice in the framing of the policies of commercial organizations and in the premises guiding the systematic analysis of actual businesses themselves.

Michael Poole
University of Wales Institute
of Science and Technology

References

Ackerman, R. W. and Bauer, R. A. (1976), *Corporate Social Responsiveness*, Reston, Virginia.

Child, J. and Kieser, A. (1979), 'Organization and managerial roles in British and West German companies: an examination of the culture-free thesis', in C. J. Lammers and D. J. Hickson (eds), *Organizations Alike and Unlike: International and Inter-Institutional Studies in the Sociology of Organizations*, London.

Davies, K., Frederick, W. C. and Blomstrom, R. L. (1980), *Business and Society: Concepts and Policy Issues*, New York.

Dore, R. P. (1973), *British Factory-Japanese Factory*, London.

Kerr, C., Dunlop, J. T., Harbison, F. H. and Myers, C. A. (1960), *Industrialism and Industrial Man*, Cambridge, Mass.

Poole, M., Mansfield, R., Blyton, P. and Frost, P. (1981), *Managers in Focus*, Aldershot.

Rose, H. (1970), *Management Education in the 1970's*, London.

Strauss, G. and Sayles, L. R. (1980), *Personnel: The Human Problems of Management*, 4th edn, Englewood Cliffs, N.J.

Thomson, G. F. (1981), *A Textbook of Personnel Management*, London.

Cliometrics

The term cliometrics (a neologism linking the concept of measurement to the muse of history) was apparently coined at Purdue University, Indiana, US, in the late 1950s. Originally applied to the study of economic history as undertaken by scholars trained as economists (and also called, by its practitioners and others, the 'new economic history', 'econometric history', and 'quantitative economic history'), more recently cliometrics has been applied to a broader range of historical studies (including the 'new political history', the 'new social history', and, most inclusively, 'social science history').

The historians' early interest in cliometrics partly reflects the impact of two important works in United States economic history. The detailed estimates by Conrad and Meyer (1958) of the profitability of slavery before the Civil War and the quantitative evaluation of the role of the railroads in economic growth by Fogel (1964) triggered wide-ranging debate, with much attention to questions of method as well as substance. While these two works, combining economic theory and quantitative analysis, attracted the most attention, two other books published at about the same time also highlighted the quantitative aspect, although in a more traditional (and less controversial) manner. A National Bureau of Economic Research conference volume, edited by Parker (1960), presented a number of important studies (by, among others, Easterlin, Gallman, Lebergott, and North) pushing back many important times series on economic variables to the early nineteenth century, an effort complemented by the publication, several years later, of another NBER conference dealing mainly with nineteenth-century economic change (1966). North (1961) combined his new estimates of pre-1860 foreign trade with a familiar regional approach to describe the basic contours of United States economic growth from 1790 to the Civil War. These works had important implications for discussions of economic growth in the United States, particularly in the period before the Civil War. The concentration of major publications within a short time period, together with the start of an annual conference of cliometricians at Purdue University (which, with several changes of venue, still continues), generated the momentum which led to major shifts in the nature of the writing of American economic history, as well as revisions of many interpretations of past developments. The late 1950s and 1960s saw similar changes in other subfields of history, particularly political and social history, although it was in economic history that the concentration on theory, quantitative data, and statistical methods was most complete.

The most general characteristics of cliometric work (in economic history) have been the systematic use of economic theory and its concepts to examine economic growth in the past, and the widespread preparation and formal statistical analysis of quantitative material. While none of this may seem to provide a new approach in historical studies (as is often pointed out in criticizing claims of novelty), the more explicit attention to theory and the more frequent reliance on quantitative materials and statistical procedures have had an important impact upon the manner in which historical questions have been approached and interpreted. However, cliometricians still differ in how they make use of quantitative and statistical methods. To some, the major work is the preparation of quantitative data, either of detailed information for a particular time period (e.g., the samples of population, agriculture, and manufacturing records drawn from the decadal federal census) or of long-period time series (e.g., national income and wealth, wages, labour force) to be used in measuring and understanding past economic changes. These estimates require imaginative reconstructions from the available samples of past data, but do not often involve sophisticated statistical tools. Others emphasize the use of more formal statistical methods, most frequently regression analysis, to test hypotheses. And some cliometricians restrict themselves to the use of economic theory to analyse institutional and economic changes, which are not described quantitatively.

Continued interest in economic (and political and sociological) theory has led to a more frequent attempt to find historical generalizations based upon social science concepts and methods than some more traditionally-trained historians seem comfortable with. Nevertheless, the ability to collect and examine data, from archival and published sources, furthered by the development of the computer, has permitted a considerable expansion in the amount of material relevant to questions of interest to historians, as well as better methods of organizing, analysing, and testing data. In recent years, the heat of earlier debates on method has apparently declined as the use of quantitative methods and theoretical constructs has become a part of the standard 'tool-kit' of historians, while cliometricians have broadened the range of questions they have discussed and the varieties of evidence utilized.

While the first cliometric studies were done principally by North American scholars and, for reasons of data availability, most frequently concerned the United States in the nineteenth century, over the past two decades the temporal and geographic scope has widened, as has the types of questions to which cliometric analysis is applied. Much work has been done on the colonial period, as well as the twentieth century, in the United States. And, not only have the interests of American cliometricians expanded to include studies of other parts of the world, but cliometric work has developed in a number of other countries, most particularly in Britain and in Western Europe. Although, as with most attempts at categorization, a sharp dividing line is often difficult to draw, cliometric history continues to emphasize the systematic application of social science theory and the use of quantitative data and statistical analysis to understand the historical past.

Stanley L. Engerman
University of Rochester

References

Conrad, A. H. and Meyer, J. R. (1958), 'The economics of slavery in the ante-bellum South', *Journal of Political Economy.*

Fogel, R. W. (1964), *Railroads and American Economic Growth: Essays in Econometric History*, Baltimore.

National Bureau of Economic Research, Conference in Research in Income and Wealth (1960), *Trends in the American Economy in the Nineteenth Century*, Princeton.

National Bureau of Economic Research, Conference on Research in Income and Wealth (1966), *Output, Employment, and Productivity in the United States after 1800*, New York.

North, D. C. (1961), *The Economic Growth of the United States, 1790–1860*, Englewood Cliffs, N.J.

Further Reading

Engerman, S. L. (1977), 'Recent developments in American economic history', *Social Science History.*

Kousser, J. M. (1980), 'Quantitative social-scientific history', in M. Kammen (ed.), *The Past Before Us*, Ithaca.

McCloskey, D. N. (1978), 'The achievements of the cliometric school', *Journal of Economic History.*

McCloskey, D. N. and Hersh, G. (1985), *The Bibliography of Historical Economics, 1957–1980*, Cambridge.

See also: *history.*

Criminology

There are two scriptural beginnings to the history of criminology, each marking out a somewhat different fate for the study of crime and its control. The first dates from the mid-eighteenth century and tells of the revolutionary contribution of Enlightenment thinkers like Beccaria and Bentham in breaking with a previously 'archaic', 'barbaric', 'repressive'. or 'arbitrary' system of criminal law. This was the classical school.

For these reformers, legal philosophers and political theorists, the crime question was dominantly the punishment question. Their programme was to prevent punishment from being, in Beccaria's words, 'an act of violence of one or many against a private citizen'; instead it should be 'essentially public, prompt, necessary, the least possible in given circumstances, proportionate to the crime, dictated by laws'. Classicism presented a model of rationality: on the one side, the free 'sovereign' individual acting according to the dictates of reason and self interest; on the other, the limited liberal state, contracted to grant rights and liberties, to prescribe duties and to impose the fair and just punishment that must result from the knowing infliction of social harm.

This 'immaculate conception' account of the birth of classicism has been challenged by revisionist histories of law and the state. Dates, concepts and subjects have been reordered. Classicism is now to be understood in terms of the broader rationalization of crime control associated with the emergence of the free market and the new capitalist order. But the preoccupations of classicism – whether they appear in utilitarianism, Kantianism, liberalism, anarchism or indeed any political philosophy at all – have remained a constant thread in criminology. This is where the subject overlaps with politics, jurisprudence and the history and sociology of the law.

A century after classicism, though, criminology was to claim for itself another beginning and another set of influences. This was the positivist revolution – dated in comic-book intellectual history with the publication in 1876 of Lombroso's *Delinquent Man*. This was a 'positivism' which shared the more general social-scientific connotations of the term (the notion, that is, of the unity of the scientific method) but which acquired in criminology a more specific meaning. As David Matza suggests in his standard sociologies of criminological knowledge (Matza, 1964 and 1969), criminological positivism managed the astonishing feat of separating the study of crime from the contemplation of the state. Classicism was dismissed as mere metaphysical speculation. The new programme was to focus not on the crime (the act) but the criminal (the actor); it was to assume not rationality, free will and choice, but determinism (biological, psychic or social). At the centre of the criminological enterprise now was the notion of causality. No longer a sovereign being, subject to more or less the same pulls and pushes as his fellow citizens, the criminal was now a special person or member of a special class.

The whole of the last century of criminology can be understood as a series of creative, even brilliant, yet eventually repetitive variations on these late nineteenth-century themes. The particular image conjured up by Lombroso's criminal type – the atavistic genetic throwback – faded away, but the subsequent structure and logic of criminological explanation remained largely within the positivist paradigm. Whether the level of explanation was biological, psychological, sociological or a combination of these ('multifactorial' as some versions were dignified), the Holy Grail was a general causal theory: why do people commit crime? This quest gave the subject its collective self definition: 'the scientific study of the causes of crime'.

At each stage of this search, criminology strengthened its claim to exist as an autonomous, multidisciplinary subject. Somewhat like a parasite, criminology attached itself to its host subjects (notably, law, psychology, psychiatry and sociology) and drew from them methods, theories and academic credibility. At the same time – somewhat like a colonial power landing on new territory – each of these disciplines descended on the eternally fascinating subjects of crime and punishment and claimed them as its own. In this fashion, criminological theories and methods draw on Freudianism, behaviourism, the Chicago school of sociology, functionalism, anomie theory, interactionism, Marxism and much else. Each of these traces can be found in any current criminology textbook; it would be difficult to think of a major system of thought in the social sciences which would not be so represented.

All the time this positivist trajectory was being established, criminologists retained their interest in the question of punishment. If, in a sense, all criminology became positivist, then also all criminology remained concerned with 'classical' matters. But instead of speculation about the limits and nature of the criminal sanction, this side of criminology (sometimes called penology) took this sanction as politically given. True, there was (and still is) an important debate about whether the subject matter of criminology should be confined to conventional legal definitions of crime or shifted to include all forms of socially injurious conduct. The punishment question, however, was largely resolved in empirical terms: describing, analysing and evaluating the workings of the criminal justice system. Research findings were built up about the police, courts, prisons and various other agencies devoted to the prevention, control, deterrence or treatment of crime. This remains today the major part of the criminological enterprise.

Little of this, however, was 'pure' empiricism. The classical tradition was alive in another sense: modern criminologists became the heirs of the Enlightenment beliefs in rationality and progress. Their scientific task was carried along by a sense of faith: that the business of crime and delinquency control could be made not only more efficient, but also more humane. As reformers, advisers and consultants, criminologists claim for themselves not merely an autonomous body of knowledge, but the status of an applied science or even a profession.

It is this simultaneous claim to knowledge and power which links the two sides of criminology: causation and control. In positivism, this is an organic link: to know the cause is to know the right policy. Recently, however, both this link and its justification in the immaculate-conception history of positivism have been questioned. Histories of the emergence of the prison in the late eighteenth and early nineteenth century have shown the dependence of control systems on theories of rehabilitation, behaviour modification and anomie well before their supposed 'discovery' by scientific criminology. To critics like Foucault (1977) criminological knowledge has always been wholly utilitarian: an elaborate alibi to justify the exercise of power.

In the general climate of radical self-scrutiny which descended on the social sciences in the 1960s, criminology, too, began to fragment a little. There were three major attacks against the positivist hegemony – each in its peculiar and quite distinct way representing a return to classical questions.

(1) Labelling theory – a loose body of ideas derived from symbolic interactionism – restated some simple sociological truths about the relative nature of social rules and the normative boundaries which they mark. Crime was one form of that wider category of social action, deviance; criminology should be absorbed into the sociology of deviance. Beyond such concep-

tual and disciplinary boundary disputes, the very nature of the conventional quest for causality was regarded with scepticism. In addition to the standard behavioural question (why do some people do these bad things?) there were a series of definitional questions: Why are certain actions defined as rule breaking? How are these rules applied? And what are the consequences of this application? At times, these definitional questions seemed to attain causal primacy: it was not that control led to deviance, but deviance to control. Social control agencies – with their organized systems of labelling, stigmatizing and isolation – were meddlesome busybodies, making matters worse for society and its underdogs and outsiders. And behind the pretentions of scientific criminology was a simple-minded identification with middle-class values.

(2) This liberal criticism of liberalism was to become harder and tighter in the second onslaught on mainstream criminology. This came from what has been labelled variously as 'conflict', 'new', 'critical', 'radical', or 'Marxist' criminology. Drawing initially on some strands of labelling theory and conflict sociology and on the classical Marxist writing about law, class and the state, these theories moved even further from the agenda of positivism. Traditional causal questions were either dismissed or made subservient to the assumed criminogenic features of capitalism. Legalistic definitions were either expanded to include crimes of the powerful (those social harms which the state licences itself to commit), or else subjected to historicist and materialist enquiry. Labelling theory's wider notion of deviance was abandoned. Law was the only important mode of control, and the focus of criminology had to be shifted to the power of the state to criminalize certain actions rather than others. The analytical task was to construct a political economy of crime and its control. The normative task (that is, the solution to the crime problem) was to eliminate those economic and political systems of exploitation which gave rise to crime. The goal was a crime-free society, possible only under a different social order and impossible with the conceptual tools of bourgeois criminology.

(3) Another critique of the positivist enterprise came from a quite different theoretical and political direction. Impressed by

the apparent failure of the causal quest and of progressive policies such as treatment, rehabilitation and social reform, a loose coalition of intellectuals appeared under such rallying calls as 'realism', 'back to justice' and 'neo-classicism'. Some of them are neo-liberals – and theirs is a note of sad disenchantment with the ideas and policies of progressive criminology. Some of them are conservatives (or neo-conservatives) – and theirs is a note of satisfaction about the supposed failures of liberalism. Both these wings harken back to classical questions; the notion of justice (or 'just deserts') allows liberals to talk of rights, equity and fairness, while it allows conservatives to talk about law and order, social defence, deterrence and the protection of society. In neither case – but particularly for conservatives – is there much interest in traditional questions of causation.

Criminology is a subject with a complicated past and a polemical present. Most criminologists are employed at the core of the enterprise: busy either describing, classifying and explaining crime or else analysing, evaluating and advocating policy. At the periphery are various fascinating intellectual disputes about the subject's true content and justification. As Jock Young has recently shown (1981), the major schools of criminological thought are divided on quite basic issues: the image of human nature, the basis of social order, the nature and extent of crime, the relationship between theory and policy. And if we move out of the Anglo-American cultures in which contemporary criminology has mainly flourished, even more fundamental differences appear (a major – and belated – recent development has been the serious comparative analysis of crime and its control).

But whether positivist or neoclassical, radical or conservative, detached intellectuals or disguised policemen, criminologists confront the same questions. All this diversity is a manifestation of a single tension: crime is behaviour, but it is behaviour which the state is organized to punish.

Stanley Cohen
Hebrew University of Jerusalem

References

Foucault, M. (1977 [1975]), *Discipline and Punish*, London. (Original French edn, *Surveiller et punir*, Paris.)

Matza, D. (1964), *Delinquency and Drift*, New York.

Matza, D. (1969), *Becoming Deviant*, Englewood Cliffs, N.J.

Young, J. (1981), 'Thinking seriously about crime' in M. Fitzgerald *et al.* (eds), *Crime and Society*, London.

Further Reading

Christie, N. (1981), *Limits to Pain*, Oxford.

Sutherland, E. and Cressey, D. (1984), *Principles of Criminology*, Philadelphia.

Sykes, G. (1978), *Criminology*, New York.

See also: *penology*.

Demography

Demography is the analysis of population variables. It includes both methods and substantive results, in the fields of mortality, fertility, migration and resulting population numbers. Demographers collect data on population and its components of change, and construct models of population dynamics. They contribute to the wider field of population studies that relate population changes to non-demographic – social, economic, political, or other – factors. In so far as it reaches into population studies, demography is interdisciplinary: it includes elements of sociology, economics, biology, history, psychology and other fields. Its methods include parts of statistics and numerical analysis. Public health officials and actuaries have had their part in its development. Most demographers have professional knowledge of one or more of these disciplines.

Population variables are of two kinds – stock and flow. The important source of information on stock variables is national censuses, whose modern form goes back to the seventeenth century in Canada, Virginia, Sweden, and a few other places, and which are now carried out periodically in nearly all countries of the world. Among the cross-sectional information collected in censuses are age and sex distribution, labour force status and occupation, and birthplace.

The flow variables, the components of population change,

include birth and death registrations, initiated before the nineteenth century in Sweden and in Britain, and now routine in all industrial countries. Efforts to attain completeness are slowly making their way elsewhere. Migration statistics, collected at national frontiers, are less available and less reliable than birth and death registrations. Much additional information, including statistics of birth expectations, is collected by sample surveys.

These four sources (censuses, vital registration, migration records, and sample surveys) differ in the ease with which they may be instituted in a new country. Censuses and surveys are the easiest to initiate. With care the completeness of a census can reach 97 per cent or more. It is true that a large number of enumerators have to be mobilized (over 100,000 in the United States in 1980, over 5 million for China's 1982 census), but that is easier to arrange than the education of the entire population to the need for birth registration. The United States first attained 90 per cent complete birth records in the first quarter of the twentieth century; contemporary poor countries are unlikely to reach this level of completeness until their residents come to have need for birth certificates. Migration statistics will not be complete as long as many of those crossing international borders can conceal their movement from the immigration authorities. Apart from illegal crossings there is the difficulty that migrants are a small fraction of those passing national boundaries, the majority being tourists, persons travelling on business, commuters, and other non-immigrants. American sentiment that people ought to be able to leave their country of residence without hindrance is so strong that outgoing residents are not even stopped at the border to be asked whether they intend to return.

What especially characterizes demography are the quantitative and empirical methods that it uses. Once data in the form of censuses and registrations are available, demographic techniques are needed for valid comparisons among these. In today's terms, Mexico has a death rate of 6 per thousand, against France's 10; this does not signify that Mexico is healthier, but only that it has a younger age distribution as a result of recent high fertility; standardized comparison consists in finding what Mexico's death rate would be if it had France's age distribution but retained its own age-specific rates.

Partly for purposes of comparing mortality, but originally more for the conduct of pension and insurance business, life tables were developed in the Netherlands and in Great Britain during the course of the eighteenth century. The first technical problem that actuaries and demographers solved was how to go from statistics of deaths and of populations exposed to probabilities of dying. With data in finite age intervals the probabilities are not uniquely ascertainable, and a variety of methods for making life tables are currently in use.

The concerns of public health have led to the improvement of mortality statistics along many lines, including drawing up the International List of Causes of Death, now in its ninth revision. Unfortunately uniformity in applying the classification among physicians in all countries is still a distant goal. One object of the International List is the making of cause-related tables. The expectation of life in the United States at the time of writing is 75 years. If all deaths from cancer were eliminated this would be increased by about 3 years; elimination of all heart disease would increase the expectation by over 15 years.

Increasing populations have lower proportions of deaths than stationary populations. In effect the age distribution pivots on the middle ages as population growth slows. A sharp drop in the birth rate does not show its full effect immediately; births remain high as the large cohorts of children already born themselves come into childbearing; population growth thus has a kind of momentum. Replacement is the condition where each child is replaced in the next generation by just one child, so that ultimately the population is stationary. After birth rates fall to bare replacement a population can still increase by 60 per cent or more.

Births are not as sensitive to the pivoting of age distribution as are deaths, since the fertile ages, intermediate between childhood and old age, are a relatively constant fraction of a population. Fast-growing countries have more children below reproductive age but fewer old people. But births are greatly affected by a bulge of individuals in the reproductive ages; births in the United States have risen from about 3.1 million in the early

1970s to about 3.6 million currently, almost entirely due to change in age distribution as the large cohorts of the 1950s reach reproduction.

The pioneer in demographic methods and models was Alfred J. Lotka, who in a series of papers extending from 1907 to 1948 showed how to answer a number of questions that are still being asked. A central one was, 'How fast is a given population really growing, as determined by its age-specific birth and death rates in abstraction from its age distribution?' Any population that grows at a fixed rate for a long period develops a stable or fixed age distribution which Lotka showed how to calculate, and its increase when it reaches this stage is its intrinsic rate.

After a long period of neglect, Lotka's work came to be applied and further developed during the 1960s. It turned out that his approach could help the estimation of birth and death rates for countries of known age distribution but lacking adequate registration data.

The techniques of birth and death analysis have been carried over to migration, especially in the form of Markov chains that describe movement or transition between countries, and other areas, just as they describe transition between life and death. Such Markov chains are capable also of representing transitions between the married and single condition, among working, being unemployed, and leaving the labour force, and many other sets of states. A literature has now been built up in which changes of state, including migration, are represented by matrices, particularly easy to handle on a computer. The first extensive calculation of this kind was due to P. H. Leslie in the 1940s.

Communities living under 'primitive' conditions grow slowly; their high birth rates are offset by high deaths. The movement of a community from this condition to one of low birth and death rates as it modernizes is known as the demographic transition. Since the fall in the birth rate lags behind the fall in the death rate, very large increases can be recorded during the transition. Britain's population multiplied fourfold between the censuses of 1801 and 1901. Contemporary less-developed countries are increasing even more rapidly.

This effect of rising income is contrary to what has often been thought: that people want children and will have as many as they can afford – a view commonly attributed to Malthus, although Malthus's writings, after the first edition of his *Essay*, are much more subtle than this. Apparently at a certain point the causal mechanism flips over: for very poor people a rise of income results in a faster rate of increase; once people are better off a further rise slows their increase.

The modernization that brings down the birth rate affects subgroups of national populations at different times. In consequence the demographic transition shows itself as differential fertility: the rich, the urban, and the educated have for a time lower birth rates than the poor, the rural, and the illiterate in cross sections taken during the transition. Such differentials close up as incomes generally rise and income distributions narrow.

Some of the most puzzling questions concern the causal mechanisms that lie behind contemporary demographic changes. In what degree the fall of fertility is due to education, in what degree to income, cannot yet be answered in a way that applies to all countries. Less developed countries today have far greater rates of increase than did the countries of Europe when these were at a comparable stage of development. To what extent is the difference due to higher birth rates among presently poor countries than among the poor countries of the eighteenth century, and to what extent to lower death rates? Population models can provide answers to such questions; they show that birth differences are much more influential than death differences.

More difficult are questions on the direction of causation between two variables clearly related to each other. In most advanced countries more women are working outside the home now than 30 years ago, at a time when their husbands are for the most part earning higher real wages; at the same time their fertility has diminished, when the income of their spouses would permit them to have more children if they wanted. Is the fall in fertility the result of women seeking jobs, and so finding it inconvenient to have children, the wish to work being primary, or, on the other hand, do they no longer wish to have children and so take jobs to fill their time? A wealth of data exists, but the techniques for answering such questions are elusive. Again, are the present low birth rates a cohort or a period phenomenon? Do they result from present generations intending to finish up with fewer births, or are they a conjunctural phenomenon due, say, to the world recession of the past decade?

A task that demographers are often called on to perform is population forecasting. Professional demographers describe their statements on future population as projections, the working out of the consequences of a set of assumptions. Users believe that the assumptions are chosen by the demographers because they are realistic, and they accept the results as forecasts. Forecasting has gone through many styles, starting with extrapolation of population numbers by exponential, logistic, or other curves. More acceptable is extrapolating the components of population – birth, death, and migration – and assembling the population from the extrapolated values of these. Sampling to ascertain childbearing intentions of women has been extensively tried. Demographers have no illusions about the predictability of the long-term future, but on the other hand estimates made by those who have studied the past are more worthy of attention than the simple-minded extrapolations that are the alternative. Some numbers on future population are indispensable for virtually any kind of economic planning, whether by a corporation or a government.

The richness of demography today is in part due to the commitment of scholars from many disciplines. Actuaries developed much of the early theory, and statisticians and biostatisticians today add to their work the techniques of numerical analysis and determination of error. Sociologists see population change as both the cause and the result of major changes in social structures and attitudes; they study the increase of labour-force participation by women, of divorce, of single-person households, the apparently lessening importance of marriage, and the decline in fertility rates. Economists see fertility rising and falling as people try to maximize utility. Biologists employ an ecological framework relating human populations to the plant and animal populations among which they live and on which they depend. Psychologists have brought their survey and other tools to the study of preferences of parents for number and sex of children. Historians, in a particularly happy synthesis with demography, are putting to use the enormous amount of valuable data in parish and other records to gain new insights on what happened to birth and death rates during the past several centuries.

Nathan Keyfitz
Harvard University
and the International Institute
for Applied Systems Analysis

Further Reading
Coale, A. J. (1972), *The Growth and Structure of Human Populations: A Mathematical Investigation*, Princeton, N.J.
Keyfitz, N. (1977), *Applied Mathematical Demography*, New York.
Petersen, W. (1969), *Population*, 2nd edn, Toronto.
Pressat, R. (1969), *L'Analyse demographique*, 2nd edn, Paris.
Shryock, H. S. and Siegel, J. S. (1971), *The Methods and Materials of Demography*, 2 vols, Washington, D.C.

Development Studies

The concept of development, like its kindred notions of growth and modernization, has its historical and intellectual roots in the period of major social changes associated with the Industrial Revolution, or what Kumar (1978) has called the 'Great Transformation', when industrial and social change in Europe became synonymous with social progress. Throughout the century that followed, and often in the face of strong countercurrents challenging this simple orthodoxy (Kitching, 1982), development in the eyes of most people (experts and laymen alike) came to be identified with some kind of stage-by-stage movement towards more 'modern', technologically and economically 'advanced' forms of society such as the industrial nations.

By the mid-twentieth century the dominant image of social change was modernization, the process by which so-called traditional social structures are transformed into those of a more modern type, along the lines of what happened at an earlier stage in Europe (Smelser, 1963; Smith, 1973). Following the

Second World War, the industrial nations, and especially those with colonies or ex-colonies, were increasingly confronted with the economic and political problems of the poorer nations. This led to a greater awareness of the need to devise strategies aimed at alleviating the poverty and raising the living standards of the populations of these more 'backward' countries. Development policies therefore stressed the importance of expanding production and modernizing the physical and social infrastructure. Development aid, of course, often indirectly benefited the Western nations as much as it did the recipients.

This interest in modernization was quickly translated into a new field of study gradually calling itself development studies, an interdisciplinary grouping of subjects focusing upon the analysis and solution of problems of development, particularly those faced by the poorer, so-called developing countries. The types of disciplines brought together in this way included economics, geography, political science, public administration, sociology, and anthropology; and they were sometimes joined by more technical subjects, such as agronomy and irrigation or civil engineering. Despite their differences in scientific interest and specific policy recommendations, they all, in the 1950s and early 1960s, shared a general belief in the efficacy of Western technological, economic and managerial practice for solving development problems. Even the anthropologists, whose professional expertise rested upon the elucidation of non-Western modes of behaviour and rationality, accepted, explicitly or implicitly, the modernization model when they sought to identify sociocultural obstacles or facilitating factors that might block or promote technological and economic change (Foster, 1962; Long, 1977).

By the mid-1960s, the stage was set for the establishment of a number of departments and special institutions which would provide the main scientific arena within which relevant development issues would be debated and investigated from both a theoretical and policy point of view. For example, the Institute of Development Studies at Sussex was founded in 1966, and the Overseas Development Group (later to form part of the School of Development Studies) at the University of East Anglia in the following year. However, almost as soon as development studies, with much promise, gained a foothold in academia, so it entered a period of growing uncertainty in development-policy thinking and in existing theories of development and social change (Myrdal, 1968; Seers, 1969). The credibility of simple growth and modernization models was shaken by the evident high environmental and human costs of such policies and by the widening gap in per capita incomes between the rich and poor nations and between classes within the developing countries.

Hence, by the late 1960s and early 1970s, the field had become a rather untidy collection of competing theoretical paradigms and policy objectives. This situation resulted in part from the devastating critiques of modernization theory mounted by the 'dependency' and 'underdevelopment' writers (Frank, 1967; Dos Santos, 1973) who argued that it was impossible to understand the processes and problems of development without locating them within the wider sociohistorical context of the expansion of mercantile and industrial capitalism to the poorer, more 'peripheral', countries. They sought to demonstrate that the fundamental problems facing the developing countries were a consequence of the emergence of this international system of economic and political domination. Genuine solutions to the problems of 'underdevelopment', then, would only come when the basic social contradictions inherent in structures of dependency were resolved 'in favour of the popular forces' (Salinas, 1977). At the same time, certain 'liberal' planners injected into the discussions of policy and strategy questions of income redistribution, equity and participation. Many development specialists now argued that the transfer of technology and organizational structures, together with economic growth strategies, were inadequate for tackling the fundamental problems of poor economic performance coupled with maldistribution of income and resources (Chenery et al., 1974).

These radical and liberal criticisms of modernization theory and policy destroyed the earlier coherence of development studies. By the 1980s, we find no real consensus about the major analytical issues to be explored, nor how to go about solving practical problems of development. A healthy scepticism prevails about the idea of progressive development, a scepticism which is reinforced by the global ecological and military threat and by the world economic recession. Development can no longer be regarded as a relatively self-generating process set off by the implantation of modern technology and values. There is also, nowadays, a more explicit awareness of the essentially political and ideological nature of development: formulating goals and means for societal change (whether from the point of view of the central planner or citizen) necessarily entails value commitments and choice. Development studies therefore can no longer be monopolized by economic, technological and administrative types of argument but must take serious account of opposing ethical, political and cultural evaluations.

Development, then, is a concept with different implications depending upon the point of view of the user. It is possible, because of its association with ideas of developmentalism and evolutionist thought, that it may be replaced by some other concept (Nisbet, 1970). However, the kind of problematic it deals with – namely the analysis of societies at critical junctures of social transition – will remain an important area for enquiry, reflection and social action. Development studies will continue to play a role in providing an important arena within which this debate can take place.

Development studies remains torn between, on the one hand, relatively detached (though possibly policy-relevant) scientific analysis and, on the other hand, a commitment to engaging in the practical business of solving concrete problems. It also faces the problem of bringing together disciplines whose theoretical interests, methodologies, epistemologies, and scientific milieux are strikingly different. It frequently gives insufficient emphasis to understanding what different development processes mean to individuals in the pursuit of their everyday lives: there is a tendency to concentrate upon macrostructural aspects to the neglect of microprocesses that provide important insights into the changing human condition in the contemporary world.

Norman Long
Agricultural University, Wageningen

References

Chenery, H. *et al.* (1974), *Redistribution with Growth*, London.

Dos Santos, T. (1973), 'The crisis of development theory and the problem of dependence in Latin America', in H. Bernstein (ed.), *Underdevelopment and Development*, Harmondsworth.

Frank, A. G. (1969), 'Sociology of underdevelopment and underdevelopment of sociology', in *Latin America*: *Underdevelopment or Revolution*, New York.

Foster, G. M. (1962), *Traditional Cultures and the Impact of Technological Change*, New York.

Kitching, G. (1982), *Development and Underdevelopment in Historical Perspective. Populism, Nationalism and Industrialization*, London.

Kumar, K. (1978), *Prophecy and Progress*, London.

Long, N. (1977), *An Introduction to the Sociology of Rural Development*, London.

Myrdal, G. (1968), *Asian Drama*: *An Inquiry into the Poverty of Nations*, 3 vols, New York.

Nisbet, R. A. (1970), *Social Change and History*: *Aspects of the Western Theory of Development*, London.

Salinas, P. W. (1977), 'A paradigmatic view of development strategies', *Cornell Sociology Bulletin Series*, 89.

Seers, D. (1969), 'The meaning of development' in D. Lehmann (ed.), *Development Theory*: *Four Critical Studies*, London.

Smelser, N. J. (1963), 'Mechanisms of change and adjustments to change', in B. F. Hoselitz and W. E. Moore (eds), *Industrialization and Society*, The Hague.

Smith, A. D. (1973), *The Concept of Social Change: A Functionalist Theory of Social Change*, London.

Economics

The Ancient Greeks who gave to us the name of this subject lacked the concept of what we now call economics. *Oeconomicus* would be 'Household management' in modern English, the domain of Mrs Beeton rather than J. S. Mill. Of course what we would now recognize as economic questions are certainly ancient, but such questions and particular answers to them amount to less than the kind of knowledge that in Schumpeter's elegant description, '. . . has been the object of conscious efforts to improve it'. In that sense, which is of a science in the broad and generous use of that term, economics is a young discipline. The term now usually employed is even younger than the modern form of the subject itself. Earlier writers described themselves as '*political economists*'. Too much can be and has been made of this distinction. In an age in which the educated knew Greek, it was pertinent to remind the reader what the term did not mean. However, any terminological distinction between economics and political economy must be questioned. The unadorned 'economic' had long been in use, and was frequently employed by Marx, while 'political economy' has continued in use into the twentieth century and has enjoyed something of a revival lately from writers wishing to advertise that their work has not treated its subject in isolation from the political system.

It is customary to associate the beginning of modern economics with the publication of Adam Smith's *The Wealth of Nations*. As this attribution sets aside more than a thousand years of economic writing, ancient, Christian and Islamic, it calls for justification. However, a study of the earlier literature will not leave the reader long in doubt concerning the claim that a radical shift of method had taken place. What we recognize in Adam Smith's work, and what sets it apart from that which had gone before, is the characteristic imprint of the eighteenth century in which the Grand Idea finds its expression in the language of exact scholarship. We recognize the same spirit in reading Gibbon's *History*.

Adam Smith's writing represents the source of a stream which runs to the present day. This is true of modern economics in general but more particularly of a style of approaching the subject which was his own. Its distinguishing characteristic is its limited use of the method of simplification and abstraction. The strengths of the method are obvious, but experience has revealed its weaknesses. Description needs a strong guiding principle if it is not to deteriorate into the unenlightening elaboration of a mass of incoherent fact. One could illustrate this point from *The Wealth of Nations* itself, where illustrations are sometimes developed to the point of tedium, but that would do less than justice to a writer whose genius generally enabled him to surmount this problem. Better illustrations of the point might be provided from much later work by the Institutionalist School which made its influence felt in Germany and in the United States in the late nineteenth and early twentieth centuries.

A problem inherent in Adam Smith's method is that it provides no guidance concerning the resolution of disagreements. The arguments make use of persuasive reasoning and examples to back them up. If the number and quality of these is overwhelming there will clearly be no difficulty, but such cannot always be the case, and as economics grew the triumph of ideas by acclamation was far from being the rule. What was required were more refined methods of economic reasoning and more powerful methods of evaluating the kinds of claim to which that reasoning gave rise. The first development preceded the second but they were ultimately seen to be closely related.

The method of studying economic questions by means of simplification and abstraction was developed, and even taken to extremes, by David Ricardo. So important was his innovation of method that writers for two generations acknowledged his influence even when they propounded conclusions quite contrary to his own. The kind of abstraction that Ricardo developed took the form of what today would be called an 'economic model'. This consists in a formal, more or less simple, invented economy which is claimed to illustrate a point or to capture the essence of the true, and of course more complicated, economy of real life. One illustration would be a numerical example. Another would be the stylized story, such as the Tribe of Hunters, by means of which Adam Smith illustrated his theory of the division of labour. The numbers of an example are not taken by their inventor to be the values of real life, while stories can be taken to be schematic accounts of true history. For the present purpose, however, this distinction is less important than the fact that both are examples of model building.

Ricardo was not the first or the only economist to employ a model in his work. What makes him stand out is that model-building was not a method to which he had occasional recourse: it was his typical and usual method of reasoning. Moreover, an examination of his arguments will show that the model is essential to the argument; it is not there to add colour or verisimilitude. Thus Ricardo's work sometimes reveals an almost mathematical quality, being concerned with the development of the logical implications of certain postulates. The apparent power and objectivity of this kind of reasoning could not fail to impress those who came to it anew.

From the beginning of the modern subject, then, certain important distinctions are already apparent, notably that between realism and abstraction, and between description and model building. The method of economics for another hundred years was to be very largely historical, historical, that is, in the sense that the kind of evidence employed and the manner in which it was made use of were both the same as would characterize historical enquiry. Ricardo used invented numbers, partly because his argument was general and not dependent upon the particular values selected, but also because the availability of statistics in his time was extremely limited and haphazard. But it would be wrong to suppose that this made economics a nonempirical subject. Malthus, for example, was certainly influenced by the observation that population was growing at an unprecedented rate in the England of his time, and the correctness of that observation cannot be questioned. He estimated that population unchecked by restraints would double every 25 years, which corresponds to an annual rate of increase of 2.8 per cent per annum. The latter estimate has stood up well for a population which is balanced in age composition at the start and then accelerates in its growth.

The work of Petty in gathering statistics is frequently cited, but it stands out more for being pioneering than for being representative. It was government that was to collect statistics, and government was still exceedingly small by later standards. A growing science normally demands measurement, if not experiment, as a young child calls for food. Economics, however, was nourished for a long time by such observations as were available to the informed citizen and chiefly by its own ideas. In this respect it resembled Greek science or modern physics when the latter has outreached the possibility of experiment. Most of all, it resembled philosophy to which its close affinity was recorded in the term 'moral sciences' for long in use in the ancient universities of Britain. One could characterize the 150 years and beyond following the publication of *The Wealth of Nations* as having been preoccupied with working out the logical implications of certain assumptions about economic reality, while at the same time those assumptions themselves were in the process of being changed and influenced by far-reaching alterations in economic institutions. This was no small task. The logical implications of economic assumptions can be rich and complex, and they readily give rise to controversy. Some have attributed these problems to the inherent difficulty of the subject, others to the powerful ideological content of the questions involved – both are partly correct.

The difficulties of economic theory do not consist simply of the intellectual demands that it makes, which do not compare with those of physics or pure mathematics. It is rather that economics requires a body of analytical tools and a technique of reasoning without which even simple questions cannot be accurately answered. The uninitiated constantly demonstrate the truth of that claim. However, the development of these tools and methods took some considerable time. One need only compare the writings of John Stuart Mill with those of some indifferent economist of the turn of the century to see what a difference the accumulation of technique had made. In Mill we see one of the finest intellects of the nineteenth century struggling to cut his way through a jungle. In the plain economist of the later years we would see an unskilled craftsman no doubt, but one working with what by then had become a thoroughly useful box of tools. There are even tasks for which the latter would be better employed.

The ideological problem is ever present. Economists have sometimes seen it as a distraction, as a diversion from the important questions on which economics could speak, but there is no justification for such a simple separation. Through experience and through the application of the same apparatus that he uses to resolve other matters, the economist is uniquely placed to say useful things about the type of political conflict which is concerned with the division of economic goods. That does not mean, of course, that he should play God, or pretend to more expertise than he has, but equally he cannot push such questions aside and say that because they are not all to do with him, they are therefore not at all to do with him.

The problem is naturally not peculiar to economics. It arises in any field in which the expert must address himself to issues concerning which people, including the practitioners themselves, their students, their employers and others, have strong feelings. Certain principles are obvious if economics is not to be sucked into the political whirlpool. The pursuit of objectivity and scholarly integrity clearly belong among them. These principles are under attack from two sides. On the one side will be some who will argue that there is no detachment, no standing apart, and that science should serve progressive forces in society, however those may be defined at the time. On the other side will be those who claim to accept these principles, only to discredit them by advancing under the guise of the objective and the detached what is patently the ideological.

Economics has been assaulted to its foundations during its still-short history by the claim that its doctrines are no more than 'false ideology'. Marx attacked what he called 'bourgeois political economy' as mere apologetics for the existing social order. He said the most wounding thing that can be said about a science – that his opponents were concerned only with the superficial, the surface appearance of things. The importance of Marx's contribution will ultimately be judged by what he put in the place of the economics which he attacked, and not by the attacks as such, memorable though their invective may be to anyone who has read them. It was Marx's political activity, and his political writing, that changed the world, as indeed they did, and not his economic theory. This is to insist on making a distinction to which the master would have strongly objected, but make it we must. Within the narrow field of economic theory he retains his followers to the present day, but Marxist economics, recent revivals notwithstanding, remains a backwater and a curiosum beside mainstream economics. The fact that it has failed to propose an alternative system to orthodoxy with anything like the same reach and the same richness, and probably could not as it is formulated, may alone explain this fact.

The last third of the nineteenth century witnesses a huge burgeoning of economic theory and the beginnings of systematic empirical investigation. The theoretical movement has been unhappily named 'neo-classical'. It was not 'neo' if that prefix means a revival of an earlier period, and it is difficult to see what meaning of the term 'classical' would usefully connect it with the early writers. Naturally, however, no movement is unconnected with the past. The use of abstraction and model-building was now freely employed, sometimes again to excess, but more fruitfully, generally speaking, than ever before. Most importantly, perhaps, the ultimately inescapable, mathematical character of economic reasoning was becoming clear. Diagrams were employed, not without resistance at first, and the concept of 'elasticity of demand' made its appearance. The 'marginalism' sometimes taken to characterize the period was more the result of the new approach than its generator. It may nevertheless be the most powerful single organizing principle that economics has yet seen.

These developments which established economics as we know it today began to change the appearance of the discipline. It came to stand apart from its neighbouring fields, not in every respect or in every part of the field to be sure, but noticeably all the same. Its employment of mathematics in particular, or mathematical-like reasoning, sometimes made it resemble physics more than it resembled law, philosophy, politics, history or sociology. On closer examination, however, economics did not seem to resemble any other discipline at all closely. The quantification of its theoretical relations, for example, without which a 'natural' science was not counted as having established itself, was still at a primitive stage of development. Still more, it was far from clear that the theoretical relationships of economics would ever attain to the status of those of physics or chemistry. The latter had arrived at powerful 'laws' which seemed to hold without exception and to a degree of approximation defined by the resolving power of the measuring instruments. True amendments to these laws were later shown to be necessary, but they were corrections and often unimportant ones. In economics few 'laws' worth stating could be expected to hold except as tendencies. Science certainly could investigate weak effects or tendencies but it liked to have a great deal of preferably reliable data to undertake this task. But reliable data was in short supply and often small in quantity.

Had economists reached the point at which they demanded a testable implication of every new theory, they would undoubtedly have become completely discouraged by the formidable difficulties which confront the testing of economic hypotheses. Fortunately, perhaps, they have not yet arrived at that point. Many economic models are seen as following in the tradition established by Ricardo and illustrated by his model of comparative advantage. They are not designed to produce a hypothesis to be compared with the observation of reality, so much as they aim to explore the implications of making a set of assumptions, simplified by intention but equally meant to be realistic enough to capture something of reality. The ultimate aim of such an exercise is to influence the way in which people think about the world. There are so many examples of what such reasoning might be doing that it is not easy to find an instance that stands for more than its own type. However, the following case is certainly encountered rather frequently. An economist, drawing on observation formal or informal, says to himself: 'I think that people behave in such and such a way. What would follow if I was right in that belief?'

Why should the economist worry about the subsidiary question, which may very well involve him in a lot of work? The answer is that it is a check on the reasonableness of his initial assumption. It is no different in kind, though surely less monumental in import, than Newton asking himself what would happen if bodies moved in straight lines at constant velocity unless acted upon by a force. Interesting assumptions need to have their plausibility tested in a throughgoing manner. Otherwise people who believe that the wealth of a nation is measured by its balance of payments surplus have too much influence.

Economic theory in the twentieth century has been altered by a major intellectual revolution, associated with the name of Keynes, of which more will be said below. However, the effect of the Keynesian revolution, important though it has been, should not be allowed to detract from certain advances which have gone on more or less continually, and not directly influenced by the new ways of thinking. Nineteenth-century economic theory was based on abstraction and on bringing economic concepts to bear on practical questions. These tendencies were continued in the twentieth century which has witnessed some of the greatest successes of formalization and generalization which the subject has known, at the same time as it has seen a growing interest in bringing economic theory to bear directly on important real matters. In an age in which econometrics was increasingly available as a research tool, the old presumptions about realism and unrealism have sometimes been upset. Mathematically rich models have sometimes, though not always, lent themselves better to empirical implementation than have homely and realistic ones. An important example of this is the new mathematical method of linear programming which has made complex maximization problems, even of large size, highly soluble.

Nineteenth-century economic theory borrowed from ethics the notion of 'utility' as measuring or representing the level of satisfaction or well-being of the household or consumer. It no doubt struck the students of the time as reasonable and sensible, as did Marshall's assumption that the marginal utility of income would be approximately constant, and it was useful in deriving simply the so-called 'law of demand'. Eventually this was too out of touch with reality for the twentieth-century taste, which had become more positivistic. How was utility to be measured? The outcome of these doubts was the realization that utility could only be an ordinal quantity, that this was all that was required to derive the consumer's behaviour, and the eventual understanding of income and substitution effects in a general framework.

The implication of this change of view did not stop with demand theory. Economic policy, or welfare economics, had previously been conceived as an application of utilitarian principles to economic questions. The application concerned, however, was a quantitative one; it supposed the measurability of utility. If that was now called into question, how were policy recommendations to be justified? A radical sceptical view said that they could only be justified as value judgements, that any claimed scientific basis to economic recommendations was unfounded. A more constructive approach set out to delineate which properties a recommendation would have to fulfil so as not to require value judgements for its validation. It was not so much that many interesting recommendations could be value-free that made this exercise of importance; rather the whole investigation greatly clarified how value judgements enter into economic reasoning and for the first time put welfare economics on a sound basis.

The earlier welfare economics of the nineteenth century was now seen to be, to a great extent, the economics of efficiency. The problem of distribution, of equity, one could say, had been treated as something separate, independent of efficiency. One of the major advances of the twentieth century, particularly the period following the Second World War, has been the development of a theory of economic policy, much closer to reality in its conception and in its method than traditional welfare economics. Efficiency has not been shown to be an irrelevant consideration – far from it – but the role that efficiency plays in a system constrained by perhaps a bad distribution of incomes, or constrained to depart from efficiency in certain directions, has been clarified. Economic policy has become the art of maximizing the possible, second-best optimization in the jargon of today's economics.

A settled interpretation and assessment of the contribution of Keynes is still elusive nearly fifty years after the publication of his great work, *The General Theory*. That this should be so is a measure partly of problems and obscurities in that work, and partly of the value which has been conceded to its ideas even by those who have undertaken to attack them. Only recently have wholehearted rejections arisen in the main countries of economic research, rejections not based simply on ideological revulsion. Many earlier critiques, notably that associated with Milton Friedman's monetarism, were more revisionist than completely counter to Keynes's method as well as to his conclusions. One reason is that Keynes posed some sharp and important questions to the then orthodoxy which it was at the time wholly unable to answer. To these questions Keynes provided answers. There are no more potent ingredients for an intellectual revolution and its rapid dissemination.

Keynesian ideas found their expression in a new field, macroeconomics. This division of economic theory into separate and largely non-communicating sectors was readily accepted at the time but was later felt to be unhealthy. While setting itself apart from much existing theory, the new ideas very easily connected with applied economics and econometrics, and the new macroeconomics was an applied subject from the outset. Economic forecasting models were constructed, sometimes of huge scale, and governments and private users began to pay for their results. Just as it was applied in spirit, so was the new theory interventionist in outlook. According to Keynesian doctrine a wise government could stabilize the economy close to full employment and avoid fluctuations and inflation. Later the numerous problems associated with such a programme became apparent. From early optimism there has been a pessimistic reaction in which stress has been laid on the powerlessness of governments to have any useful influence in a world whose individual actors have become more sophisticated and far-seeing. It is too early yet to forecast where these latest ideas themselves will lead, but one may note a development which is unlikely to be harmful in the end. The apparently well-established division between macroeconomics and microeconomics is breaking down. On the one hand, macro-theorists are no longer willing to accept that agents act in not very intelligent rule-of-thumb ways when it comes to determining employment and wages and asset prices, or assessing the influence of government policies on their futures, while attributing considerable sophistication to those agents when discussing price determination in individual markets. On the other hand, microeconomic theorists are more interested in building models of the price rigidities and rationing that sometimes seem to characterize markets, rather than dismissing such cases as freaks.

Meanwhile, at the practical level, economists are in a state of intellectual ferment, which manifests itself to the outsider as chaotic disunity, concerning fundamental questions of macroeconomic management. On the basic question of the consequences of a large government deficit, for example, reputable spokesmen can be found to claim that the deficit as such is unimportant, that only the supply-side, somehow defined, matters; that the deficit matters only if translated to excessive growth in the money supply; or that the deficit is expansionary, if not perhaps in the most healthy manner. The world and the profession must derive what comfort it can from the fact that such widespread disagreements tend to resolve themselves, usually as the result of the accumulation of new evidence, but sometimes of new ideas as well. Modern economics has huge resources in its techniques and in its methods of evaluating empirical evidence. These should eventually enable it to emerge from the present 'crisis of confidence' stronger and in better shape. If, as seems likely, the public never quite recovers an excessive confidence which it may have placed in the pronouncements of economists, there will be no harm in that.

Economics began as a British subject and remained so for many years. Today it is an international discipline including scholars from most countries of the world and from all regions. Its chief centre is in the US, and papers originating from there account for a sizeable proportion of those appearing in the major journals. Economists everywhere advise governments and private institutions, and they frequently write in newspapers and appear on the radio and on television. Another important development, particularly since the Second World War, has been the use of economics in new and unexpected fields. Thus the economics of medicine, to cite one example, has now become a specialism with its own practitioners and its own journals. Through optional courses at universities, more people now have some exposure to economics than ever before. While co-operating well with workers from other disciplines in applied work, economists still stand apart when it comes to theory, and fruitful cross-disciplinary co-operation, while it happens, is not at all common. A growing tendency towards specialization within the field has been evident. Few scholars are economists and econometricians, for example, and many define their field of interest surprisingly narrowly. In part this state of affairs is imposed by the huge amount of literature now appearing in every field which demands the attention of the serious worker. While it would be rash to predict the future of the subject very far ahead, it is interesting to note that the loss of an excessive confidence in economists' abilities to pronounce the truth has not been accompanied by a loss of interest in employing them. Although academic openings in the 1980s compare unfavourably with the rich possibilities of the 1960s, many other employment opportunities continue to attract economists.

Christopher Bliss
University of Oxford

Further Reading

Blaug, M. (1980), *The Methodology of Economics, or How Economists Explain*, Cambridge.

Friedman, M. (1969), *The Optimal Quantity of Money and Other Essays*, Chicago.

Keynes, J. M. (1931), *Essays in Persuasion*, London.

Keynes, J. M. (1936), *The General Theory of Employment, Interest and Money*, London.

Koopmans, T. C. (1957), *Three Essays on the State of Economic Science*, New York.

Little, I. M. D. (1982), *Economic Development: Theory, Politics and International Relations*, New York.

Luce, R. D. and Riaffa, H. (1967), *Games and Decisions*, New York.

Meade, J. E. (1975), *The Intelligent Radical's Guide to Economic Policy: The Mixed Economy*, London.

Robinson, J. (1966), *An Essay on Marxian Economics*, London.

Samuelson, P. A. (1958), *Economics: An Introductory Analysis*, 4th edn, New York.

Schumpeter, J. S. (1952), *Ten Great Economists*, London.

Schumpeter, J. S. (1954), *History of Economic Analysis*, Oxford.

Sen, A. K. (1982), *Choice, Welfare and Measurement*, Oxford.

Shackle, G. L. S. (1967), *The Years of High Theory*, Cambridge.

Education

Although recently dominated by psychology, the field of educational research was once largely restricted to the general discipline of philosophy. Today other disciplines such as anthropology, economics, political science and sociology have been increasingly prominent.

The status of education as an applied field makes it difficult to identify any specific method or conceptual domain which would single it out from other fields. For most scholars and researchers, however, the study of education has meant investigating activities related to learning, usually within the context of the schools. The problems studied and the method employed vary a great deal, depending largely on the training and background of the researchers. However, in contrast to the earlier, philosophical, studies which focused on the *aims* of education, the prominence of the behavioural and social sciences has signalled a shift in concern to questions of *means*.

As an applied field of study, the problems investigated in the area of education tend to follow closely the concerns articulated by leaders in business, government and the media. For example, in the late 1950s and early 1960s when American political leaders were primarily concerned with the space race with the Soviet Union and the so-called missile gap, a series of reports by the well-known educator, James B. Conant (1959) focused on the lagging academic quality of education in the United States. Educational research in that country then turned towards developing curriculum units, teaching strategies, school procedure and design that would produce more scientists and engineers. In this period, for example, the 'New Math' flourished, and influential educators, such as the psychologist Jerome Bruner, proposed the teaching of science, mathematics and other academic programmes in the lower grades (Bruner, 1960).

In the mid-1960s, social pressure built up over the civil rights issue, and the concern of much of the educational research community again shifted towards issues related to equality of opportunity. The work of Jean Piaget provided the intellectual basis for curriculum researchers in Britain and the US who argued for relaxing the structure of the curriculum by allowing more room for the individual expression of interests. Some opposed these moves because they were too permissive, but the intention was to create a fruitful interaction between the developmental patterns found among children and the structure and pacing of curriculum knowledge. However, the apparently reduced emphasis on a hierarchy of knowledge (with science, maths and other college preparatory subjects at the top and vocational subjects at the bottom), and the renewed recognition of the importance of the interest of the individual child as a major factor in the learning process, appeared to be consistent with the wider concern for equality of opportunity.

Equality has continued to be a major issue in educational research and debate in a number of different areas. For example, James Coleman's (1968) analysis of data from thousands of American schools explored the extent to which different variables affect school achievement across racial lines. His finding that the class and racial characteristics of the student body had an important influence on individual achievement was rapidly used as intellectual support for the busing of children across racially distinct neighbourhoods in an effort to achieve greater racial balance. At the same time other studies explored the effectiveness of pre-school programmes in raising the achievement levels of Blacks and other children from lower socio-economic classes.

At the time that educational research was exploring the pedagogical factors involved in maintaining inequality, the traditional meaning of equality of opportunity was first challenged. Coleman (1973), in an important article on equality of educational opportunity, suggested that the extent to which this ideal has been realized should be measured not in terms of equality of input – the resources spent on different children – but rather in terms of equality of results – whether or not the pattern of achievement is similar among different racial groups and minorities. Had this conception of equal opportunity been widely accepted, it would have significantly changed the rules of the game. This proposal would thus have mandated the allocation of unequal resources in some cases in order to achieve equal results.

Coleman's proposed conception was never fully accepted (Coleman, himself, only offered it tentatively). However, educational policy makers and politicians in the US did begin to assign federal resources to special groups, such as the handicapped, Blacks, women and non-native speakers of English;

legal efforts were increased to redress racial imbalance in schools; and affirmative action programmes tried to increase the opportunities for minority students and women in universities and professional schools.

Even prior to Coleman's attempt to redefine the concept of equal opportunity, there had been other challenges to compensatory policies. The most publicized was an article in 1969 by Arthur Jensen which claimed that most compensatory programmes had failed, and therefore children of different intellectual ability should be taught differently. Children with high IQ scores, Jensen argued, should be taught conceptually by problem-solving methods. Children with low IQ scores should be taught through associative or rote methods. Jensen's article was controversial because of three propositions. These were: IQ tests measure intelligence; in a population intelligence is eighty percent explained by genetic factors; and Blacks as a population score on the average consistently lower than Whites on both standard IQ tests and culture-fair tests. Jensen concluded that environmental enrichment programmes were severely limited in their ability to raise IQ scores, and that educators would better spend their time and resources identifying conceptual and associative learners and teaching them through the methods appropriate to their learning style. Jensen himself believed that when IQ tests were appropriately refined to identify the two types of learners, Blacks and other minority students would be more fairly treated. He also believed that teaching style would become more consistent with learning style and that conceptual learners from these groups would be less likely to fall victim to the prejudicial judgement of a few teachers. However, he also strongly implied that because of genetic factors Blacks would continue to achieve at a lower rate than Whites.

An uproar followed the publication of Jensen's article. The twin studies on which he had built much of his case for the prominence of genetic over environmental factors were discredited. Questions were raised about the whole concept of measurement as applied to intelligence and about the appropriateness of such tests for culturally distinct, minority children. In addition, Jensen's argument traded on the ambiguity of the claim that 'IQ tests measure intelligence'. The claim could mean that a conceptual limit exists beyond which an individual cannot reach and an IQ test measures it, or it could mean that IQ tests measure the speed at which different individuals learn. This ambiguity is especially significant when it is understood that Jensen's view of associative and conceptual learning is inaccurate in at least one important respect. He believes that children can learn essentially the same basic material either through associative or conceptual methods, depending upon the learning style of the child. But, in fact, the children would be learning the same skills in only the most superficial sense. They might be learning how to translate symbols on a page into oral sounds, or learning to repeat number facts, thus giving the *appearance* of learning the same thing. However, each group also would be learning something about learning. One group would be learning that learning is a rote affair, while the other would be learning that it is essentially a conceptual and problem-solving activity. Jensen's article provides no evidence to support the view that such learning styles were irreversible, even though his own proposal seemed to rest upon this assumption.

The debate over Jensen's article was significant for a number of reasons. One of these went to the very heart of the question of equality of opportunity. For if equality of opportunity means that everyone is to be given the same chance, then presumably ability differences should be the sole determinant of outcomes. However, if the major measure of ability, that is, IQ tests, is put into question, so too is the justification for different outcomes.

Some scholars, while dismissing the significance of IQ tests, continued to justify differential outcomes and to argue against 'extraordinary' measures to achieve educational equality. These arguments were often based on the view that governmental intervention creates unrealistic expectations and increases frustration and, possibly, violence. Environmental factors were considered important, but the most significant aspect of environment, the habits, discipline and foresight developed through class culture, were thought extremely difficult to change. Because these studies took 'class-culture' and the habits and attitudes associated with it as an independent variable, they failed to examine the relationship between a student's habits, attitudes and achievement, and the work structures that were available to children from certain social classes.

This enlarged focus came only with a renewed interest in Marxist scholarship and, especially, with the work of two economists, Bowles and Gintis (Bowles and Gintis, 1976). Their study concluded that schooling provided very little mobility, even when research controlled for IQ scores, and that schools largely served to reproduce and legitimize the personality characteristics required by the hierarchical relations found in advanced capitalistic countries.

The findings of Bowles and Gintis were challenged on a number of methodological grounds. However, one of the more significant effects of their work for educational scholarship was to reintroduce a Marxist perspective into the study of education in the US. This perspective continued a tradition that was already established in England, Western Europe, Australia, and in a number of Third-World countries. In effect Marxists have shifted some of the focus of educational research from the individual to the larger social, historical, cultural and political context of schooling (Apple, 1982).

There is no uniform Marxist perspective. For example, the Brazilian educator, Paulo Freire, draws on Marxist literature for many of his insights, but he also draws on French existentialism, phenomenology, and upon Christian theology (Freire, 1973). Some analysts have adopted a structural approach and have examined the limits placed on the educational system by a hierarchical mode of production. Others, utilizing an ethnographic methodology, have explored the way in which a critical working-class consciousness is both developed and blunted in schools. There have been insightful studies on the reproduction of classroom knowledge for different social classes, on the production of educational materials and texts, and on the dilemmas created by radical educational thought for teacher education (Apple, 1982; Giroux, 1981).

While Marxist-oriented research represents a significant redefinition of the problem of education, it has remained a largely critical movement which only occasionally penetrates mainstream thinking about education. When inequality was a major issue for the educational community and the wider public, Marxism was able to gain a reasonable hearing. However, as unemployment rates in the United States, Britain and Western Europe hit post-depression records, educational policy makers steered the agenda away from the issue of equality and towards the educational needs of the 'high technology revolution'. Educational research is following suit as more concern is expressed about developing 'computer literacy', and about increasing the pool from which future scientists and engineers can be drawn. There have been calls to tighten up the curriculum, increase standards for admission into and matriculation out of higher education, and to reduce the 'frills' in the public schools. These concerns seem to signal a return to the era dominated by Conant. However, the applied nature of educational research and its inability to develop a reasonably independent research programme makes any prediction about the future direction of educational scholarship dependent upon uncertain political and economic developments.

This point raises a deeper issue about the nature of educational research and its potential for developing a research programme that involves more than simply the application of methods drawn from other disciplines to problems as they are defined by immediate political forces. The last attempt to provide an independent focus for the study of education was developed by the American philosopher, John Dewey. Since Dewey, educational philosophy has taken a different turn, one that emphasizes the anaylsis of concepts and linguistic clarity. Yet the deeper questions about education involve the understanding of intergenerational continuity and change and the normative concerns that guide the process of social and cultural reproduction. While little systematic effort has been undertaken to explore the process and patterns of social identity, it is possible to specify some of the factors that such a research programme would involve. They would include an analysis of the kind of knowledge that is prized by a given society, the institutional arrangements to protect and carry on such knowledge, the methods used to identify and train those who will bear that knowledge in the future, and the way in which knowledge is distributed among different groups in the society. Such a programme would maintain the interdisciplinary character of educational studies but would provide a focus that has been lacking. It would also provide a critical point from which to appraise present educational practice.

Walter Feinberg
University of Illinois
Champaign-Urbana

References

Apple, M. (1982), *Education and Power*, London.

Bowles, S. and Gintis, H. (1976), *Schooling in Capitalist America: Educational Reform and the Contradictions of Economic Life*, New York.

Bruner, J. (1960), *The Process of Education*, Cambridge, Mass.

Coleman, J. S. (1968), 'The concept of equality of educational opportunity', *Harvard Educational Review*, 38.

Coleman, J. S. (1973), 'Equality of opportunity and equality of results', *Harvard Educational Review*, 43.

Conant, J. B. (1959), *The American High School Today*, New York.

Freire, P. (1973), *Pedagogy of the Oppressed*, New York.

Giroux, H. A. (1981), *Ideology, Culture and the Process of Schooling*, Philadelphia.

Jensen, A. R. (1969), 'How much can we boost I.Q. and scholastic achievement?', *Harvard Educational Review*, 39.

Further Reading

Bourdieu, P. and Passeron, J.-C. (1977), *Reproduction in Education, Society and Culture*, London.

Feinberg, W. (1983), *Understanding Education: Toward a Reconstruction of Educational Inquiry*, Cambridge.

Sharp, R. and Green, A. (1975), *Education and Social Control; A Study in Progressive Education*, London.

Epidemiology

The most widely accepted definition of epidemiology is probably that of Brian MacMahon *et al.* (1960): 'Epidemiology is the study of the distribution and determinants of disease prevalence in man.' In contrast to clinical medicine, in which attention is focused on individual patients, epidemiology is primarily concerned with populations, or large groups of persons. Epidemiology is the basic science on which preventive medicine is based. Epidemiologists investigate how disease occurs in the population – who gets the disease and who does not – and what are the reasons or causal factors that explain the patterns of occurrence. In the analysis of population data, statistical methods, both simple and complex, are used extensively. The underlying assumption of epidemiology, that diseases do not occur randomly in populations, has been repeatedly verified.

Although epidemiology did not become a relatively organized and self-conscious scientific profession until the twentieth century (particularly the last few decades), epidemiologic reasoning and investigation go back to antiquity. The ancient Greek physician, Hippocrates, wrote in 'On Airs, Waters and Places' that anyone who wished to investigate medicine properly should consider the climate and geographic situation of a locality, the waters that the inhabitants use 'and the mode in which the inhabitants live, and what are their pursuits, whether they are fond of drinking and eating to excess, and given to indolence, or are fond of exercise and labour'.

Epidemiologic investigations of various sorts have been carried out in more recent centuries. A classic example in the nineteenth century was John Snow's investigations of cholera epidemics in London. Although other explanations had been offered for the occurrence of cholera epidemics (e.g. climatic conditions), Snow and others believed that person-to-person transmission was responsible, because cholera epidemics spread in the direction of, and never faster than, human travel; because persons in contact with cholera victims frequently developed cholera themselves, and because the disease was associated with filth, poverty, and crowded living conditions. Snow hypothesized that cholera was frequently transmitted through the water supply and that this explained why some parts of London were much more affected than others. His careful investigation and determination of the rates of occurrence of disease in defined subgroups of Londoners showed that cholera was frequent in persons who obtained water from the Broad Street pump and in persons living in homes that obtained water from a particular company whose water supply came from a contaminated section of the Thames River. These findings led to control measures for the disease even before the specific causal agent, the cholera vibrio, was identified. While some scientists are not satisfied that they have identified a cause of disease until the detailed mechanism down to the molecular level has been elucidated, epidemiologists often take a more global and pragmatic view: if a factor can be identified, which if reduced will lead to a reduction in the occurrence of a disease, the factor can be assumed to be causal while we await a fuller explanation of the biochemical details. Of course, epidemiologists would not accept a supposed cause of disease if it is inconsistent with biological knowledge.

Until the mid-twentieth century most epidemiologic studies were directed at infectious diseases, which had been the main causes of death until modern times. The work 'epidemic' from which 'epidemiology' is derived, means the occurrence of a disease in a proportion of the population of a community or geographic area far in excess of the usual or expected proportion. Now that many infectious diseases have been brought under control in relatively affluent industrialized societies, epidemiologic attention is being increasingly paid to chronic non-infectious diseases that are now the leading killers, such as heart disease and cancer. It is clear that some societies are experiencing epidemics of such diseases as coronary heart disease (heart attacks) and cancer of the lung, in that these diseases are occurring far in excess of what is observed in other societies. Thus, epidemiologic attention is directed at explaining the nonrandom distribution of these conditions in the world in the hope that methods of prevention and control will be found.

Epidemiological studies may be subdivided into the descriptive and the analytic. Descriptive studies measure the occurrence of disease in various major subgroups of the population. (The commonest epidemiological measures of disease occurrence are prevalence – the proportion of a group with the disease at a given moment, and incidence – the proportion developing the disease per unit of time.) So, for example, a descriptive study might compare the incidence of a disease in men and women, in persons of various ages, races and occupations, in one geographic area against another, or in one time period against another. These exemplify the major axes of classification found in descriptive studies, that is, person (who, or what type of person, is more apt to get the disease?), place (where does it occur more frequently?), and time (when does or did it occur more frequently?). For example, an interesting descriptive observation about place concerns Japanese who have migrated to the United States compared to those living in Japan. The migrants experience a higher incidence of breast cancer and a lower incidence of stomach cancer than their non-migrant counterparts. This has suggested hypotheses concerning dietary and other environmental factors that might play a role in causing these two types of cancer.

Investigation of specific hypotheses is the purpose of analytic studies. In these one attempts to determine whether persons exposed to a particular suggested causal factor (for example, dietary fat intake, cigarette smoking, exposure to X-rays or to a chemical at work, infection by a particular micro-organism, crowding, intense sunlight, and so on) have a higher incidence of disease than those not so exposed. For practical reasons, epidemiologists sometimes will not tackle this question directly by following up persons through time, but will conduct a backward-looking 'retrospective' or 'case-control' study in which they determine whether persons with the disease under study were more often exposed to the factor in question than those free of the disease.

A special form of analytic study is the experiment. An experiment involves some intervention on the part of the investigator rather than simply collecting and analysing data as is done in the usual observational study. For example, an experimental field trial may be carried out in which an active vaccine is administered to one group of people while another, otherwise comparable, group receives a 'dummy' or placebo. The object is to determine whether the incidence of the disease to be prevented is lower in the group receiving vaccine. Most analytic epidemiological studies are observational because of the practical difficulties involved in conducting controlled experiments on free-living humans. Sometimes ethical considerations rule out an experiment, particularly when exposure to a suspected disease-causing agent or substance is involved. But experiments are generally accepted as being more rigorous and believable demonstrations of cause-and-effect than can be achieved through observational studies. The findings of the latter are sometimes suspected of entailing guilt by association. When an exposed group has a higher incidence of a disease, it may be some characteristics of the group other than the exposure itself that is responsible. Epidemiologists devote considerable effort to investigating whether associations between proposed causal factors and diseases may really be due to other 'confounding' factors.

Recent major accomplishments of epidemiology include the demonstration that cigarette smoking is the main cause of lung cancer and that several personal characteristics, such as serum cholesterol level, blood pressure, cigarette smoking and obesity, are highly predictive of who will develop ischemic heart disease, the leading killer of adults in industrialized societies. The field of epidemiology continues to broaden as it did in the past, when non-infectious diseases became as important to society as infectious diseases. Now the analytic skills of epidemiologists are becoming involved in other pressing health-related matters, such as improving the delivery of medical care while limiting its economic costs.

Gary D. Friedman
Kaiser-Permanente Medical Care Program
Oakland, California

Reference
MacMahon, B., Pugh, T. F. and Ipsen, J. (1960), *Epidemiologic Methods*, Boston.

Further Reading
Friedman, G. D. (1980), *Primer of Epidemiology*, 2nd edn, New York.
Lilienfeld, A. M. and Lilienfeld, D. E. (1980), *Foundations of Epidemiology*, 2nd edn, New York.

MacMahon, B. and Pugh, T. F. (1970), *Epidemiology: Principles and Methods*, Boston.

Morris, J. N. (1975), *Uses of Epidemiology*, 3rd edn, Edinburgh.

Roueché, B. (1982), *The Medical Detectives*, New York.

Ethology

Konrad Lorenz defined ethology as 'the discipline which applies to the behaviour of animals and humans all those questions asked and those methodologies used as a matter of course in all other branches of biology since Charles Darwin's time'. Ethology is concerned with causality and the functions of behaviour, and it tries to establish the influence on behaviour of genetic, physiological and ecological variables. Ethologists also ask how and why forms of behaviour develop in interaction with the environment in the ontogeny of the individual, as well as how behaviour could have developed phylogenetically. Behaviour is thus interpreted as a contribution to adaptation to a particular environment. The methods of ethology involve primarily observation of a species in their natural environment. Having collected the data, ethologists then develop an 'ethogram', an inventory of behaviour of a species. This step is followed by systematic experiments and interspecific comparisons.

The origins of ethology can be traced back to Darwin. His book, *On the Origin of Species* (1859), established the basis for the concept of instinct, while even more important was his theory that natural selection underlies the behaviour of an animal as well as its morphology and physiology. In 1898 Whitman also claimed that an evolutionary perspective on behaviour was necessary, and independently of Whitman, Heinroth (1910) discovered the existence of 'patterns of movements' which, like morphological structures, are comparable between species. Through such comparisons, particular behaviours could be called homologous and could be traced back to a common ancestor.

Another antecedent of ethology is 'purposive psychology' developed by McDougall in *An Outline of Psychology* (1923) and later by Tolman in *Purposive Behavior in Animals and Man* (1932). Both postulated a factor called 'instinct' and noted that the behaviour of animals follows a 'purpose' governed by this instinct. Craig (1918) differentiated the end of a chain of behaviours (the consummatory act) from its beginning (appetitive behaviour). Appetitive behaviour is a specific seeking behaviour for a stimulus situation in which the consummatory act can begin.

Modern ethology dates back to 1931 with Lorenz's 'Contributions to the study of the ethology of social *corvidae*'. This article and others that followed represented a synthesis of previously isolated efforts in ethology and led to a new model of animal behaviour. Lorenz stressed that the interpretation of animal behaviour is only possible after detailed observation of the animal in its natural environment, and that it is necessary to compare behaviours of different species.

Lorenz used a hydraulic model to describe the interaction between internal and external factors, and he redefined Craig's 'consummatory act' as the 'fixed action pattern' (F.A.P.); the preliminary 'appetitive behaviour' was the phase leading to the performance of the F.A.P. Appetitive behaviour causes the animal to look for a configuration of stimuli which release the F.A.P. These stimuli are recognized innately according to a hypothetical mechanism, the 'innate releasing mechanism'. These signals are not only objects in the environment but also signals emitted by other members of the species, in which case signals serve a social function and are called 'releasers'. Releasers are not always equally efficient: this is because the efficiency is modulated by an 'action specific energy' which is diminished by the execution of an F.A.P. If only a little of the action specific energy is present, then the F.A.P. can only be executed incompletely and thus becomes an intention movement. When the F.A.P. has not been executed for a long stretch of time, the threshold for the execution decreases and the F.A.P. can be released even by a weak or inadequate stimulus; Lorenz termed this a 'vacuum activity'.

Lorenz's model was often criticized because it was so simple. Niko Tinbergen elaborated on Lorenz's original model. He expanded the techniques of observation through simple but ingenious experiments, and he evolved more sophisticated notions of releasers and instincts. He defined instinct as a 'hierarchical organized nervous mechanism which reacts to priming, releasing and directing stimuli of either endogenous or exogenous character. The reaction consists of a coordinated series of movements that contribute to the preservation of the individual and species'. Tinbergen worked mainly on the reproductive behaviour of the stickleback and through his findings expanded our understanding of the hierarchical organization of instincts. His experiments were mostly concerned with motivational conflicts, redirected activities, ambivalent behaviour and displacement.

Following Lorenz's and Tinbergen's seminal work, ethology spread rapidly all over Europe and, at a slower rate, to the US. Progress was halted during World War II and commenced again in the 1950s with the first international publication of Tinbergen's *The Study of Instinct* (the first ecology textbook) in 1951, and Lorenz's *King Solomon's Ring*, a popularized account of ethology, in 1952.

With the growth of ethology came a major conflict between two opposing views of behaviour. American experimental psychology adopted a behaviourist orientation that stressed the influence of environment and learning factors; they carried out laboratory experiments using rats, cats, dogs and apes as models for humans. On the other hand, ethology, with its systematic observation of species in their natural setting, tried to discover evolutionary and adaptive mechanisms underlying animal behaviour – the genetic basis for behaviour. Unlike experimental psychologists, ethologists studied many and diverse species, thus strengthening their case for innateness and instinct. The neglect of learning by ethologists provoked a strong reaction against the discipline from members of the opposing camp, notably by Lehrman (1953) who based his criticisms on the work of Kuo (1932).

The innate versus acquired dichotomy resulting from the debate seems somewhat sterile and false today. Innate and learned are no longer regarded as exclusive categories. Contemporary ethologists would agree that behaviour develops ontogenetically through the interaction between genetic information and environment. This does not imply that an apparently innate characteristic is really learned, or that every phylogenetically pre-programmed behaviour must be adaptively modifiable through learning. But everything learned must have as its foundation a phylogenetically provided· programme if appropriate and adaptive behaviour patterns are to be produced. It seems logical to postulate that certain behaviour elements – those which conduct learning processes – should never be modifiable through learning. Learned behaviour does contain genetic information, to the extent that the basis of learning is a physiological apparatus which evolved under the pressure of selection. Lorenz termed this mechanism the 'innate school-marm'. Thus the question is not whether behaviour patterns are innate or acquired but rather how behaviour can be modified, or what can be learned, and when.

From the beginning, ethology was also interested in aspects of social behaviour such as territorial behaviour, group structure, and communication. A milestone in the ethological study of communication was the development of the concept of 'ritualization' (Huxley, 1966), referring to the modification of a behaviour pattern by natural selection in order to serve a communicative function. Such expressive movements mostly occur in courtship and in displays of aggression or submission. Their social function is largely to channel aggression – thus ritualized fighting or submissive behaviour hinders escalation of a fight. Bonding is another function of ritualized behaviour.

Ethologists also investigated ranking as an aspect of social behaviour. Schielderup-Ebbe (1935) found that among a flock of hens a few enjoyed privileges during feeding and had first access to the feeding site and pecked at other, lower-ranking, hens. This led on to the study of dominance, defined as having priority access to scarce resources, and measured by the number of conflicts won. This concept is now generally limited to description of relationships, while other forms of behaviour are referred to in the construction of social hierarchies where high-ranking individuals are the focus of attention of other group members.

Other areas of interest to ethologists are the relationship between social organization and ecology (DeVore, 1965); play behaviour; 'imprinting', or how individuals become attached to other members of the group, first observed by Lorenz in birds and studied by Hess (1973) and others. Ethologists have also considered the link between behaviour and the nervous system. Holst and St Paul (1963) elicited different behavioural reactions in hens through electrical stimulation of the brain, and Delgado (1967) was able to control aggressive behaviour using similar techniques. Neurophysiological research led to the discovery of neurons in the brain that are responsible for the control of different aspects of behaviour (Ewert, 1976).

A new development in ethology is sociobiology. Sociobiologists propose a global theory of behaviour which derives from the 'selfish interest' of the gene to reproduce itself; this selfishness leads to the concept of kin-selection, for related individuals share a determinable number of genes. Sociobiology's primary tools are intriguing mathematical models that consider phylogenetic adaptation and ecological pressures. When, in certain situations, different possible behaviours exist, pressures result in the development of evolutionary stabile strategies (E.S.S.) of behaviour. Sociobiology tries to include the social sciences in a modern synthesis of evolutionary theory, arguing that all forms of social organization – in animals ranging from termites to primates, including man – can be described using the same parameters and the same quantitative theory. Sociobiologists are criticized for their overemphasis on genetic determinism and for their analytical models which are strongly reminiscent of the Social Darwinism of the early twentieth century. Nevertheless they can provide new insights into the structure and organization of individuals and their behaviour, and their importance is acknowledged in the study of insects, fish and birds. But the general applicability of sociobiological laws to primates and humans has yet to be proved.

The originality of the ethological approach in the study of human behaviour was in its methods of systematic observation and qualitative description, its considerations of phylogenetic roots, and the functions of behaviour deduced from a comparative approach. Human ethology in turn influenced areas of anthropology, psychology and sociology. However, the construction of an appropriate theoretical framework still remains a problem for the human ethologist.

Development of speech is a distinguishing primary characteristic of human behaviour. This made it possible to transmit information between generations by non-genetic means. Cultural evolution then assumed a major role in the adaptation of the species. It is possible that cultural evolution follows rules comparable to those which govern phylogenetic evolution, and also leads to the modification in behaviour. Moreover, humans are capable of altering their environment, thus changing selective pressures. These possibilities make it more difficult to determine the genetic adaptive value of a behaviour, and blur the distinction between phylogenetic and cultural traits. Finally, human ethologists have tended to neglect the adaptive modification of behaviour, that is, learning processes.

Several popular books on human ethology – Ardrey's *The Territorial Imperative* (1966), Lorenz's *On Aggression* (1963), Morris's *The Naked Ape* (1967) and Wilson's *On Human Nature* (1978) – brought the subject to the attention of a wider public. These authors tried to present a biological explanation for human behaviour, but they often worked with naive analogies and simplistic comparisons. At the same time, however, an authentic human ethology was being developed. Research focused on human-ethological interpretations of child development (child ethology), as in the work of Blurton-Jones (1972) and McGrew (1972); others described children's relationships and resulting group structures. Intercultural comparisons were made in the work of Eibl-Eibesfeldt on non-verbal behaviour (1972), who also observed the expressive behaviour of children born deaf and blind (1973). These studies have shown the complexities and the multidimensional nature of ontogeny, as well as confirmed the existence of invariant transcultural traits in human behaviour, such as expressive behaviour and its ritualization.

Human ethology has moved away from its descriptive beginnings and no longer restricts itself to investigating phylogenetic adaptations in behaviour: cultural patterns are also studied in relation to adaptation, and already a number of universal social interaction strategies have been observed through cross-cultural comparison. Their apparent variation can be attributed to the fact that phylogenetic and cultural patterns can be substituted as functional equivalents for one another, or they can be verbalized. Nevertheless, the underlying structural rules remain the same. This opens the way for the study of a grammar of human social behaviour encompassing verbal and nonverbal strategies. Such an approach could provide a theoretical framework and together with the empirical research in progress could give human ethology the refinement of animal ethology.

The results of human ethological studies could have an important impact on social questions, and the dangers arising from the neglect of human nature should be clear. While the modifiability of human behaviour, especially through educational programmes, is limited, this knowledge should not be used to justify a freeze on social changes, as extreme conservatives have already suggested. Indeed, this view was only possible because of the oversimplification of the field by popular writers. Rather, the universals identified by human ethology, especially in communication and in mechanisms of group cohesion and seclusion, could be the basis for shared concern and a common understanding and could provide a means to overcome ethnocentric political strategies.

Karl Grammar
Max-Planck Institut für Verhaltensphysiologie
Forschungsstelle für Humanethologie, West Germany

References

Blurton-Jones, N. G. (1972), *Ethological Studies of Child Behaviour*, Cambridge.

Bowlby, J. (1969), *Attachment and Loss: Vol. 1 Attachment*, London.

Craig, W. (1918), 'Appetites and aversions as constituents of instincts', *Biographical Bulletin*, 34.

Dawkins, R. (1976), *The Selfish Gene*, London.

Delgado, J. M. R. (1967), 'Aggression and defense under cerebral radio control', in C. D. Clemente and D. B. Lindsley (eds.), *Aggression and Defense*, Berkeley and Los Angeles.

DeVore, I. (1965), *Primate Behavior: Field Studies of Monkey and Apes*, New York.

Eibl-Eibesfeldt, I. (1972), 'Similarities and differences between cultures in expressive movements', in R. A. Hinde (ed.), *Non-Verbal Communication*, London.

Eibl-Eibesfeldt, I. (1973), 'The expressive behaviour of deaf and blindborn', in M. von Cranach and I. Vine (eds), *Non-Verbal Behaviour and Expressive Movements*, London.

Ewert, J. P. (1976), *Neuro-Ethologie*, Berlin.

Heinroth, O. (1910), 'Beitrage zur Biologie, insbesondere Psychologie und Ethologie der Anatiden', *Verh. J. Int. Orthin. Kong.*, Berlin.

Hess, E. H. (1973), *Imprinting: Early Experience and the Development of Attachment*, New York.

Holst, E. V. and St Paul, U. V. (1963), 'On the functional organization of drives', *Animal Behaviour*, 11.

Huxley, J. S. (1966), 'A discussion on ritualization of behaviour in animals and man', *Philosophical Transactions of the Royal Society*, London, 251.

Kuo, Z. Y. (1932), 'Ontogeny of embryonic behavior in Aves I and II', *Journal of Experimental Zoology*, 61.

Lehrman, D. S. (1953), 'A critique of Konrad Lorenz's theory of instinctive behaviour', *Quarterly Review of Biology*, 28.

McGrew, W. C. (1972), *An Ethological Study of Children's Behavior*, New York.

Schielderup-Ebbe, T. (1935), 'Social behavior of birds', in A. Murchinson (ed.), *A Handbook of Social Psychology*, New York.

Tinbergen, N. (1942), 'An objective study of the innate behavior of animals', *Biblioth. Biotheor.*, 1.

Whitman, C. C. (1989), 'Animal behavior', *Biol. Lect. Mar. Lab.*, Woods Hole, Mass.

Further Reading

Bateson, P. P. G. d Hinde, R. A. (eds) (1976), *Growing Points in Ethology*, London.

Eibl-Eibesfeldt, I. (1975), *Ethology: The Biology of Behavior*, 2nd edn, New York.

Lehner, P. N. (1979), *Handbook of Ethological Methods*, New York.

See also: *evolution; sociology.*

Evolution

The term evolution implies transformation through a sequence of stages. Although the term is a general one which is used in many fields of study (Lewontin, 1968), in biology it is a fundamental unifying theory. Biological evolution specifically refers to *genetic* transformation of populations through time which results primarily from changes in the interactions between organisms and their environment (Dobzhansky *et al.*, 1977). The fact that life evolved is accepted by almost all modern biologists, although the exact mechanisms by which organic evolution occurs are the subject of intense research today.

Principles

The bench mark for the beginning of research on biological evolution is the 1859 publication of Charles Darwin's *The Origin of Species*, although evolutionary ideas were common before that date. Darwin and Alfred Russel Wallace independently developed the idea of natural selection as the chief mechanism of causing life to evolve. The key feature of natural selection is that it is indirect: inherited variability exists in all species and the best adapted variants tend to leave more offspring, so that through time there is gradual change. In this view, evolution is not directed by the processes that create the inherited variability, but rather by how that variability is shaped or pruned through time by natural selection.

Natural selection is a major feature of the synthetic theory of evolution, a term used to describe the modern view of the mechanisms of organic evolution. This synthesis was forged in the first half of this century by combining the theory of natural selection, Mendelian genetics, and other features to explain how life evolves. There has never been complete agreement on all aspects of the synthetic theory, however, with current controversy centring on topics such as the importance of random processes, the mechanisms of speciation, and the extrapolation from observable genetic changes over a short time span to patterns of phylogeny (Gould, 1982).

At the core of the synthetic theory of evolution are the processes that result in genetic transformation from generation to generation. These processes occur in two phases: (1) The production and arrangement of genetic variation by gene mutation, chromosomal changes, genetic recombination, and gene migration. (2) The reduction of genetic variation by natural selection and genetic drift. Genetic variability is ultimately produced by gene mutation, which is a chemical change in the DNA molecule. Most mutations are deleterious or relatively neutral to the survival of the organism. Mutations with small effects probably accumulate and eventually have a greater role in evolution than macromutations. Mutation rate has little relationship with evolutionary rate. Genetic recombination is also a source of genetic variation, but at a different level. Whereas gene mutation is a change in the DNA molecule, genetic recombination is the formation of different combinations of genetic factors that occur during the sexual cycle from the formation of the sex cells to fertilization. Theoretically, this process can create nearly an infinite number of different organisms simply by reshuffling the immense amount of genetic differences between the DNA of any two parents. Gene migration or flow is a source of new variability at the population level. A local population, for example, can undergo profound genetic change by the introduction of genes from other populations.

The second phase of genetic transformation is the reduction of genetic variation which is done primarily by natural selection. Since far more sex cells are fertilized than can possibly survive and reproduce, there is immense loss of potential life at each generation. In humans it is estimated that only about 12 per cent of all fertilized eggs survive, grow to adulthood and reproduce. The loss is probably mostly selective: genetic variants that do not survive to reproduce are lost because of deleterious mutations or combinations of genetic factors that tend to decrease vitality. Even resistance to disease often has a genetic component that can be selected. Simple chance may also be a factor in loss of genetic variability from generation to generation, a process called genetic drift. The importance of this random factor in evolution has been controversial ever since Sewall Wright proposed it in the 1930s.

The formation of new species involves mechanisms which reproductively isolate populations that were once part of the same species. In animals this usually requires physical isolation and no gene flow between populations that then undergo divergent genetic change. Naturalistic studies show that this can occur relatively rapidly in small isolated populations. Alternatively, changes in chromosomal structure between local populations may lead to their reproductive isolation and speciation.

A common misunderstanding of evolution is that it occurs because of mutations that arise and directly change the genetic composition of a species through the generations. This view, called the mutation theory of evolution, was common in the early part of theory, but is now discredited for complex organisms. Genetic variability in species is immense, and recent biochemical research has shown that a large percentage of genetic loci have one or more mutant variants. According to the synthetic theory, the direction of genetic change is determined by the selection and random loss of this vast store of existing genetic variability.

Another common misunderstanding of the synthetic theory of evolution is that it explains why the organic world evolved in the way it did. The *pattern* of evolution revealed in the fossil record and, by inference, from living organisms cannot be predicted by the processes of production and reduction of genetic variation any more than human history can be explained by the processes by which individuals learn from birth to death.

Human Evolution

There are eighteen living orders of mammals. The one in which humans are classified (Primates) may have originated in the late Cretaceous (roughly 70–65 million years ago) but only by Eocene times (54 to 35 million years) do primates of the modern aspect appear (Szalay and Delson, 1979). These Eocene forms resemble modern lemurs and tarsiers. By Oligocene times (35 to 24 million years) there are primates which share some derived characteristics seen in the group containing modern monkeys, apes and people (Anthropoidea). Not until the Miocene (24 to 5 million years) are there fossils which have traits shared uniquely with the superfamily containing apes and people (Hominoidea). Although some middle to late Miocene (roughly

16 to 8 million years) hominids have a chewing apparatus that looks like early members of the human family (Hominidae), the resemblance is probably due to the fact that the common ancestor of the great apes and people also shared these traits. The earliest fossils that can be linked unequivocally and uniquely to modern humans are grouped in the genus *Australopithecus* and date back at least to 3.7 and probably to 5 or 5.5 million years (McHenry, 1982). The earlier date is from a fragment of jaw which appears to share unique characteristics with later and better-known members of *Australopithecus*. All members of this genus are confined to Africa.

The earliest fossil species that is undoubtedly a member of the human family is *Australopithecus afarensis* known in East Africa from geological strata dating between 3.7 and 3.0 million years ago. Its dentition shows many derived traits in common with later hominids, but it also retains numerous generalized characteristics of the ape-human common ancestor, such as distally worn upper canine teeth, obliquely set lower first premolars with small inside cusps, sloping chin, and a space between the upper incisors and canines. It had relatively very large cheek teeth and well developed chewing muscles like later species of *Australopithecus*. The brain size relative to body size is much closer to modern apes than to modern people, being less than one half the relative size of *Homo sapiens*. The body below the head (postcranium) is completely reorganized away from the common plan seen in all other primates and shares the uniquely human bipedal pattern. Some primitive traits are retained in the post-cranium such as long and curved toes, which may imply a retention of greater tree climbing ability than that seen in *Homo sapiens*. By about 2.5 million years ago many of the primitive dental and cranial features of *A. afarensis* are lost and another species is recognized, *A. africanus*. Relative cheek tooth size remains large and relative brain size remains diminutive. The postcranial skeleton is only partly known, but appears to be very similar to *A. afarensis*. By about 2 million years ago two species of hominid appear in the fossil record, *A. robustus* and *Homo habilis*. The former (*A. robustus*) continues and exaggerates the trend to heavy chewing adaptation with an emphasis on grinding. The latter (*H. habilis*) shows the first signs of relative brain size increase and dental reduction. Stone tools first appear at about this time. In African strata dated to about 1.6 million years ago hominids appear which resemble very closely the well-known Asian *H. erectus*. Relative brain size is further increased and stone tool technology becomes much more elaborate.

The first appearance of human populations outside of Africa may precede 1 million years, but certainly by about 0.9 million years ago *H. erectus* occupied parts of tropical Asia. The exact chronology is still uncertain, but some time after this and before 0.5 million years ago some populations had adapted to life in the temperate climatic zone of Asia and Europe. The appearance of *H. sapiens* depends on the definition, but by 0.3 million years ago the fully modern brain size had evolved, although the skull still retained many *H. erectus*-like traits. These archaic *H. sapiens* persisted in most areas of Eurasia until about 35,000 years ago. The earliest traces of anatomically modern *H. sapiens* are in Africa perhaps as early as 130,000 years ago, although in Eurasia this form becomes abundant only after 35,000. By at least 30,000 years ago Australia was inhabited by anatomically modern *H. sapiens* (yet archaic forms persisted until at least 10,000). America was settled by immigrants from Asia who migrated across a landbridge connecting Siberia and Alaska perhaps at 20,000 to 15,000 years ago. People first reached some of the Pacific islands several thousand years ago from the east, reaching the Marquesas Islands by about AD 300 and New Zealand by about AD 900.

Technological development in human evolution appears to be erratic in pace, but it certainly shows a pattern of acceleration. Relatively crude stone tools persist for over 1.5 million years. Finely worked blade tools are much more recent. Humans have had agriculture, cities, and writing for less than one quarter of one per cent of their evolutionary development as a separate mammalian lineage.

Behaviour

Human locomotor behaviour probably evolved from an ape-like ancestor with a short back, a flat chest, and a highly mobile shoulder and forelimb adapted to climbing and suspending the body below tree branches (McHenry, 1982). Like modern apes (but unlike monkeys) this hypothetical ancestor was relatively awkward and energetically inefficient at walking on the ground either quadrupedally or bipedally. But as has happened to many other primate groups, terrestrial travel was increasingly adopted. Why our ancestors took up bipedality instead of quadrupedality is unknown, but certainly the unique ape-like body plan made either gait equally efficient in terms of energetic cost at normal speeds. Free hands for carrying makes bipedality more advantageous. Fossil evidence at about 3.5 million years ago shows that bipedality had been established in the human evolutionary lineage, but before that time the paleontological record is not yet complete enough.

The evolutionary history of human feeding behaviour is documented by fossil dental remains spanning millions of years. The earliest hominids were quite different from modern African apes, having thick molar enamel, exceptionally large cheek teeth, and powerful chewing muscles. Microscopic studies of dental scratches show that these early humans were probably not eating seeds and grass, nor were they crushing bones. By about 2 million years ago meat eating was certainly practised, as evidenced by bone remains with stone tool cut marks. Relative cheek tooth size reduces fairly gradually from 2 million years ago to the present which may be because extra-oral food preparation to some extent took over the function of the grinding teeth.

Many other aspects of human behavioural evolution are related to the fact that absolute brain size tripled and relative brain size more than doubled over the last 2.5 million years of human evolution. Human fossils dating between about 3.5 and 2.5 million years ago have endocranial volumes the size of modern chimpanzees, although relative to body size they are slightly larger.

The biological evolution of most aspects of human behaviour are much more difficult to document. The basic method of inquiry involves comparisons with other living animals. From this perspective it is clear that spoken symbolic language is the most unique human attribute in the organic world. Recent field studies of monkeys reveal that they possess a form of vocal symbolic communication, but there is a vast quantitative gap in speech capabilities between human and nonhuman primates.

The chief difficulty of studying the biological evolution of human behaviour is determining the genetic component of behaviour. Often the only genetic component is genetically conditioned developmental plasticity. There is a genetic basis for the development of the neurophysiology required for speech, for example, but a great deal of plasticity in the kind of language that is learned. There is a genetic basis for most aspects of human sexuality, but an enormous flexibility in how it is expressed. One method for approximating the extent of genetic contribution to specific behaviours is by comparing differences between identical twins (and hence genetically identical individuals) with the differences among unrelated individuals. Twin studies are complicated by the fact that most twins are raised in the same environment and that the sample of identical twins raised apart is still very small.

One theoretical breakthrough in the study of behavioural evolution came in 1964 with the publication of W. D. Hamilton's 'The genetical theory of social behavior'. He suggested that even genetically controlled behaviours that were detrimental to an organism's survival could be favoured by natural selection because of what has become known as kin selection. Kin selection refers to the '. . . selection of genes because of their effect in favouring the reproductive success of relatives other than offspring' (Barash, 1982). Kin selection theory has been successfully employed to explain several aspects of the social behaviour of nonhuman animals, especially social insects, but application of this and other sociobiological theories to the evolution of human social behaviour has not yet resulted in universally accepted principles. The enormity of human behavioural plasticity makes the search for evolutionary principles difficult, but a great deal of research on this topic is currently being pursued. Even more difficult, if not impossible, is the search for any behavioural evolutionary divergence between human groups that have a genetic basis.

Henry M. McHenry
University of California, Davis

References
Barash, D. P. (1982), *Sociobiology and Behavior*, New York.
Darwin, C. (1859), *On the Origin of Species by Means of Natural Selection*, London.
Dobzhansky, T., Ayala, F. J., Stebbins, G. L. and Valentine, J. W. (1977), *Evolution*, San Francisco.
Gould, S. J. (1982), 'Darwinism and the expansion of evolutionary theory', *Science*, 216.
Hamilton, W. D. (1964), 'The genetical theory of social behavior', *Journal of Theoretical Biology*, 12.
Lewontin, R. C. (1968), 'Concept of evolution', *International Encyclopedia of the Social Sciences*, New York.
McHenry, H. M. (1982), 'The pattern of human evolution: studies on bipedalism, mastication, and encephalization', *Annual Review of Anthropology*, 11.

Further Reading
Futuyma, D. J. (1979), *Evolutionary Biology*, Sunderland, Mass.
Nelson, H. and Jurmain, R. (1982), *Introduction to Physical Anthropology*, 2nd edn, St Paul.
See also: *race; sociobiology.*

Geography

The range and internal diversity of geography make definition problematic. I suggest two definitions, one elaborated, the other concise. Long definition: Geography seeks and refines deductive laws concerning the changing spatial patterns and relationships of terrestrial phenomena viewed as the world of man at varying scales of study. Short definition: Geography is the scientific study of changing relationships of terrestrial phenomena viewed as the world of man (Bird, 1973).

Geography is a social science, but it is also more than a social science. Within 'physical geography' fall such fields as cartography, climatology, parts of biogeography, and geomorphology (the study of the nature and processes of the evolution of earth surface features). These treat phenomena that can be expected to obey the cause and effect laws of physics. The subject has perhaps a dangerously diverse agenda, but geography derives its unity from its constant attempt to see *zusammenhang* between the spatial relationships of terrestrial features. Here are four different dimensions of the subject.

(1) Geographers have been driven to seek ever more profound description of the world of man in maps, numbers and words, and in that endeavour they have naturally wanted to know how contemporary spatial patterns evolved. Why not look at past patterns (historical geography) to seek an explanation not only of these, but perhaps also of the present in their light via a true scientific cause and effect sequence over time? Any success in this search must lead to an understanding of processes. So why not let that process run on beyond the present, leading to possibilities of prediction, perhaps as an aid to planning?

But planning for whom? The world perceived by whom? As soon as man is studied as a vital constituent of earth-space patterns, we encounter all the problems of perception. The actions taken by man in shaping his environment (physical and social) are so taken in the light of his behavioural values and attitudes. That is the subject matter of behavioural geography. The guiding view is that man's actions are not determined directly by the environment, but rather by what he thinks the environment (again physical and social) constrains him to do. He then modifies his view of the world as he perceives the results of his actions.

(2) A second dimension is made by dividing the subject in two different ways: there is the worldwide study of a narrow range of phenomena – systematic geography; and there is regional, 'total' geography of manageable areas, treated as variations upon regional models. This twofold division, supported by courses in techniques, particularly in the physical geography laboratory, in computation, and in cartography, is often used as the framework for the undergraduate curriculum. A key problem related to these subjects is that of scale. The study of one world implies the ability to slide from one scale to another appropriate scale in view of the study objective. The 'appropriate' scale is where the phenomena under study deviate most from randomness.

(3) A third dimension of the subject has to do with its relation to other environmental and regional sciences. In university curricula geography is often combined with other environ-

mental sciences (commonly geology and biology), or it may form part of a training in regional science, when it is taught together with mathematics (statistics) and economics. This integrated approach is particularly useful at postgraduate level, where there is a greater emphasis on problem-orientation than on 'discipline servitude'. Three broad headings for geography's contribution to an integrated attack on problems are spatial analysis, ecological analysis and regional complex analysis.

(4) A fourth dimension of geography has to do with the internal tension between its natural science and social science poles. This contrast occurs *within* geography (as it does in medicine) as either a basic weakness or a source of strength. If geographers are able to allow one method to act as a continual critique of the other, it may provide deeper insights. Areas of the subject tending towards the 'harder' pole are more likely to use some form of positivistic thinking; areas tending towards the other pole are likely to employ some form of behaviouralism.

A useful umbrella phrase to describe what the geographer seeks in both his desk and field studies is a 'search for spatial relationships', bearing in mind that this includes physical as well as man-made modifications of the earth surface, the spatial relationships of these modifications and man himself, and the spatial relationships of man with man. If these are difficult objectives, they are nevertheless vital questions for a modern society attempting to manage the distribution of resources: land-use planning (*aménagement de la territoire, Raumordnung*), is practised in some form everywhere, as competing claims turn spaces into places exhibiting environmental pressures. Planning becomes at once more sophisticated, as the citizens on whose behalf plans are promulgated become more environmentally informed, and also more difficult as expectations rise.

Having emphasized that research in geography is problem-oriented, I turn to one or two problems that preoccupy geographers today. In physical geography there is an emphasis on process-landform relationships, with time seen as an important variable. The tendency for pioneer geomorphologists to see landform shaping in a 'compartmented' sequence of mountain building, followed by discrete periods of degradational erosion, has given way to a perspective which sees change in the landscape as more continuous, with perhaps contemporaneous mountain-building and erosion. There is continual refinement of mathematical modelling principles in order to understand and predict the changes in the landscape, an objective with obvious applied importance.

In physical and in human geography, there is the constant striving to produce concepts, models and laws. (For a list of fifty 'basic concepts' in behavioural geography worked on by geographers see Hurst, 1974.) Geographers have moved away from regarding areal differentiation as a prime objective and have begun to worry less that the scientific rigour of the natural sciences has never been approached (will never be?) by the social sciences aspects of geography. In the face of many possible research strategies in human geography, from micro case studies to macro aggregate models, from positivistic to humanistic geography, a current response has been to suggest that what is believed to be the most appropriate strategy for the problem in question (in itself a subjective choice, but to be more objectively judged by its results) should be made subject to the critique of alternative strategies.

Since 1954 there have been behavioural geography theories that the causal sequence of spatial relationships is basically as follows: political idea, decision, leading to movement over a designated field of operation or political area, giving the projection of ideas on to space, as power in the political field and as property in the economic field. Behavioural geography also grew because of progressive dissatisfaction with the fruits of the positivistic locational analysis school of human geography of the 1960s. It was even realized that physical environmental hazards were best studied in the light of the way the decision maker on the ground perceived the hazard, rather than via the perspective of some supposed objective principles from within physical geography. The supplantation of optimizing economic men by satisficers was accompanied by an interest in the spatial diffusion of innovations and, more broadly, by the time-space geography of the Swedish school of geographers led by Torsten Hagerstrand, where time and space are seen as scarce resources and their attempted optimum allocation by individuals builds up to the spatial relationships of societies.

Geographers have tried to keep abreast of work by psychologists as to whether perceptions are hypotheses and only hypotheses, or whether the relationship between perceiver and perceived is something like the symbiotic relationship between predator and prey. A celebrated tool of the geographer, the map, is now seen as a perceptual filter imposed upon our observation of space that is too large to be individually observed at one moment of time. A whole sub-subject of mental maps has arisen wherein questionnaire fieldwork survey compares individuals' ideas of spatial patterns with some external standard representation.

J. H. Bird
University of Southampton

References
Bird, J. H. (1973), 'Desiderata for a definition: or is geography what geographers do?', *Area*, 6.
Hurst, M. E. E. (1974), *A Geography of Economic Behaviour*, London.

Further Reading
Holt-Jensen, A. (1981), *Geography: Its History and Concepts*, London.
Johnston, R. J. (1979), *Geography and Geographers: Anglo-American Human Geography Since 1945*, London.

History

History has long had an uneasy relationship with the social sciences. It is the natural tendency of an historian to think first of what has been, rather than what now is. Few historians can ignore the world in which they live, just as few economists or sociologists can ignore the way in which past events have determined the economy and society which they study; nor would most wish to do so. Yet historians turn first to the past, to seek precedents or to examine the evolution of ideas and institutions, and they see such an examination as an essential preliminary to serious study, whether of an event in the past or of an event in the present.

History is, as Marc Bloch put it, 'le science des hommes dans le temps' (Bloch, 1949), and it is the sense of time and of the apparently infinite variety of human experiences in time which creates much of the uneasiness which has characterized the relationship between history and the contemporary sciences of man. To Bloch, one of the founders of the French *Annales* school of historians, which has been the most coherent and most influential force on historical writing since the Second World War, the enormous amount of information that survives to us from the past was a challenge and a boon; time has given to us a range of knowledge which, if our vision is broad enough and our analysis thorough enough, can reveal the 'structures' and 'conjunctures' underlying the 'events' which have been the concern of most historians of past generations. Such a revelation can come only through the use in historical study of the methods or insights of the other social sciences and, in its turn, the study of history is fundamental to the future development of those methods.

The confident assertion by the *Annales* school of the unity and interdependence of history and the social sciences was a reaction to earlier views of history that had been sceptical of newer disciplines. These doubts were based on two contradictory beliefs; the first, held by many historians in the late nineteenth century, was that history was pre-eminent in its ability to give an objective account of the past which would be useful in the present and the future; the second, characteristic of the German historicist school, was that history was concerned, as Barraclough has put it, with 'the realm of the unique, of the spirit and of change' (Barraclough, 1979). In other words, the very diversity of human experience which to the *Annales* school was a source of strength, led earlier historians to reject generalizations and to exalt intuition in the study of individual action.

Of these two views, the historicist emphasis on the study of individual experience and the rejection of generalization from such experience was the more influential in driving a wedge between history and the emergent social sciences. If generalization was impossible, then history was there to be studied for its own sake, evaluated and re-evaluated as more facts came to light, but serving no purpose other than that of satisfying curiosity or, perhaps, training the mind. Moreover, the exercise of the historian's intuition, his empathy with people in the past, could not be based explicitly on knowledge of how people behave in the present, since by definition events and people's reactions to them are unique. The historian could not, therefore, approach his subject with questions or hypotheses, but had to allow the documents to speak for themselves.

Historicism thus narrowed the scope of history, for its emphasis on intuition in the close study of individual experience prevented historians from taking account of many economic and social phenomena, or from studying the behaviour of crowds or groups. Kings and generals might make fascinating subjects, but, particularly to an age which had experienced the Russian Revolution and the rise of Fascism, a wider historical view seemed necessary.

Such a wider view came both from the *Annales* school and from the increasing influence in the years around the Second World War of Marxist history. While some early Marxists exhibited an extreme economic determinism that was as stultifying as the individualism of their fiercest opponents, this extremism was soon modified both by the influence of *Annales* and by historians such as E. J. Hobsbawm, E. P. Thompson and Christopher Hill who had been trained in a British empirical tradition. Thus Marxist history in Britain, and its counterpart, 'radical history' in the United States, developed a blend of the Marxist categorization of historical and particularly economic forces, with an emphasis on social, intellectual and cultural forces.

This widening of the scope and the methods of historical investigation enlarged the impact of the social sciences upon history. The process was encouraged by the increasing tendency of historians, in the 1950s and 1960s, to develop subdisciplines with their own organizational structures. Economic history had been such a distinct entity in some countries since the 1930s, but it was followed by social history, cultural history, and by many smaller groupings. Although, with the principal exception of the 'new' economic historians in the United States, most of the members of these new disciplines had been trained as generalist historians, they naturally tended to look for ideas and methods to the cognate social science disciplines. The closest links which were forged in this way, mainly during the 1960s and 1970s, were in the fields of economic history, historical demography, social history and historical geography. In all these cases, there was an increased awareness of the potential of social science theory and quantitative methods and a consequent desire to borrow whatever seemed useful.

The 'new' history, as it was called with arrogance by its proponents and derision by its opponents, was first manifest in economic history. There have always been close links between economics and economic history, particularly in Britain and the United States. Marx, Marshall, Keynes, Kuznets and many other economists have used historical material or written works of economic history, while economic historians such as Clapham, as early as 1926, emphasized the reliance of economic history on economic theory and on statistics. Clapham, too, saw the need for historians to fill the 'empty boxes' of the economists (Clapham, 1922). The 'new economic history' which developed in the 1960s, beginning with two studies of the impact of the building of the railways on the economy of the United States (Fogel, 1964; Fishlow, 1965), was thus within an old tradition, but it was new in its emphasis on the quantitative evaluation of hypotheses based on neoclassical economics

The 'new' economic history was accepted with ease by most economists, particularly in the United States – most of its early adherents had been trained there as economists – but was viewed with suspicion or outright hostility by most historians. Suspicion sprang from wariness about the use of methods of multivariate statistics, in particular, regression analysis; hostility sprang from the behavioural assumptions which underlay the economic models and from an apparent innovation in historical study, the 'counterfactual'.

Students of history had long been warned of the danger of hypothetical history, of imagining what would have happened if Cleopatra's nose had been less beautiful. They were aghast to discover that the most striking of the first studies in the 'new' economic history was based on asking the question: what would have happened to the American economy if the railways had not been built? It was even more alarming that Robert Fogel, the author, should argue that discussion of historical causation must be based, explicitly or implicitly, on 'hypothetico-deductive models'. That is, the historian must construct a model of the interaction of the variables that determine the outcome which he is studying, the historical 'fact', and examine its causation by imagining changes in the independent or determining variables.

The 'new' economic history expanded very rapidly in the late 1960s and soon became the predominant form of economic history in the United States. The expansion was marked by controversy, particularly after the publication of Fogel and Engerman's *Time on the Cross* in 1974. The arguments surrounding this discussion of the economics of American Negro slavery took place among 'new' economic historians, as well as between them and more traditional historians, and they were fuelled by the availability of computer tapes containing the data on which Fogel and Engerman had worked. This was paradoxical, since one of the earliest criticisms of the 'new' history had been that its findings were impossible to check just because they were quantitative and based on computer-held data. Moreover, the arguments about the findings of *Time on the Cross* were widely misunderstood by historians who professed to see the 'new' historians falling out and discrediting themselves; in fact, the arguments were based on a shared assumption of the superiority of the 'new' methods.

Despite the arguments, the 'new' economic history is now firmly established as the predominant method within the subject, even if many doubts still remain about its adherence to neoclassical economic assumptions. A similar success for new methods derived from the social sciences has been achieved in the field of demographic history, although in this field opposition was less intense. French scholars working in the 1960s, in particular Louis Henry, developed new methods for the analysis of population history, of which the most novel was 'family reconstitution' – the reconstruction of family trees for entire communities. This method, followed in Britain by the Cambridge Group for the History of Population and Social Structure, and by others in Scandinavia, has not yet justified its immense cost, but other new methods of 'aggregative' analysis of records of baptisms, marriages and deaths have done so. Most notably, Wrigley and Schofield's *Population History of England* (1981) has rewritten the demographic history of England over four centuries.

Perhaps because so much effort has gone into describing population change, demographic history is still weak in analysing the causes of that change. However, it is the area of history in which most progress has been made with computer simulation of historical processes, in particular those concerned with family and household formation (Wachter, 1978). This topic has also been of particular interest to the growing number of social historians who now increasingly interact with a once derided group, genealogists or family historians; it is now recognized that many social processes can only be understood by attention to microlevel data, tracing and linking families or other social groups over long periods. A notable example of such work has been the study conducted by Alan MacFarlane, an historian and social anthropologist, of the many different records of an English village over four centuries (1980–1). But social historians have also studied social and geographical mobility through microlevel data – as in the work of the social and urban historians in the Philadelphia Social History Project.

The methods of political science have contributed to the 'new' political history. The pioneer in this field was W. A. Aydelotte (1971), but he has been succeeded, particularly in the United States and in West Germany, by historians who have made especially good use of the voluminous voting records of the two countries (Kousser, 1980).

In political as in economic and social history, much innovative historical research during the last two decades has been quantitative in method and has relied on the collection of large quantities of data. Contemporary social scientists are often ignorant of the enormous volumes of evidence which lie unused in archives, evidence which can provide sample sizes far larger than are dreamed of in current studies. The effort to use this material has produced new problems and enforced new methods of work for historians. Group research, once almost unknown in a profession where the individual scholar reigned supreme, has now become commonplace. Historical research has become much more expensive, as armies of research assistants are marshalled to tackle archives. Computer terminals are now to be seen in archives. Most strikingly, the use of quantitative methods from the social sciences has changed the vocabulary of history. Books and journals are now replete with regression coefficients and factor scores, where hitherto intuition and the telling quotation had prevailed.

The initial tendency of the 'new' history was fissiparous; economic, social and demographic historians emphasized their separate skills and interests. Recently, however, researchers have begun to realize that such divisions are stupid. Consequently, there has been a new emphasis on the uniting qualities of the new methods, leading to the foundation in the United States of the Social Science History Association.

Yet social science history does not have a monopoly of new styles of history. French historians, led by Emmanuel le Roy Ladurie, have been particularly successful in developing the history of 'mentalités', the evocation of past modes of thought and behaviour. Ladurie's most famous and popular book, *Montaillou* (1978), described the life of a medieval French village through the records of the Inquisition. The work of Philippe Ariès has also shown the potential of psychological investigation of the past (1962).

Most striking, however, has been the growth in many countries, particularly in Western Europe, of 'people's history'. In reaction both to the concentration of traditional historians on élite behaviour and to the apparently arcane methods of the new social science historians, 'people's historians' such as the History Workshop group in Britain or the adherents of *'Alltagsgeschichte'* in Germany emphasize the history of working people written by and for working people. These groups of historians have been particularly successful in drawing a large number of nonprofessionals into historical study.

These new methods, and those of the social science historians, are still challenged. The most popular English text on historical method, G. R. Elton's *The Practice of History* (1967), argues in traditional vein, for example, that the historian must be 'the servant of his evidence of which he will, or should, ask no specific questions until he has absorbed what it says. . . . The mind will indeed soon react with questions, but these are the questions suggested by the evidence . . .' Many also agree with another leading historian, Lawrence Stone, that the time has come to revive narrative history and to reject the expensive model building of the social science historians (1979).

In spite of these disagreements and in spite of its use of new methods, history retains its identity, part science and part art, its coherence stemming from its role as discoverer and interpreter of the past. Its power to stir and even to inflame is constantly shown by the use and misuse of historical parallels in political argument; the most emotive of academic disciplines, its passion and rhetoric disturb and confuse social scientists. The power of social science to simplify and generalize is its greatest gift to the historian. Yet the lesson of the variability and unpredictability of human behaviour is perhaps the greatest lesson that social science has to learn from history.

Roderick Floud
Birkbeck College, University of London

References

Aydelotte, W. A. (1971), *Quantification in History*, New York.

Ariès, P. (1962), *Centuries of Childhood*, London.

Barraclough, G. (1979), *Main Trends in History*, New York.

Bloch, M. (1949), *Apologie pour l'histoire*, Paris. (English translation, *The Historian's Craft*, New York, 1964.)

Clapham, J. H. (1922), 'On empty economic boxes', *Economic Journal*, 32.

Elton, G. R. (1967), *The Practice of History*, London.

Fishlow, A. (1965), *American Railroads and the Transformastion of the Ante-Bellum Economy*, Cambridge, Mass.

Fogel, R. W. (1964), *Railroads and American Economic Growth*, Baltimore.

Fogel, R. W. and Engerman, S. L. (1974), *Time on the Cross*, New York.

Kousser, J. M. (1980), 'Quantitative social science history', in C. Kammen (ed.), *The Past Before Us: Contemporary Historical Writing in the United States*, Ithaca, N.Y.

MacFarlane, A. (1980–1), *Records of an English Village: Earls Colne 1400–1750*, Cambridge.

Ladurie, E. le Roy (1978), *Montaillou*, Paris.

Stone, L (1979), 'The revival of narrative', *Past and Present*, 85.

Wachter, K. W. (1978), *Statistical Studies of Historical Social Structure*, New York,

Wrigley, E. A. and Schofield, R. S. (1981), *The Population History of England, 1541–1871*, London.

Further Reading

Landes, D. S. and Tilly, C. (eds) (1971), *History as Social Science*, Englewood Cliffs, N.J.

Lorwin, V. R. and Price, J. M. (eds) (1972), *The Dimensions of the Past*, New Haven.

Marwick, A. (1970), *The Nature of History*, London.

Tilly, C. (1981), *As Sociology Meets History*, New York.

International Relations

In the most general sense international relations have existed ever since men formed themselves into social groups, and then developed external relations with groups like themselves. Relationships were most frequently conflictual or warlike, although occasionally they were co-operative; but they took place in a system of anarchy and not within the framework of any political or legal or customary rules. These peculiar relationships were little considered by writers in the Western world before Machiavelli, but from the seventeenth century onwards international law (Grotius, Pufendorf, Vattel) and the problems of war and peace (Rousseau, Kant) began to attract attention. These historical origins, combined with the horror of the First World War, led to the subject's emergence as a policy-making, prescriptive and normative study: war was an intolerable evil, its recurrence must forever be prevented, and the duty of international relations scholars was to show how to achieve this. It was assumed that nobody could want war, so if states were democratic and governments were accountable to their peoples, and if the system's anarchy were ended (hence the League of Nations), war might be banished.

The diagnosis was too simple. The aspirations and actions of

Hitler, Mussolini, the Japanese, and the Bolsheviks in Moscow showed the truth of the dictum of Morgenthau (1948) that peace and security is the ideology of satisfied powers. Scholars now turned their minds away from study of ways to achieve a supposedly universal goal to study of how things in the international arena in fact were. The modern subject of international relations was born. From the outset, though at first not explicitly, the subject was approached by different scholars from two different points of view. The first sought to establish why the significant units (or actors) on the international stage behaved in the ways they did: most such scholars saw states as the significant actors, and this branch of the subject became foreign policy analysis. The second group focused on the arena within which relations occurred, and was concerned to identify the mechanisms by which patterned relationships with a fair degree of stability and order were able to be maintained in conditions which, formally at least, were anarchical. The 1950s and 1960s saw a burgeoning of methodological experimentation and quasi-theoretical speculation, and a proliferation of journals. The behaviouralist revolution in the United States invaded international relations, as it did other social sciences, and a great debate with the so-called traditionalists raged through the 1960s and early 1970s, and is not yet concluded. But in the last decade, disappointment at the relative lack of success in the creation of theories with explanatory power for real-world problems has led to some redirection of attention towards substantive questions, to smaller-scale analyses and to theorizing over limited ranges of phenomena.

Foreign policy analysis is the branch of the subject in which most practical advances have occurred. Many conceptual frameworks have been developed, the most comprehensive probably being that of Brecher et al. (1969), but the central components of such frameworks are now widely agreed. States are conceived as having objectives of various kinds – political/security, economic, ideological. Objectives are not consistently compatible one with another, and a short-term objective may be inconsistent with a long-term goal. Objectives are ranked differently by different groups, organizations, and political leaderships within states, and rankings change over time. Explanation of policy-decisions thus requires understanding of political interplay and bureaucratic process. But the determination of policy is conditioned also by states' capabilities – economic, demographic, political, military – and by decision makers' perceptions of the comparative efficacy of their own capabilities as against those of the other state(s) with which they are dealing, all in the context of support relationships (alliances, economic aid) and of respective commitments elsewhere in the system. Most, if not all, relationships have elements of conflict and common interest, and are essentially of a bargaining character; but the conflictual element usually predominates, and the concept of power is thus central to the analysis. A check-list of such considerations affecting foreign policy decisions enables rudimentary comparisons of foreign policies to be made, but also makes possible greater awareness among policy makers of the likely consequences of their decisions. enable rudimentary comparisons of foreign policies to be made, but also makes possible greater awareness among policy makers of the likely consequences of their decisions.

The purposes of studies at the second or system level are to determine the factors that make the stability of the system more or less probable, and the effect on international outcomes of the system's structure. Essential structural components are the number of significant units (or actors) in the system, the nature, quality and quantity of interactions among the units, the distribution of capabilities among them, and the degree to which realignment of relationships is easy or is constrained (a system that is ideologically highly polarized, for example, is relatively inflexible). Analysis at the system level is commonly more highly abstract than analysis of state behaviour: this makes possible theory construction of a more rigorous kind, but by the same token makes application of theory to the real world more difficult.

At both levels statistical and mathematical techniques are used, as well as more traditional methods relying on historical and verbally described data. The distinction between the levels is, of course, analytical only. To take just one example of interdependence: at the unit behaviour level the extent to which states are economically, militarily or ideologically interdependent will very greatly affect the policy choices that are open; at the system level the extent to which the realignment of units is impeded by their interdependence will fundamentally affect both outcomes and the stability of the system. Mention of interdependence calls attention to the fact that while states are widely accepted as still the most significant actors in the international arena, there are now many other actors, including intergovernmental organizations (the International Monetary Fund), and nongovernmental organizations (guerrilla groups, multinational corporations). The roles of these, in interplay with the behaviour of states, and as components of international systems, all form part – and some would say an increasingly important part – of the study of international relations.

P. A. Reynolds
University of Lancaster

References
Brecher, M., Steinberg, B. and Stein, J. (1969), 'A framework for research in foreign policy behaviour', *Journal of Conflict Resolution*, 13.
Morgenthau, H. J. (1948), *Politics Among Nations*, New York.

Further Reading
Carr, E. H. (1939), *The Twenty Years' Crisis 1919–1939*, London.
Holsti, K. J. (1977), *International Politics*, Englewood Cliffs, N.J.
Reynolds, P. A. (1980), *An Introduction to International Relations*, London.
Rosenau, J. N. (1971), *The Scientific Study of Foreign Policy*, Glencoe, Ill.
Smith, M., Little, R. and Shackleton, M. (1981), *Perspectives on World Politics*, London.
Waltz, K. N. (1979), *Theory of International Politics*, Reading, Mass.

Labour Relations

Labour relations, or industrial relations, are the terms most commonly used to refer to study of the social relations between employers and employees, management and workers, or their representatives. These relations have attracted the interest of those with a variety of disciplinary backgrounds – economics, history, law, political science, psychology and sociology, as well as students of business and management or of labour movements; consequently the study of labour relations has always been multidisciplinary. Each of these disciplines has tended to see different aspects of labour relations as problematic: economists, for example, have been interested particularly in the determination of the price of labour, lawyers in the possibilities and limitations of legal regulation, and sociologists in the nature and consequences of industrial conflict. Much of the research and writing on labour relations, however, has been descriptive, concerned with elucidating often very complex social situations, and drawing on and contributing to the various disciplines in a fairly atheoretical way.

The most notable attempts to establish the study of labour relations as an intellectual discipline in its own right have been those within a 'systems' framework (Dunlop, 1958). In an important contribution, Flanders (1970), for example, argued that the system of industrial relations constituted 'a system of rules' (legislation, collective agreements, custom and practice, and so on), regulating the relations between the enterprise and its employees, and among employees; and that the study of industrial relations could be described as 'the study of the institutions of job regulation'. Such claims to disciplinary independence have not been widely accepted, though industrial or labour relations is often the concern, and title, of separate university departments or research institutes; but in a more descriptive sense the notion of an industrial relations 'system' has been very influential.

The ways in which labour relations are analysed and interpreted depend in crucial respects on the 'frame of reference' adopted (Fox, 1966, 1973). A *unitary* perspective conceives of the industrial enterprise as a team in which all have the same underlying interests in commercial success. Symptoms of conflict, such as strikes or grievances, are attributed to inadequate management and/or to workers' irrationality, and there is no agreed place for trade unions or other interest groups. A *pluralist* perspective acknowledges that different sectional groups within the enterprise have legitimately conflicting interests, particularly in the outcome of the market relations which determine wages and in the exercise of managerial authority over employees. These conflicts of interest are manifest in a variety of ways, through 'organized' action (strikes, lock-outs, working to rule) and 'unorganized' individual behaviour (absence, sabotage); but such conflicts can be contained within procedures for negotiation and bargaining which produce acceptable compromises. A *radical* perspective, which draws heavily on Marxist social theory (Hyman, 1975), emphasizes that the relations between capital and labour are inherently asymmetrical and exploitative; labour relations are class relations and the interests of the subordinate, working class can only be realized by a fundamental transformation of the whole pattern of ownership and control of industry. Few social scientists now adopt a unitary perspective, but debates between adherents of the other two approaches continue unabated.

Richard K. Brown
University of Durham

References
Dunlop, J. T. (1958), *Industrial Relations Systems*, New York.
Flanders, A. (1970), *Management and Unions*, London.
Fox, A. (1966), 'Industrial sociology and industrial relations', *Research Paper* no. 3, Royal Commission on Trade Unions and Employers' Associations, London.
Fox, A. (1973), 'Industrial relations: a social critique of pluralist ideology', in J. Child (ed.), *Man and Organisation*, London.
Hyman, R. (1975), *Industrial Relations: A Marxist Introduction*, London.

Further Reading
Clegg, H. A. (1979), *The Changing System of Industrial Relations in Great Britain*, Oxford.
Hyman, R. (1977), *Strikes*, Glasgow.
Nichols, T. (ed.) (1980), *Capital and Labour*, Glasgow.

Law

Conceptions of what law is are culturally and historically specific. But legal 'theories' often claim for themselves a univer-
salism that they do not really have. When scholars from the
Western European legal tradition study the laws and legal
institutions of other cultures, what they look for are norms and
institutions that are either in form or function analogous to
those in their own heritage. The category 'law' they proceed
from is a Western cultural construct (Berman, 1983).

Many of the arguments about what law is or should be are
organized around a single dichotomy: whether the basis of law
is a moral consensus or a matter of organized domination. Law
is sometimes interpreted as an expression of cultural values,
sometimes as a rationalized framework of power. In ethnographic fact it is usually both. Separating the two absolutely
creates a false opposition. Friedman (1975) has argued that 'the
function of the legal system is to distribute and maintain an
allocation of values that society feels to be right . . . allocation,
invested with a sense of rightness, is what is commonly referred
to as *justice*'. Society is thus anthropomorphized as a consensual
entity having common values. But Friedman's more extended
discussion indicates a clear awareness of social stratification,
and sharp differences of interest and power. His social science
approach tries to embrace both consensus and domination in
the same analysis.

In the jurisprudence of the West there have been a number
of competing scholarly paradigms of law. The four principal
schools of thought with roots in the nineteenth century (and
earlier) are conventionally designated: (1) natural law theory;
(2) analytical jurisprudence (or legal positivism); (3) historical
jurisprudence (or legal evolutionism); and (4) sociological jurisprudence. The various modern social science perspectives on
law have been shaped by this intellectual history, as have
modern works on jurisprudence and legal history. Current work
is best understood in the light of earlier ideas.

(1) Natural Law Thinking
In its various forms this dominated Western ideas about justice
through the eighteenth century, and has not fully disappeared,

being perhaps most evident today in current arguments about universal human rights. It was once closely associated with the idea of divine law. Natural law theory postulates the existence of a universal, underlying system of 'justice' and 'right', which is distinguishable from mere human enactments, norms and judgements. The content of this natural law was thought to be discoverable by human beings through the exercise of reason. To be just, human laws should conform to natural law, but they do not always do so. Human law can be unjust.

(2) Legal Positivism

This was a nineteenth-century development that continues in new forms to the present, and attacked natural law thinking on the ground that it was unscientific, that it was grounded on a mythical entity, and that it confused law with morality. The notion was that only law *as it is* can be the subject of scientific inquiry, that the province of what law ought to be was not a matter for science, but for philosophers and theologians. It was Bentham's follower, John Austin, who first generated 'the science of positive law'. Austin's science was a 'conceptual jurisprudence' occupied with discovering the key doctrines and ideas actually used in the existing formal legal system.

Austin's most cited formulation is one in which law is treated as command, the source of law as 'the sovereign person or body' that sets it within a particular 'political society'. And, consistent with this position, Austin argued that international law was 'improperly so-called' because it was neither set nor enforced by a political superior. He invented a category, 'positive morality' to contrast with 'positive law' to accommodate the law-like quality of international law without having it disturb his model that associated law with sovereignty.

Later positivists were critical of Austin, and developed modifications. Hans Kelsen generated an analysis which he called 'the pure theory of law' in which he asserted that law consists of a hierarchy of norms to which sanctions are attached. The validity of lower-level norms is derived from higher norms, until ultimately at the top of the hierarchy is the 'basic norm' on which the whole structure depends. The effect of that basic norm is to require people to behave in conformity to the legal order. It defines the limits of that order.

Another major positivist critic of the Austinian perspective is H. L. A. Hart who also has reservations about the artificiality of Kelsen's idea of the basic norm, and proposes an alternative. Hart (1961) rejects a conception of law based on coercive order as one too much derived from the model of criminal law. He argues that in fact law does many more things than prohibit or command and punish. It also can empower persons to act, and can define the conditions under which such actions are legally effective. Hart points to three troublesome issues that frequently recur in the attempt to define the specifically legal and distinguish it from other domains: the relationship between law and coercive orders, between legal obligation and moral obligation, and the question whether law is to be understood as a set of rules. Plainly there are coercive orders, binding obligations and rules that are not matters of law, yet all three elements also are central to legal systems. How are these to be distinguished? Hart's resolution of this problem is to describe law as a set of social rules divided into two types: primary rules of obligation and secondary rules of recognition, change and adjudication. The secondary rules sort the legal from other rule orders. Since legal validity is established by formal criteria, according to Hart's definition, an immoral law can be legally valid. Original and elegantly formulated as Hart's discussion is widely acknowledged to be, it has been criticized for its exclusive focus on rules at the expense of other important dimensions of legal systems, particularly the fact that it is a formal internal definition that turns away from questions about the socioeconomic context, the institutional framework and cultural ideas that inform law in action. His is very much a formalist lawyer's definition, and emphatically not a sociological one. Much of the sociological perspective has emerged as a reaction against this kind of legal positivism.

(3) The So-Called Historical School
Here renamed evolutionist, this developed as another nineteenth-century reaction to natural law thinking. It is much more society-conscious and culture-conscious than positivism.

In Germany this took the form of an almost mystical conception of the cultural unity of a people. This was coupled with the idea that there was an organic mode in which a people's inherent destiny unfolded over time. For Savigny, law was the expression of the spirit (*Volksgeist*) of a particular people, the notion of *Volksgeist* being ambiguously associated with race as well as culture. In this interpretation, custom was the fundamental form of law since it originated in the life of the people. Legislated law was only significant when grounded in popular awareness, a kind of codification and refinement of legal ideas already in the popular consciousness.

In England, Maine (1861) constructed a very different historical approach. He rejected Savigny's idea of the *Volksgeist* special to each people, and tried to generalize about the evolution of law and legal ideas in universal terms. Using comparative examples of the legal institutions of a few peoples, he endeavoured to show the sequential steps in the legal development of 'progressive' societies. His idea was that in the shift from kin-based to territorially-based polities, collective family property faded out and private individual property came in, that there was a change in the conception of certain wrongs which ceased to be treated as torts and came to be treated as crimes, and that much of the law affecting persons shifted from status to contract. Many of these generalizations have been criticized in later work, but the questions they raise remain issues of importance.

Marx, though only peripherally concerned with law, has had such a profound effect on social thought that his ideas about law must be taken into account in any review of these matters. He resists compartmentalization but could be suitably placed within the historical school, as his is a theory of sequential developments. Since in his model of history class struggle is the principal dynamic of change, law is a dependent variable, not an independent force. In Marx's thought, the mode and relations of production constitute the 'base' of any social formation, and politics, law and ideology are part of the 'superstructure' of ideas and practices which maintain a given set of class relations. The state and law are seen essentially as instruments of class domination, and reflections of it. In the twentieth century, the expansion of the Welfare State, largely the product of legislation, has often been referred to in order to call into question some of these ideas of Marx's about law, but some Marxists see no contradiction in the matter and argue that what has happened is simply that class domination has taken new forms.

Marxist and neo-Marxist ideas are extremely important in the development of current critical legal theory. Marxist themes can be seen in the work of Abel (1982), Kennedy (1980), and Balbus (1977) among others. They interpret law as a mode of maintaining the inequalities inherent in capitalist economies, however seemingly ameliorative reformist laws sometimes appear on their face.

(4) The Sociological School

By contrast, from the start, this school was wedded to the idea that progress could be made to occur through legal reform. Today, a major species of legal sociology interprets law as the means of solving social problems. Jhering thought of society as an arena of competing interests, and that the function of law was to mediate among them. The purpose was to produce 'the security of the conditions of social life' as a whole. The good of the whole was to come above special interests. Pound (1911–12) came to be very much influenced by Jhering's ideas as he considered the function of law in a democracy. He added his own conception that the task of law was one of 'social engineering'. In order that law achieve a scientifically informed efficacy in this role, he urged that sociological studies be made of any social field to be regulated, and also of the actual impact of existing legal institutions, precepts and doctrines.

Ehrlich, another member of the sociological school, stressed the gap between law on the books and the 'living law', the actual conventional practices of a people. For Ehrlich (1926 [1913]) social practice was the true source of viable law. This 'living law' could come to be embodied in formal statutes and decisions, but law that did not have that anchoring lacked the social vitality to be just and effective. Consequently Ehrlich exhorted lawyers and jurists to make themselves aware of existing social conditions and practices in order to bring formal law into harmony with society. This explains Ehrlich's broad definition of law as 'the sum of the conditions of social life in the widest sense of the term'. 'Law' included rules made and enforced by private associations. His was not a definition focused on 'government', but on 'society'.

Ehrlich's contemporary, Weber (1954 [1922]), conceived of law equally broadly. Law, he said, involved a 'coercive apparatus', the purpose of which was norm-enforcement within a community, corporate organization or an institution. Thus law-like norms could be 'guaranteed' by a variety of social bodies, not only by the state, although the state differed from the others in having a monopoly on 'coercion by violence'. Weber made it clear that, despite the coercive apparatus, the motive for obedience to norms was not necessarily the existence of such a system of physical coercion. The motive could be 'psychological'.

In his models of government and society, his 'ideal types', Weber identified the bureaucratic state with a 'legal order' of 'rational' rules. As he saw it, the evolution of law was marked by a movement from formal and substantive irrationality to rationality. In this sense rationality meant a logically coherent system of principles and rules. Legal irrationality was the use of means other than logic or reason for the decision of cases. Ordeals and oracles were examples of formal irrationality. Arbitrary decisions in terms of the personal predilections of the judge constituted substantive irrationality. In his ideal types Weber postulated a consistency between the type of overall political organization of a society (its mode of 'imperative co-ordination'), its values and ideology, and its type of legal system.

Weber's ideas continue to influence the work of theorists of law. One of the recent revisionist writers is Unger (1976), who borrows 'ideal types' from Weber and postulates a multiplicity of them in historical sequence. But not only do his types differ from Weber's, but he sees as the principal impetus to change an awareness of the dissonance between ideal and real in a particular social order. His is a very orderly, very personal vision. In his view, the problem of our time is the reconciliation of freedom and community.

Like Weber's, Durkheim's (1960 [1893]) legal theory had an evolutionary theme. He thought that primitive societies were held together by 'mechanical solidarity', a coherence produced by a homogeneity of culture and a sameness of all social units, while the cohesion of complex societies was one of 'organic solidarity' founded on the division of labour in society and a system of complementary differences. Associated with each of these was a type of law. He regarded punitive retribution as the mode of dealing with wrongs in primitive society, while restitutive justice was appropriate to repair many wrongs under conditions of 'organic solidarity'. While Durkheim's interpretation of law in primitive societies was quite wrong, as the anthropologist Malinowski (1926) later showed, the direction of his inquiry, the question to what extent law is an aspect of social cohesion, remains cogent.

Today, social scientists approach law with a distilled and selective recombination of many of these classical ideas of nineteenth-century and early twentieth-century scholars. They use these transformed paradigms in combination with new methods, new information and new preoccupations. These have been generated in a very much altered politico-economic setting. Statistical studies have become an essential concomitant in many analyses of law and its effect in mass society. Quantitative methods have also been applied to the study of legal institutions themselves, to the behaviour of courts, lawyers, and administrative agencies. Legal arguments and rationales are not taken at face value, but are studied as texts, both as they reveal and as they obscure values and interests. Economic dimensions and consequences have loomed increasingly large in the study and evaluation of legal norms. The costs of 'justice' and the nature of access to 'justice' have become major issues. The high-flown values that legal principles express are examined by legal economists in the light of their 'efficiency' and their social effect, not just their self-defined moral content.

Anthropologists have substantially enlarged the existing body of knowledge regarding the social order of non-Western societies, simple and complex. Ethnographic materials collected through direct observation have made plain the ways in which order is maintained without government in small-scale systems, and the way disputes are negotiated in oral cultures. These works are pertinent to the operation of subsections of large-scale, complex societies. A knowledge of such subsystems illuminates the peculiar relation between national laws and local practices in many parts of the world.

The importance and widespread existence of plural legal systems has been acknowledged in the post-colonial world as never before. All the theories founded on a notion that consensus and common values necessarily underlie all effective legal systems have been brought into question in the many instances in which power, rather than consensus, underpins particular laws. The role of law in relation to dissensus and conflict, cultural pluralism and class stratification is an increasingly urgent question for social theorists. The difference between the way law is conceived in the West and elsewhere has also become important as the greater interdependence of all countries is manifest. The question whether there are overarching commonalities that are or could be embodied in international law bears on everything from international commerce to the rights of refugees.

Variously conceived by the professions that generate, apply and enforce it, law is obviously quite differently approached by those who observe, analyse and teach it. Thus there is the law of lawyers and judges, of governments, of legislators and administrators, the formal legal system, its concepts and doctrines, its institutions and workings. In a related, but not identical, territory is the law of legal theorists and legal scholars and social scientists, many of them teachers. Beyond that is the way that the legal order impinges on ongoing social life.

Social scientists study all of this wide range, with a great variety of purposes and perspectives. Some are occupied with assembling information which will be the basis for proposed reforms. Others are engaged in trying to understand the relation between the actual workings of legal institutions and the self-explanations that form its ideology, without any immediate application in mind, rather with the idea of enlarging knowledge, and refining theory. In the broadest sense, one might say that there are two general streams of modern research. One is a social problems/social engineering approach that proceeds from the assumption that law is a consciously constructed instrument of control which has the capacity to shape society and to solve problems, an instrument which can itself be reformed and perfected towards this end. Research is seen to serve these practical purposes. In contrast is the social context approach which assumes that law is itself a manifestation of the existing structure (or past history) of the society in which it is found, and tries to know, understand or explain its form, content and institutions by showing contextual connections. Instead of just one 'social science approach' to law, there are many.

Sally Falk Moore
Harvard University

References

Abel, R. (1982), 'The contradictions of informal justice', in R. Abel (ed.), *The Politics of Informal Justice, Vol. I: The American Experience*, New York.

Balbus, I. D. (1977), 'Commodity form and legal form: an essay on the "relative autonomy" of the law', *Law and Society Review*, 571.

Berman, H. J. (1983), *Law and Revolution; The Formation of the Western Legal Tradition*, Cambridge, Mass.

Durkheim, E. (1960 [1893]), *The Division of Labour in Society*, Glencoe, Ill. (Original French edn, *De la Division du travail social*, Paris.)

Ehrlich, E. (1936 [1913]), *Fundamental Principles of the Sociology of Law*, tr. Walter L. Moll, Cambridge, Mass. (Original German edn, *Grundlegung der Soziologie des Rechts*, Munich.)

Friedman, M. (1975), *The Legal System, A Social Science Perspective*, New York.

Hart, H. L. A. (1961), *The Concept of Law*, New York.

Kennedy, D. (1980), 'Toward an historical understanding of legal consciousness: the case of classical legal thought in America 1850–1940', *Research in Law and Sociology*, 3.

Maine, H. (1861), *Ancient Law*, London.

Malinowski, B. (1926), *Crime and Custom in Savage Society*, London.

Pound, R. (1911–12), 'The scope and purpose of sociological jurisprudence', *Harvard Law Review*, 24 and 25.

Unger, R. (1976), *Law in Modern Society*, New York.

Weber, M. (1954 [1922]), *Max Weber on Law in Economy and Society*, ed. M. Feinstein, Cambridge, Mass. (Original German edn, *Wirtschaft und Gesellschaft*, Tübingen.)

Further Reading

Black, D. (1976), *The Behavior of Law*, New York.

Cain, M. and Hunt, A. (1979), *Marx and Engels on Law*, London.

Friedman, L. M. and MacCaulay, S. (eds) (1977), *Law and The Behavioral Sciences*, 2nd edn, Indianapolis.

Nader, L. and Todd, H. F. (eds) (1975), *The Disputing Process – Law in Ten Societies*, New York.

Nonet, P. and Selznick, P. (1978), *Law and Society in Transition*, New York.

Linguistics

Linguistics can be defined as the science of language. Language, however, may be approached from a number of different perspectives, and it plays such a central role in human life that many disciplines are concerned with language in one way or another. Indeed every science contains one linguistic component at the very least, the language of its theory and observations with which it may at times be concerned. What then distinguishes linguistics from other sciences?

There is one field which is particularly close to linguistics, and that is the study of literature, since its very material is verbal. However, even in this case the preoccupation with linguistic matters is different from that of linguistics itself. In all other fields, language is a means to an end; only in linguistics is it studied as an end in itself.

Like so many other sciences, linguistics took its modern form as a separate academic discipline in the nineteenth century, although, it has a long prehistory. In particular it was preceded by national philologies, which arose in literate societies such as those of India, China and Greece. Modern linguistics developed in Europe on the basis of the Graeco-Roman tradition with minor contributions from Semitic sources in the Renaissance. The most theoretically sophisticated of these national philologies was that of India, and yet it only became known to Europe in the nineteenth century while an appreciation of its significance is even more recent.

Although the philological studies of the grammarians is the chief source for linguistics in the Classical tradition, two other pursuits are worthy of mention. One is the philosophical concern with the nature of language. The main question was whether the relation between sound and meaning is natural or conventional and the most important discussion is Plato's *Cratylus*. The second source is rhetoric, the effective use of language in public speaking and writing. Some of the earliest analyses of linguistic phenomena, such as Protagoras' distinguishing of the various moods of the verb, grew out of this applied interest.

The most important, though, was the philological tradition of the grammarians which developed in the Alexandrian period. In common with other national philologies it displayed the following features. The study of languages has as its goal the understanding of certain highly valued texts, sacred or, in the case of the Greeks, profane, namely the Homeric poems. It involves concentration on a single language and a valuation of it as superior to all other forms of speech including the contemporary spoken language which inevitably, in the course of linguistic change, has come to differ from it. It views historic change not as a rational process but as a haphazard degeneration from a formerly ideal state. This in turn involves the notion of prescriptivism, an attempt to restore a particular norm which is contrary to existing usage. The concentration on written texts also makes the written form primary *vis-à-vis* the spoken, since sounds are merely the momentary realizations of the apparently stable and fixed written norms. That language is not here studied for its own sake is very strikingly expressed in the *Technē Grammatikē* (attributed to Dionysius Thrax around 100 BC), itself the model of numerous subsequent grammars. After enumerating the various subdivisions of grammar, the last mentioned is 'the appreciation of literary composition which is the noblest part of grammar'.

Nevertheless this tradition made lasting contributions. It provided a comprehensive model for describing language which was well suited to Latin and Greek and is the source of a large part of current linguistic terminology. It may be called the word-paradigm model. The sentence consists of words which are divisible on the basis of form and function into a small number of classes, the parts of speech. Further, each part of speech can be considered from two points of view, internal variabililty of form (morphology) and functional relation to other words in the speech chain (syntax). In the area of morphology the lasting achievement was the discovery of the paradigm, literally 'example'. Inflectional parts of speech such as the noun vary according to a set of categories, for example, case and number, and the number of distinct models is very small. For instance, all Latin nouns of the first declension have similar variations of form and any one noun, such as *puella*, 'girl', can be viewed as an example to follow for the rest. This was no mean achievement and grew out of the dispute in the Alexandrian period between the analogists, who stressed regularity in language, and the anomalists, who denied it. It was the search for regularities by the analogists that revealed the existence of comprehensive patterns, namely paradigms.

In syntax, there was the classification of types of relationship among words such as government, as when a verb requires and hence 'governs' a particular case, and agreement, as when two words agree in having the same categories, for example, the adjectives agreeing with nouns in gender, number and case.

One further feature of this model should be mentioned. It involved a hierarchy of levels. Sounds made up words; words made up sentences. On this basis there were two main levels, the phonological and grammatical, the latter divided, as has been seen, into morphology and syntax. Such a notion of levels has remained as part of linguistic theory. In particular the existence of phonological and grammatical levels, even though there are relationships between them, seems to be fundamental to any theory of language.

The model just described was not all discovered at once by

the Greeks. It developed considerably in the Roman, medieval and the post-medieval periods. In particular the rise of *grammaire générale*, largely but not exclusively French, in the seventeenth and eighteenth century (though without medieval predecessors) deserves mention. It employed the word-paradigm model but sought to explain its structure by reference to universal reason and the very nature of the world and of thought as shown by metaphysics and logic. Thus the difference between nouns and adjectives mirrored the difference between substances and their qualities. Moreover, a number of languages were often compared on the assumption that such categories, inherent in human reason, must exist in all languages.

The nineteenth century was not marked merely by the rise of linguistics as a separate discipline but involved a revolution in the conception of language. As a result of exploration and colonization, Europe became acutely aware of the vast number and diversity of human languages. The traditional explanation was the biblical story of the Tower of Babel, and at first the main question was what language was spoken before the confusion of tongues, the *lingua Adamica*. However, it began to be noticed that the differences in language were not haphazard; they fall into groupings such as the Romance, Germanic and Semitic languages.

The basic explanation which developed about the turn of the nineteenth century was that just as Spanish was like Italian because they were both changed forms of an originally homogeneous language, Latin, so where the original language was not recorded, the explanation had to be similar. There must have been a 'Proto-Germanic' and a 'Proto-Semitic' and so on. Moreover this process of differentiation of an ancestral language was not confined to the most obvious groupings. In particular the discovery of Sankrit, the sacred language of India, with its obvious resemblance to Latin, Greek and other European languages, led to the hypothesis of an original Indo-European language which had branched into Latin, Greek, Indo-Iranian, Germanic, Slavic and so on, which then in most instances differentiated once more in a more recent period. The metaphor was that of a family tree.

The historical-comparative method that dominated nineteenth-century linguistics had as its goal the reconstruction of the original ancestral language and of the subsequent changes in it, which gave rise to later language. It was mainly applied to Indo-European but was also employed in the study of other language families. This way of looking at language was in many ways diametrically opposed to the traditional one inherited from Classical philology. Change is not a haphazard degeneration but follows rational patterns, indeed, becomes the central object of linguistic science. Changes on the phonological level are understandable in terms of articulatory and auditory similarity. Hence the written form is equally valuable since change is not degeneration, and the logical basis for linguistic prescriptivism is destroyed.

During the nineteenth century and up to about 1920, the inherited pattern of grammatical description, though often modified, continued its sway because the focus of interest was historical change. However, in the late 1920s another basic revolution in linguistics occurred, which we may call the structural. The first articulation of this was in 1915 in the posthumous *Cours de linguistique générale* (English translation, *Course in General Linguistics*, 1959) of Ferdinand de Saussure of Geneva. De Saussure, himself a historical linguist by training, introduced a terminology which has become general in the social sciences. Language can be studied diachronically in its aspect of historical process, or synchronically in terms of the internal relations within a state as abstracted from change. There were a number of structural schools, differing in many respects but united in finding in the synchronic structure of language the central object of linguistic science. An important factor was the work of anthropologists on non-Western languages where both the profound differences from Western languages and the usual absence of historical records combined to concentrate attention on synchronic structure.

The nature of these new methods can be most easily illustrated from phonology, which was in fact the earliest area of interest for the structuralists. A mere enumeration of the sounds of the language without regard to their functional relations was unenlightening. Thus two languages might both have *p* and *b* sounds which were phonetically identical but, if a rule could be formulated that told us when *p* occurs and when *b* in terms of other sounds, there could never be a functional meaning contrast. This is the case for the Algonkian languages. In English, on the other hand, *pat* and *bat* are different words. For the Algonkian languages *p* and *b* belong to the same phoneme or functional unit, while in English they are two contrasting units.

Similarly, methods were extended to the grammatical level leading to the positing of functional units like the morpheme. Thus the English phonemic variants of the plural -*s*, -*z* and -*əz* are predictable on the basis of the final phoneme, the stem, and hence are members of the same functional unit.

In 1957, Chomsky's *Syntactic Structures* ushered in the period of generative grammar. The basic concept uses not functional units but rules. Moreover, grammar was constructed not as in the American structural school of observation by induction from the bottom up, morphemes consisting of phonemes and so on, but from top down – from syntax, particularly relations among whole sentence patterns (transformations) with appeals to native intuitions of grammaticality. The whole grammar was not unlike an axiomatic system. The basic formulas often called deep structure such as Subject + Predicate occurred first and by rule-governed substitutions, and transformations ended up as strings which would then be realized as actual utterances by phonological rules. After some years it became apparent that describing languages with this basic approach also leads to differing theories as in structuralism, and at the time of writing no one version holds the field.

A basic question raised by both the structuralist and generative revolution was the role of interlinguistic comparisons. Historical linguistics was essentially comparative, but was it possible to compare structures ahistorically? Did one just end up with an indefinitely large number of non-comparable individual descriptions? The American structuralist school seemed on the whole content with these results. The only universals of the dominant view were those of methodology. Languages could differ to any degree so that no cross-linguistic generalization was possible. The Prague school stressed the possibility of comparing structures and made some beginnings, especially in phonology. Chomsky had by 1965 (*Syntactic Structures*) moved to the notion of universal grammar and indeed hailed *Grammaire générale* as a predecessor. All grammars had identical deep structures and these reflected a universal genetically based human endowment. This viewpoint ultimately had to be abandoned to be replaced by universal constraints on the forms of grammars. Finally there were those who approached language universals by noting the existence of recurring and limited sets of types based on observations close to the surface, for example, in word order. Such constraints were frequently in the form of implicational relationships. For instance, language of the VSO type (with basic order verb-subject-object) always had the dependent genitive after the noun, but not necessarily *vice versa*. There were also non-restricted universals, such as that all sound systems have at least two vowel levels and two series of stop sounds based on the point of articulation.

Linguistics is at present divided into a considerable number of subfields, some of which are interdisciplinary. Some linguists pursue historical comparison whose legitimacy has never been seriously questioned by structuralists, usually specializing in some particular historical family, or subfamily, of languages. Others, particularly anthropological linguists, concentrate on the synchronic description of unwritten languages often with an areal specialization and some historical-comparative interests. On the basis of linguistic structure, some specialize in phonology frequently involving laboratory phonetics. Others work on grammatical level, particularly the syntactic, and may have connections with computer science. Still others are chiefly interested in semantics, often in alliance with philosophy. More purely interdisciplinary fields include psycholinguistics, involving an analysis of the psychological processes at work in language use, acquisition of language by the child or second-language learning. A further important interdisciplinary area is sociolinguistics, commonly divided into macro-sociolinguistics, for example, language in relation to ethnicity with its accompanying social, political and education problems, and micro-sociolinguistics, which is concerned with conversational interaction as related, for example, to situational factors and the relative social status of the participants.

Since the 1950s linguistics, usually a minor speciality in other departments, has had an almost explosive growth, particularly in the United States, with a corresponding expansion in the number and size of independent departments and reflecting both the intellectual development of the field itself and its numerous connections with other disciplines.

Joseph Greenberg
Stanford University

Further Reading

Greenberg, J. H. (1977), *New Invitation to Linguistics*, Garden City, New York.

Greenberg, J. J. (ed.) (1978), *Universals of Human Language*, 4 vols, Stanford, Calif.

Lyons, J. (1968), *Introduction to Theoretical Linguistics*, 2 vols, London.

Newmeyer, F. J. (1980), *Linguistic Theory in America*, New York.

Robins, R. H. (1968), *A Short History of Linguistics*, Bloomington, Ind.

Sampson, G. (1980), *Schools of Linguistics*, Stanford, Calif.

Vachek, J. (1964), *A Prague School Reader in Linguistics*, Bloomington, Ind.

Mass Media

Mass media together comprise a new social institution, concerned with the production and distribution of knowledge in the widest sense of the word, and have a number of salient characteristics, including: the use of relatively advanced technology for the (mass) production and dissemination of messages; the systematic organization and social regulation of this work; the direction of messages at potentially large audiences who are unknown to the sender and free to attend or not. The mass media institution is essentially open, operating in the public sphere to provide regular channels of communication for 'messages' of a kind determined by what is culturally and technically possible, socially permitted and in demand by a large enough number of individuals.

It is usual to date the beginnings of mass media from the first recognizably modern newspaper, in the early seventeenth century, which in turn was a new application of the technology of printing, already in use for over 150 years for the multiple reproduction of book manuscripts. The audiovisual forms which have subsequently been developed, mainly since the end of the nineteenth century, have caused existing media to adapt and have enlarged the total reach of media, as well as extended the diversity of their social functions.

This history of media development is, nevertheless, more than a record of technical advance and of increasing scale of operation. It was a social innovation as much as a technological invention, and turning points in media history are marked, if not caused, by major social changes. The history of the newspaper, still the archetypal as well as the first, mass medium, illustrates the point very well. Its development is linked to the emergence to power of the bourgeois (urban-business-professional) class, which it served in cultural, political and commercial activities. It became an essential instrument in subsequent economic and political struggles, a necessary condition for economic liberalism, constitutional democracy and, perhaps also, revolution and bureaucratic centralism. Its development thus reflects political and economic forces on the one hand and major social and cultural changes on the other. The latter include: urbanization; rising living standards and the growth of leisure; the emergence of forms of society which are, variously, democratic, highly organized, bureaucratic, nationalistic and committed to gradual change. Consideration of newer media, especially film, radio and television, would not greatly modify this assessment, and these media have not greatly widened the range of functions already performed by the newspaper as advertiser, entertainer and forum for the expression of opinion and culture.

Early social science views of mass media reflect some of these historical circumstances. Commentators were struck by the immense popular appeal of the new media and by the power which they might exert in society. Beyond that, views divided sharply on whether to welcome or regret the new instruments of culture and information, and a division between pessimists and optimists has been an enduring feature of assessments of mass media, only starting to fade as the inevitability and complexity of the media are accepted. The pessimistic view stems partly from the pejorative connotations of the word 'mass', which includes the notions of vast scale, anonymity, impersonality, uniformity, lack of regulation, mindlessness. At the extreme, the media were regarded, sometimes by conservative and radical critics alike, as instruments for manipulation, a threat to existing cultural and spiritual values and to democracy. But optimists saw the mass media as a powerful means of disseminating information, education and culture to the previously excluded classes and of making feasible a genuine participatory democracy. By the 1930s some circumstantial evidence and enough theory supported both 'sides', but there was little systematic investigation.

The first period of scientific investigation of mass media undertaken between the mid 1930s and the late 1950s resulted in a much more modest estimate of media effects than was previously assumed, even a new 'myth' of media powerlessness. The earlier stimulus-response model of influence was replaced by a model of indirect influence, according to which the media were seen to be subject to mechanisms of selective attention, perception and response, such that any effects would be more likely to reinforce existing tendencies than to cause any major change. Further, the working of media was seen to be subordinate to the existing patterns of social and personal influence and thus not well conceived of as an 'external' influence. While the evidence reassured many critics and discomfited prophets of doom, it seemed to lead to no slackening of efforts to use media, in ever more subtle ways, for political and commercial ends. Since the 1960s there has been further development in the assessment of mass media effects in the direction of a renewed belief in their potency.

The earlier research, despite its reassuring message, left open the possibility that media effects could be considerable under certain conditions: (1) where there exists a monopoly or uniformity of message content; (2) where the messages seem to concern matters beyond immediate experience or direct relevance; (3) where there is a cumulation over a long period of time of similar messages. Research attention has thus shifted from the search for direct, short-time, effects on individuals and towards the following: structures of ownership and control of media; patterns of ideology or culture in messages and texts; professional and organizational contexts in which media knowledge is 'manufactured'. Experts assessing the influence of mass media nowadays emphasize what people 'learn' from the media, thus cognitive effects in the widest sense. We may learn from the media what is normal or approved, what is 'right' or 'wrong', what to expect as an individual, group or class, and how we should view other groups or nations. Aside from the nature and magnitude of media effects on people, it is impossible to doubt the enormous dependence of individuals, institutions and society as a whole on mass media for a wide range of information and cultural services.

If the mass media play an essential part in mediating a wide range of relationships within societies, they have also come to be seen as playing a comparable part in mediating relations between nation states and world blocs. The flow of information and culture by way of mass media does much to establish and confirm patterns of perception, of hostility and attraction and also the relations of economic dependence and latent conflict between the different 'worlds' of East and West, North and South. While mass media still largely consist of separate national systems, the increasing internationalization of networks and content is now interesting researchers.

The history of mass media has so far been fairly short and very eventful, but it already seems on the point of a new and significant departure which may change the essential character of mass communication. The most important developments are of smaller-scale, point-to-point and potentially interactive media, employing cable, satellite or computer technology. It is likely that there will be a move away from centralized and uniform media of distribution towards a more abundant and functionally diversified provision of messages based on receiver demand. The boundaries between mass communication and the emerging new forms of information transfer are likely to become even more blurred in what is being hailed as an emerging 'information society'. Nevertheless, the issues which shaped early debates about mass media are still somewhat relevant in the new conditions, especially those which concern the contribution of mass communication to equality or inequality, order or change, unity or fragmentation.

Denis McQuail
University of Amsterdam

Further Reading
McQuail, D. (1983), *Mass Communication Theory, An Introduction*, London.
Curran, J., Gurevitch, M. and Wollacott, J. (eds) (1977), *Mass Communication and Society*, London.

Mental Health

The categories of mental health and mental illness have to be understood against the backdrop of the social institutions and practices which gave rise to them; and to do this, we need to set the whole in historical context.

Mental illness replaced earlier nineteenth-century concepts of 'madness' or 'insanity'. This was not primarily because of changing beliefs about the cause of mental disturbances, but because the medical profession had gained control of their management. Psychiatry arose hand in hand with the asylum system, but at the outset the latter was conceived as a social remedy for a social problem: if anything, doctors captured this territory *despite* their association with physical theories and treatments, not because of it. Thus, the concepts of mental health and illness were not closely tied to a physical approach to mental disorders. In the nineteenth century, indeed, the most significant feature of mental illness was not its cause but its treatment – incarceration in an asylum. Mental patients at this time were defined as a group primarily by the danger they were seen to pose to themselves or others, a danger which could not be contained in any other way.

The asylum became in practice a last resort when no hope remained for the patient, but in this century the fight against mental illness was taken outside its walls and into the home, workplace and school, where interventions could be made before problems had become intractable. The invention of psychological theories and treatments, in which Freud played a key role, greatly facilitated this spread. Treatment moved from the asylum to the consulting-room, and the meanings of mental illness and mental health shifted accordingly. A new range of illnesses (most importantly, the neuroses) was recognized, and a new range of professions – social work, psychotherapy and the various branches of psychology – arose alongside psychiatry.

Rather than being seen as dangerous, the mental patient was now primarily someone who could not cope with his allotted tasks in life: mental illness was seen as partial and reversible (Armstrong, 1980). Mental health, in the rhetoric of the influential 'mental hygiene movement' founded in America in 1909, became equated with productiveness, social adjustment, and contentment – 'the good life' itself.

The promise of this approach as a panacea for all human ills, coupled with the enormous potential market it opened up to professionals, led to a huge increase in mental health services by the middle of this century. A key factor in the creation of this 'therapeutic state' was the adoption by the mental health professions of a 'scientific' image: in this way, their interventions came to be seen as applications of a value-free, ideologically neutral technology, after the fashion of Comte's 'positivism'.

Social scientists have approached mental health in two main ways. The first is to explore the connection between mental illnesses and aspects of the social environment. Classic studies in this mould are those of Hollingshead and Redlich (1958), who found an increased incidence of mental illness in lower social classes; Brenner (1973), who associated mental illness and economic cycles; and Brown and Harris (1978), who identified predisposing and precipitating factors in women's depression. Though this approach can be seen as merely an extension of the psychiatric enterprise, it nevertheless suggests that to treat environmentally-related conditions as cases of individual malfunctioning may be a form of 'blaming the victim' (Ryan, 1972). In this light, the role of psychiatrists emerges as a fundamentally conservative one: to alleviate the stresses inherent in the social order, while removing any threat to that order itself. It is implicit in the psychiatric concept of 'maladjustment' that it is the individual who has to adapt to society, and not the other way round.

Nevertheless, in the heyday of psychiatric expansionism in the US (the 1950s and early 1960s), some psychiatrists argued that the reform of adverse social conditions was a valid part of psychiatry's mandate after all. Yet financial cutbacks, professional inhibitions, and a political shift to the right soon nipped this 'preventive' psychiatry in the bud.

The second approach adopted by social scientists challenges the very notion of mental illness, and questions the motives that lie behind professional interventions. (Such questioning is invited by the seemingly arbitrary variations in psychiatric nosology, diagnosis and treatment between different times, places and practitioners.) One line of argument focuses on the way in which the field has been shaped by professional self-interest and financial or political factors (for example, profiteering by the drug companies): this critique runs parallel to that made by Illich (1977) and Freidson (1970) of physical medicine. Such an approach has been adopted by historians who have set out to correct the 'triumphalist' picture which professions tend to present of their own history – a picture in which the cumulative victories of reason and humanity culminate inevitably in the achievements of the present.

Other commentators, however, take the argument a step further: they treat mental health as an ideological concept, concealing highly problematic notions about how people should live, and regard the professions that deal with it as agencies of social control. This critique came to the fore in the 1960s, via the work of Foucault (1961), Szasz (1961), Goffman (1961), Scheff (1966) and 'anti-psychiatrists' such as Laing (1960). These writers were not simply claiming that the labelling of certain conditions as 'pathological' was value-laden and culture-bound, for, as Sedgwick (1982) pointed out, the same is true of physical conditions. The critique of psychiatry went further, in claiming that the so-called 'symptoms' were in fact meaningful and freely-chosen acts.

This criticism seems warranted when psychiatry stops people from doing what they want, by means of physical or chemical intervention – for example, political dissidents in the Soviet Union, homosexuals in the West, or (according to Shrag and Divoky, 1975) the million or so American schoolchildren kept under permanent sedation to prevent 'hyperactivity'. Such an analysis seems inapplicable, however, when treatment is actively sought by people anxious to get rid of their 'symptoms'. Moreover, some treatments (especially psychotherapy) claim to increase autonomy, not to diminish it. To treat mental illness as deviance pure and simple is to ignore essential distinctions between 'mad' and 'bad' behaviour – chiefly, the fact that the former is regarded as not making sense, and not under the control of the individual. A straightforward social control model of the mental health professions is therefore limited in its applications.

This is not to say, however, that the remaining instances lack any political significance and are purely therapeutic in character. Behind the concept of mental health lie numerous presuppositions about norms of work, education and family life; and the mental health professions are probably instrumental in maintaining these norms, by influencing not just problem cases but our way of making sense of the world. (Feminists, for example, have argued that psychiatry powerfully reinforces women's traditional role in society (Chessler, 1972).) But if this is a social control mechanism, it is one which has been largely internalized by the population itself. Foucault (1980) goes further, arguing that the power of this mechanism is not 'repressive' but 'productive', since it actually *creates* forms of subjectivity and social life.

Plenty of instances still remain of repression in the name of mental health – as the activities of civil rights organizations and patients' groups testify – and the most convincing analysis is perhaps that of Castel *et al.* (1982), who see the 'hard' and 'soft' methods of treatment as an ensemble, each depending on the other to be fully effective. Although this idea has obvious validity, it is doubtful whether an adequate understanding of the place of mental health in modern society will ever be achieved by trying to impose the same model on such diverse phenomena as lobotomy, forcible incarceration, marital counselling, psychoanalysis and encounter groups.

David Ingleby
University of Utrecht

References

Armstrong, D. (1980), 'Madness and coping', *Sociology of Health and Illness*, 2,

Brenner, H. (1973), *Mental Illness and the Economy*, Cambridge, Mass.

Brown, G. and Harris, T. (1978), *Social Origins of Depression*, London.

Castel, F., Castel, R. and Lovell, A. (1982), *The Psychiatric Society*, New York.

Chessler, P. (1972), *Women and Madness*, New York.

Foucault, M. (1971), *Madness and Civilization*, New York. (Original French, *Histoire de la folie*, Paris, 1961.)

Foucault, M. (1980), 'Truth and power', in *Power/Knowledge: Selected Interviews and Other Writings 1972–1977*, Hassocks.

Freidson, E. (1970), *Professional Dominance*, New York.

Goffman, E. (1961), *Asylums: Essays on the Social Situation of Mental Patients and Other Inmates*, New York.

Hollingshead, A. B. and Redlich, F. C. (1958), *Social Class and Mental Illness*, New York.

Illich, I. (1977), *Disabling Professions*, London.

Laing, R. D. (1960), *The Divided Self*, London.

Ryan, W. (1972), *Blaming the Victim*, New York.

Scheff, T. (1966), *Being Mentally Ill: A Sociological Theory*, London.

Sedgwick, P. (1982), *Psycho Politics*, London.

Shrag, P. and Divoky, D. (1975), *The Myth of the Hyperactive Child and Other Means of Child Control*, New York.

Szasz, T. (1961), *The Myth of Mental Illness*, New York.

Further Reading

Ingleby, D. (ed.) (1980), *Critical Psychiatry: The Politics of Mental Health*, New York.

See also: *psychiatry*.

Penology

Penology is the study of penalties (from the Greek ποινή: penalty), although in its broadest sense it is also concerned with the consequences and merits of attempting to deal with various kinds of conduct by criminal prohibition ('criminalizing'). It includes the study of penal codes of law, but also investigation of the ways in which such penal codes are applied by courts in practice, and the manner in which each type of penal measure is applied. For example, even when a penal code appears to oblige courts to pronounce a sentence (such as imprisonment for 'life' in the case of murder), there are ways of avoiding this (such as convicting the offender of a less serious charge of homicide); and most penal systems provide legal devices by which a sentence of imprisonment can be terminated before its nominal end. Penologists are interested in all such expedients, and in the criteria which are used by courts, administrators and other personnel to make distinctions between offenders, whether for such purposes or for other reasons. Other reasons may include the belief that certain types of offender are more likely than others to respond to certain regimes, or on the other hand that some prisoners are so 'dangerous' that they must be given special sentences, detained longer than is normal for the offence, or given freedom only under specially strict conditions.

An important task of penologists is to provide answers to the question 'How effective is this (or that) measure?' Effectiveness is usually assessed by reconvictions or rearrests, although this is not without problems. For example it cannot take account of offences of which the offender is not suspected; the follow-up period must be substantial; in some jurisdictions rearrests or reconvictions for minor offences are not recorded centrally. The most serious problem, however, is the difficulty of being sure that offenders who remain free of rearrests during the follow-up period would not have remained free if otherwise dealt with: for example, if merely discharged without penalty. In consequence, follow-up studies must usually be content with *comparing* the reconviction rates after different measures. Even so, they have to take into account the fact that courts are selective, and do not allocate offenders randomly to different measures (a few 'random allocation studies' have been achieved, but only for rather specific groups of offenders or offences: see Farrington, 1983). The criteria used to allot offenders to different measures may themselves be associated with higher or lower reconviction rates. For instance, the more previous convictions in a man's record, the more likely he is to be reconvicted, quite apart from any effect which a sentence may have on him. Again, offenders whose offences usually involve theft, burglary, drunkenness or exhibitionism are more likely to be reconvicted than those who commit serious sexual offences or personal violence. Statistical devices have to be used to allow for this, for example, by subdividing samples into 'high-' 'medium-' and 'low-risk groups'. It is often said that when such precautions are taken the differences between reconviction rates following such different measures as imprisonment, fines and probation tend to disappear, and that the choice of sentence therefore makes no difference to a person's likelihood of reconviction, or not enough difference to justify expensive measures: but this is probably an oversimplification (as was eventually conceded by the chief exponent of the 'nothing works school' in the 1970s, Martinson, 1974, 1979).

In any case, other possible aims of penal measures have to be taken into account. Psychiatrists, for example, usually regard themselves as primarily concerned with the mental health of those committed to their charge by criminal courts; and social workers – including many probation officers – regard their clients' financial and family problems as more important than their legal transgressions.

Whether these views are accepted or not, some penal measures are valued as general deterrents, in the belief that even if they do not often affect the conduct of those who have experienced them, they discourage potential offenders who have not yet committed offences (Beyleveld, 1980). The efficacy of general deterrents has been exaggerated, for example by the supporters of capital punishment: statistical comparisons of jurisdictions which have abolished or retained the death penalty, or of decades in the same jurisdiction preceding and following abolition, suggest that the substitution of long periods of imprisonment for the death penalty does not affect rates of intentional homicide. In plain terms, potential murderers who think before they kill are as likely to be deterred by 'life' as by death. Whatever the penalty, however, its deterrent efficacy depends to a great extent on people's own estimates of the probability of being detected and punished. For some people this seems immaterial; but they tend to be those who commit impulsive or compulsive crimes.

Another aim of some penal measures is simply to protect other people against a repetition of the offence by the offender concerned, usually by some degree of incapacitation. Incapacitation may take the form of long detention, disqualification from certian activities (such as driving or engaging in certain occupations), or surgery (for example, castration for rapists). The more severe types of incapacitating measure are controversial, the chief objection being that the probability of the offender's repeating his offence seldom approaches certainty, and is often less than 50:50 (Floud and Young, 1981).

This illustrates a more general tendency in recent years to acknowledge the relevance of jurisprudence for penology. Scepticism about the efficacy of corrective or deterrent measures, together with the excessive use of very long detention in the name of therapeutic treatment, has revived the classical emphasis on the need for penalties to reflect the culpability of the offender. The underlying Kantian morality of this was never quite abandoned by jurists in West Germany; but the revival of it in the US and Scandinavia is an important phenomenon, although lacking the sophistication of German jurists (Von Hirsch, 1976).

English judges – and, quite independently, Durkheimian sociologists – have contributed yet another notion. Without necessarily accepting the retributive view (which has both difficulties and dangers) they hold that penalties have an important 'expressive' or 'symbolic' function, declaring publicly the moral disapproval with which most people regard harmful offences (Walker, 1978). Some English judges have even stated that an important task of sentencers is to lead public opinion, although this seems to exaggerate the attention and respect which the public pay to sentences (Walker and Marsh, 1984). More tenable is the proposition that sentences *reflect* people's disapproval: the question is whether sentencers are selected or trained so as to be sure of reflecting the views of the law-abiding public, particularly in societies with heterogeneous moralities.

Other subjects in which penologists have interested themselves are the rights of offenders, especially those recognized by conventions (such as those of the United Nations or European Economic Community); the protection of offenders against avoidable stigma; and the rights of victims to compensation, whether from the State or the offender, and to other forms of care.

Nigel Walker
University of Cambridge

References
Beyleveld, D. (1980), *A Bibliography on General Deterrence Research*, Westmead.
Farrington, D. P. F. (1983), 'Randomised experiments on crime and justice', in M. Tonry and N. Morris (eds), *Crime and Justice*, Vol. IV, Chicago.
Floud, J. and Young, W. (1981), *Dangerousness and Criminal Justice*, London.
Martinson, T. (1974), 'What works?', *Public Interest*, 35.
Martinson, T. (1979), 'New findings, new views', *Hofstra Law Review*, 7.
Von Hirsch, A. (1976), *Doing Justice, the Choice of Punishments: Report of the Committee for the Study of Incarceration*, New York.
Walker, N. (1978), 'The ultimate justification', in C. F. H. Tapper (ed.), *Crime, Proof and Punishment: Essays in Memory of Sir Rupert Cross*, London.
Walker, N. and Marsh, C. (1984), 'Do sentences affect public disapproval?', *British Journal of Criminology*.
See also: *criminology*.

Policy Sciences

The policy sciences are concerned with understanding the decision processes of public and private institutions, and with assessing the significance of all knowledge for purposes of decision. The term policy sciences was introduced after World War II (Lerner and Lasswell, 1951) to refer to the emergence of this common frame of reference among specialists in many disciplines. Subsequent development of the policy sciences has been marked by the refinement of conceptual tools, their application to a variety of policy problems, and by the establishment of policy-sciences centres in universities, government agencies and the private sector. Policy scientists in the aggregate have only begun to develop a distinctive professional identity and an understanding of the roles they may play in the evolution of our civilization.

Policy scientists are traditionally graduates from academic schools or departments of public or business administration, political science, political economy, jurisprudence, and the like. In recent decades, the physical and natural sciences, as well as the cultural sciences, have also produced policy scientists. These disciplines have had little contact with traditional policy theory but a great deal to do with the policy problems of our time. In a typical career pattern, a scientist in a laboratory or research institute discovers latent interests and talents in an initial attempt to relate his specialized knowledge to the broader environment. The political and social environment may nurture and reinforce these initiatives to the extent that knowledge is expected to pay. The budding policy scientist soon learns to sustain this expectation through delivery of partial results, and to justify further science and scholarship in terms that the environment rewards: security, profits, political advantage, health and social welfare, prestige and many other objectives. This career pattern broadens the attention frame and the circle of contacts beyond one's disciplinary origins.

Policy scientists tend to converge on a common outlook, despite their diversity of origins. One element of the common outlook is contextuality. Scholarship that restricts consider-ations of realism and worth to those of a single discipline may be acceptable to manuscript editors who enforce disciplinary standards. However, it is less likely to be acceptable to a decision maker who must grapple with a broader range of considerations and is unimpressed by the traditional academic division of labour. In the search for knowledge pertinent to the decision process and problem at hand, partial approaches tend to become more contextual. A second element is a problem orientation, which includes all the intellectual tasks logically entailed in the solution of any problem. For example, a choice among policy alternatives entails the postulation of goal values. The 'value free' connotation of 'science', as propagated in some disciplines, gradually becomes attenuated as policy scientists discover the value implications of their research and develop competence in normative analysis. (The connotation of 'science' as the 'pursuit of verifiable knowledge' is retained.) Conversely, philosophers and other specialists in normative analysis learn to describe trends, to clarify factors conditioning trends, and to project future possibilities in the process of relating normative principles to specific decisions. A third element is the synthesis of diverse methods. Each method of observation or analysis tends to divert attention from some potentially important aspects of the problem at hand. The use of multiple methods is an important means of compensating for such blind spots.

Evidence of convergence can be found in the development of concepts for contextual, problem-oriented, and multi-method research. Lasswell (1956; 1971) and his collaborators (Lasswell and Kaplan, 1950; Lasswell and McDougal, 1971) have refined the most comprehensive set of conceptual tools, but approximate equivalents are persistently rediscovered, often independently, by others. A contextual approach leads to an explicit conception of the decision process as a whole. Among other things, it identifies the multiple points at which decision outcomes might be affected, and thereby facilitates the rational allocation of analytical and political resources. Workable conceptions have been proposed by Anderson (1975), May and Wildavsky (1978), and Brewer and deLeon (1983). A contextual approach also leads to an explicit conception of the broader social process. Among other things, it directs attention to the otherwise unnoticed or discounted costs and benefits of decisions that impact on society. The social indicator movement (Bauer, 1966) and general systems theory (Isard, 1969) have spawned a number of social process models. The intellectual tasks entailed in problem-oriented research have been conceptualized in nearly equivalent ways by Simon (1968), Allison (1971), and many others. Finally, conceptions of 'economic man' and invariant 'behavioural laws' have turned out to be limited for purposes of the policy sciences. The explanation or interpretation of human acts requires attention to the simplified cognitive 'maps' used by the actors in question to respond to their environments. Essentially equivalent concepts for this purpose are Lasswell's 'maximization postulate' and Simon's (1957) elaboration of the 'principle of bounded rationality'.

Such conceptual tools ideally formulate and conveniently label the principal distinctions that have turned out to be useful across broad ranges of experience. They do not provide general answers to particular problems, as theory is sometimes purported to do. Rather, they provide principles of procedure (or heuristics) to guide a systematic search for data and insights pertinent to a specific decision problem; and they provide principles of content that outline elements of a satisfactory solution and help bring to bear the knowledge cumulated from different times, places, and cultural contexts. As short lists of interrelated concepts, they anticipate or implement findings of cognitive psychology showing how information can be processed efficiently (Simon, 1969; 1979). Command of these conceptual tools enables a policy scientist to maximize the potential for rational decision within the constraints of time, resources and the nature of the situation.

Applications of the policy sciences approach are numerous and diverse. Good examples illustrating the range of applications have addressed problems of administration and governance in a psychiatric hospital; public services for handicapped children; social development at the community level; defence analysis; income redistribution at the national level; public order of the world community, and global political transformations. Among authors of these studies alone, the disciplinary origins include anthropology, economics, law, medicine, political science, public administration and psychiatry.

The professional identity of the policy scientist tends to be in flux. Ideally, the policy scientist perceives himself as an integrator of knowledge and action. Complications arise, however, when other scientists perceive him as an ex-scientist and current politician. Moreover, decision makers may not know what to make of a scientist who nevertheless appears to know how to operate in the policy arena. Further complications arise from the question of whose interests are served. The rich and powerful are in a position to acquire his services, but knowledge may also be used to improve the position of the weak, the poor, and others who are disadvantaged. The situ-

ation is complex, and the policy scientist may share the ambiv-
alences he perceives in his relationships with others.

From a broader perspective, there is little doubt that the
scientific revolution has failed to modify the political structure
of a militant and divided world, or to abolish zones of poverty
amidst prosperity. In principle, the fruits of knowledge are
available to all. In practice, knowledge is often selectively introduced and used for the benefit of the few. One of the continuing
tasks of the policy sciences is to appraise its own impact on
policy and society. The search for authoritative criteria can be
guided by the Universal Declaration of Human Rights.

Ronald D. Brunner
University of Colorado, Boulder

References

Allison, G. (1971), *Essence of Decision: Explaining the Cuban
Missile Crisis*, Boston.
Anderson, J. E. (1975), *Public Policy-Making*, New York.
Bauer, R. A. (ed.) (1966), *Social Indicators*, Cambridge, Mass.
Brewer, G. D. and deLeon, P. (1983), *The Foundations of Policy
Analysis*, Homewood, Ill.
Isard, W. (1969), *General Theory: Social, Political, and Regional
with Particular Reference to Decision-Making Analysis*,
Cambridge, Mass.
Lasswell, H. D. (1956), *The Decision Process: Seven Categories of
Functional Analysis*, College Park, Maryland.
Lasswell, H. D. (1971), *A Pre-View of Policy Sciences*, New York.
Lasswell, H. D. and Kaplan, A. (1950), *Power and Society*, New
Haven.
Lasswell, H. D. and McDougal, M. S. (1971), 'Criteria for a
theory about law', *Southern California Law Review*, 44.
Lerner, D. and Lasswell, H. D. (eds) (1951), *The Policy Sciences*,
Stanford.
May, J. V. and Wildavsky, A. B. (eds) (1978), *The Policy Cycle*,
Beverly Hills.
Simon, H. A. (1957), 'Rationality and administrative decision
making', in H. A. Simon (ed.), *Models of Man*, New York.

Simon, H.A. (1968), 'Research for choice', in W.R. Ewald
   (ed.), *Environment and Policy: The Next Fifty Years*, Bloomington.
Simon, H. A. (1969), *The Sciences of the Artificial*, Cambridge,
   Mass.
Simon, H. A. (1979), *Models of Thought*, New Haven.

Political Science

Although the study of politics is an ancient pursuit, it is only
in the last few decades that the discipline of political science
became truly established, not perhaps so much because the
fundamental problems which had intrigued the authors of the
past have been superseded or even radically changed, but
because new political processes, new techniques of government
and, above all, a greater variety of studies have broadened
markedly the fields of inquiry.

Traditionally, political science was essentially concerned with
the purpose, character, and organization of the State. The great
classics, Hobbes and Locke in the seventeenth century, Rousseau in the eighteenth, for instance, were primarily preoccupied
with determining the goals of civil society and describing the
institutions which appeared best-suited to achieving these goals.
In the nineteenth century, the tradition was developed and
amplified as new political institutions were set up in most
Western-European countries and in America: the main preoccupation of some of the most prominent political scientists of the
period, the constitutional lawyers, was to elaborate the ways in
which these institutions could be firmly established and thus
give the modern State a stable organization.

While political science analysis was thus focusing on the
organization of the State, it was doing so on the basis of a
twofold concern which remains a fundamental distinction to
the present day. On the one hand, thinkers had a normative or
prescriptive purpose: they wished to present the general principles on which the organization of government *should* be based.
For political science is in large part born out of the desire to
'improve' political life and thus to reflect on the goals of government which would be most appropriate to bring about the 'good
life'. Of course, this type of inquiry necessarily reflects the
values of the thinkers themselves. Most political scientists of

the past undertook their inquiries because of deeply felt views about human nature in politics; these views consequently differed profoundly from one thinker to another, with the result that the models of society are often in sharp contrast. Hobbes, for example, started from the hypothesis that man is a beast to man, and that the function of political organization is to make more liveable a society which would otherwise be 'nasty, brutish, and short'; Locke and Rousseau, on the contrary, had a more optimistic view of human nature and basically believed that the ills of society came from malorganization rather than from defects inherent in individuals.

On the other hand, alongside a desire to present the goals for a better society, political scientists had also to devote their attention to the examination of the 'facts'; they had to assess what was wrong with a situation they wished to alter and explain why their proposals would achieve the desired results. Political science has thus always included a study of the 'objective' characteristics of government, as well as a prescriptive or normative inquiry. The great classical writers often described in detail the existing arrangements and their drawbacks; they compared institutions in one country with those of another. Similarly, nineteenth-century constitutional lawyers looked for workable arrangements relating to elections, the structure and procedures of parliaments, the relationships between executive and legislature, thereby relating the political goals to the reality.

Political science is, consequently, both concerned with what should be and with what is. This is one reason why some believe that the term 'science' should not be taken too literally in the context of the study of politics, as political science is more than a science in the normal sense of the word: it is both descriptive examination and prescriptive philosophy. Improvements are studied and presented in the form of arguments, rather than by the analysis of data alone.

Naturally enough, although political science does incorporate both aspects, some political scientists are more inclined in one direction than in the other. Especially in recent years, when the discipline grew rapidly and became increasingly specialized, the political philosophers (sometimes known, albeit wrongly, as political 'theorists' – because there are also other political theorists) and the students of the 'facts' of political life (occasionally referred to as empirical political scientists) have often clashed, each group claiming to be superior.

The Problem of Definition

For a very long period, extending to the end of the nineteenth century, political science studied the State. There seemed little need to go beyond this simple definition of the scope of the subject, as the State appeared paramount and other organizations seemed to depend on it; indeed, as years went by, the involvement of the State in the daily life of citizens appeared to be on the increase.

Yet, while the State was becoming more pervasive, governmental decisions were increasingly subjected to the pressure of many groups operating within the State. The growth of political parties, of trade unions, of employers' organizations and, indeed, of large numbers of other associations, was challenging if not the legal sovereignty of the State, at least its practical supremacy. Political scientists in this century could clearly not confine their analyses to State institutions and to the goals of these institutions; they had to broaden their inquiries to include the bodies which were involved in the many pressures brought upon the State. Moreover, 'political' activities similar to those taking place within the State were occurring within other groups – in the life of the parties, of trade unions, and of pressure groups in general.

Thus political science ceased being concerned exclusively with the State and became more broadly conceived. For this to happen, the subject-matter of the discipline had to shift from a specific area of inquiry – the State – to an activity – politics. But what, then, is politics? From the 1920s, many political scientists tried to establish the basic features of the activity which they were studying. In the 1930s and 1940s, especially under the influence of Lasswell, the operative concept was power, as politics does indeed appear to be closely related to the ability of some men to induce others to act (Lasswell and Kaplan, 1950; Barry, 1976).

But this approach gradually gave way to a more flexible and wider definition, as the scope of politics seemed to go beyond power and include many instances of 'natural' obedience which could not easily be defined as uses of power, at least in the normal sense of the concept. Politics thus became viewed as the activity concerned with the elaboration and implementation of collective decisions, through a variety of mechanisms involving power, to be sure, but also legitimacy, automatic acceptance, and basic loyalty. The definition proposed by Easton in the 1950s was widely adopted and suggests that political activity relates to the 'authoritative allocation of resources' in a community (Easton, 1953).

Such a definition of politics is intellectually more satisfying than the one which relates the field of study to the activities of the State. The effect was to enable political scientists to broaden markedly the scope of their analyses. If, for instance, the study of politics is concerned with the pressures on the government to take a particular decision, it follows that political scientists should also be concerned with examining the features of such pressures and, in particular, with the bodies involved in these pressures. While constitutional lawyers mainly studied assemblies, executives or courts, modern political scientists found it natural, indeed necessary, to look at groups of all kinds, not only political parties, but also other pressure groups in the decision-making process such as trade unions, churches, employers' organizations and others.

The Concern with the Systematic Analysis of Reality and the Development of Behaviourism

In the course of their inquiries, political scientists became increasingly aware of the gap between what constitutions proclaimed and what actually occurred. For example, it was simply not the case that parliaments and even governments were able to exercise the 'sovereignty' which was said to be theirs in liberal democratic systems: that sovereignty was in fact shared by the various groups involved in the decision process. Thus, not only was the scope of empirical inquiries broadened, but there was a disaffection from – and at times a rejection of – the analysis of legal and institutional devices; in its place the emphasis was on the 'true' reality of political life. The new school of thought which pressured for greater realism was called *behaviourism* (Dahl, 1963; Storing, 1962; Meehan, 1971).

The behavioural approach in political science, started in the United States, was widely adopted in the 1950s and 1960s, and later extended to many other academic centres. This approach seemed particularly appropriate at a time when, both in Eastern Communist States and in many parts of the Third World, the gap was increasing between constitutional formulas and the reality of government. Even in Western liberal democracies, the constitutional approach appeared inadequate since parties and interest groups had strikingly modified the characteristics of political life. Thus one major area of political science – the comparative analysis of political systems pioneered by Aristotle over 2500 years ago – benefited from the behavioural approach at a time when so many new systems of government emerged throughout the world.

Quantification, 'Positivism' and the Crisis of Behaviourism

Behaviourism was not only a demand for a more realistic approach to the study of politics: it also included two other claims that were to lead to many controversies and ultimately contributed to its decline in the 1970s. First, behaviourism became closely associated with a desire, in itself eminently justifiable, but in practice often difficult to bring about, to give empirical studies a 'truly' scientific basis. It tried to ensure that conclusions were not drawn merely from a few examples or from impressionistic remarks, but were the result of systematic examination of facts. This new trend in political science was indeed paralleled by similar developments in other social sciences, especially in economics, psychology, and, though to a somewhat lesser extent, sociology. It advocated a systematic presentation of the facts and the testing of hypotheses, in particular, the use of quantitative techniques. Many political scientists anxiously sought indicators that could be expressed numerically, and they achieved significant results in a variety of fields in which large masses of numerical data could be used. This was obviously the case in electoral studies, which for at least a decade was to be the leading area of development of quantitative political science. Helped by the increased sophistication of survey techniques, political scientists were able to do complex analyses of the relationship between voting patterns and social, economic, and psychological characteristics of electors, both at a given moment and over time.

But there were problems. Not all aspects of political life were as readily quantifiable as electoral behaviour: much of the life of governments and groups appeared at least *prima facie* to have to be described in a less 'rigorous' manner. Moreover, an undue emphasis on quantification might lead to an exaggerated reliance on some types of indicators, because they were quantified, and to the neglect of other aspects, such as cultural factors, not as easily amenable to mathematical treatment. Nevertheless, the quantification process increased in political science during the 1960s and 1970s: parties, interest groups, legislative activity, governmental structures, court pronouncements and certain aspects of the decision-making process were examined more rigorously; but it also became clear that the goal of general quantification was very distant.

Meanwhile, interest began to shift from the problem posed by quantification to the underlying philosophical implications of behaviourism. The supporters of the behavioural approach did not only wish to be more factual and realistic; they also wanted political science to become more scientific. They hoped to develop theories that could be tested systematically through hypotheses; these, in turn, needed the backing of a 'general theory'. This suggested a move towards a positivistic type of inquiry, which was to cause major controversies. Behaviourists pointed out that political science had so far been concerned almost exclusively with normative theories and with the detailed examination of specific situations. They argued that what was needed was a systematization of the data through the search for overall explanatory frameworks which would account for the wide range of political phenomena hitherto presented in an unconnected manner.

Such a goal was logical in the context of a move designed to improve the scientific character of the discipline. But it was at best premature, and it proved to be contentious. It was clearly impossible to elaborate general theories, akin to those in the natural sciences, that could effectively explain all varieties in political life. Some models were advanced, such as systems analysis or structural-functionalism, but these had at best the status of frameworks which might guide the scholar in his inquiries; they were not testable theories accounting for reality. But these models pointed to the interconnection between the many political institutions present in a 'system'; they showed the need to look for the role (or functions) of the various institutions (structures), as this role was not necessarily the same from 'system' to 'system'. But this scarcely amounted to a general theory.

The models also proved contentious as soon as they claimed to be more than a 'guide for research': they tended to emphasize – even overemphasize – the need for 'stability' and 'system maintenance' in the development of political life. Critics argued that, far from being 'scientific' and 'objective', these models were truly ideological in the manner of the normative theories of the classical writers of the past. Marxists were not alone in stressing the part played by values in the analyses which scholars undertake in a field such as political science where the ideas of the 'good society' cannot easily be disentangled from the examination of the 'facts'.

As a result of this conflict, fewer scholars believed it possible to establish rapidly (if at all) a body of general theory from which one could deduce characteristics of political life.

The nature of reality is too complex. This is one reason why in the 1970s more emphasis came to be placed on 'middle-range' analyses of political phenomena, that is, studies of one particular aspect of the political system such as party development, legislative behaviour, or governmental structure and activity. If a general theory is to emerge, this can only be after a long process, especially since political science is not, and cannot be, merely the study of what is, however this is defined: it is also the study of what ought to be. Norms and prescriptions are part of the study of politics, whether this is consciously recognized or not.

Such a recognition does not make political science 'unscientific'; but it has the effect of leading to the conclusion that political science has to develop, alongside the other social sciences, in its own special way. Ideology and values will always play a part in the analysis of politics. Perhaps a new form of scientific methodology needs to emerge if all aspects of the discipline are to be fully interconnected; meanwhile, progress will have to take place both through normative and through empirical analyses, with, where it proves useful, the help of quantitative techniques.

J. Blondel
University of Essex

References
Barry, B. (1976), *Power and Political Theory*, London.
Dahl, R. A. (1963), *Modern Political Analysis*, Englewood Cliffs, N.J.
Easton, D. (1953), *The Political System*, New York.
Lasswell, H. D. and Kaplan, A. (1950), *Power and Society*, New Haven.
Meehan, E. J. (1971), *The Foundations of Political Analysis*, Homewood, Ill.
Storing, H. (1962), *Essays on the Scientific Study of Politics*, New York.

Further Reading
Blondel, J. (1981), *The Discipline of Politics*, London.
Jouvenal, B. de (1963), *A Pure Theory of Politics*, Cambridge.
Sabine, G. J. and Thorson, T. L. (1973), *A History of Political Theory*, New York.
Seliger, M. (1976), *Ideology and Politics*, London.
See also: *political theory*.

Political Theory

Political theory is a subject which is more easily defined ostensively than formally. It is simple enough to point to the intellectual tradition which runs from Plato and Aristotle through to Marx, Mill and beyond, but less simple to point to the common elements in their thought which enable us to say that they were all in some sense engaged in the same enterprise. Perhaps the best approximation is to say that political theory is an attempt to understand political and social relationships at a high level of generality, and in the light of that understanding to advocate a certain practical stance towards them. At one extreme, a theory may portray existing relationships as the perfect embodiment of rationality and consequently recommend conserving them in their entirety; at the other extreme, a theory may highlight the gulf between existing institutions and rational principles, and describe in some detail an alternative social and political order which would better realize the principles in question. The way in which this common project has been carried out, however, has varied a great deal. Some theories have started from a conception of the human individual, and asked what political and social arrangements would best satisfy his needs and desires. Others have interpreted existing institutions as part of an overall pattern of historical development – either as the culmination of that pattern, or as a transient stage destined to be replaced by something higher. Others again have begun by asking what kind of knowledge is possible in political matters, and gone on to defend institutional arrangements which give people tasks in proportion to their capacity to carry them out. Political theorists have been just as diverse in their methods as they have in their practical conclusions.

Because political theory aims to be prescriptive as well as explanatory, questions inevitably arise about its relationship to the practical outlooks of ordinary men and women, especially those relatively systematic world-views often referred to as ideologies. Political theory is best seen as an attempt to render these outlooks more adequate by reflecting on their underlying assumptions – discarding assumptions that are untenable, and providing more solid foundations for those that remain valid. It is differentiated from ideology by the fact that ideologies take for granted beliefs that political theory puts in question. Thus an ideology might incorporate the belief that social inequalities were the proper result of differences in individual merit. A political theorist would need to ask both about the extent to which the distribution of benefits in society actually corresponded to personal merit, and about the meaning of the notion of merit itself – say about the features in virtue of which one person could be described as more meritorious than another. It would be wrong, however, to harden this contrast into a rigid distinction. No political theorist is able to subject all of the beliefs that enter his theory to critical examination; some he has simply to take for granted. We may therefore refer to the ideological components of political theories, and say of a theory such as Locke's that it embodies elements of liberal ideology, or of Marx's that it embodies elements of socialist ideology. Indeed, we may wish to think of political theory as an activity that can be carried on at different levels, according to the extent to which received ideological beliefs are put in question. At the lowest level, there will be theories that are little more than the systematic expression of an ideology; at the highest level, theories that are very much more reflective, in the sense that a high proportion of their component beliefs have been subjected to critical examination.

In our own century, the very idea of political theory has been called into question by the widespread acceptance of positivism as a philosophical standpoint. Positivism denies that there is any logical connection between empirical propositions describing the world as it is and normative propositions telling us how we ought to act. Acceptance of this view implies that political theory as traditionally conceived rested on a mistake. The mistake was to combine explanations of social and political relationships with recommendations about how those relationships should be carried on. On the positivist view there are two distinct enterprises: political science, which aims at the empirical explanation of political phenomena, and political philosophy, which starts from certain political values such as democracy and equality and draws out their practical implications. Although, as we shall see later, this view is open to challenge, its popularity has been such that a distinction is often now drawn between three types of political theory:

(1) *Empirical political theory.* This term is commonly used to refer to the theoretical parts of political science. Political scientists are interested in describing and explaining particular political events, but they are also interested in developing broader explanatory theories which draw together a wide range of phenomena under a single heading. They have, for instance, tried to explain in general terms why revolutions occur, or why some democracies are dominated by two large parties while

others generate many small ones. The issues that are considered are often similar to those addressed in the older tradition of political theory, but much greater use is typically made of quantifiable evidence. Thus someone seeking to produce a theory about the causes of revolution would characteristically begin by looking for correlations between the outbreak of revolutions and other phenomena, such as the extent of economic inequality in the societies under consideration.

(2) *Formal political theory*. This burgeoning field overlaps considerably with 'social choice theory', 'public choice theory', and so on. The approach here is to model a political system by assuming certain procedural rules and actors with designated goals, and then to investigate formally (on the assumption that each actor pursues his goals rationally) what the final configuration of the system will be. Two major applications are to collective decision procedures and to party competition in a representative democracy. In the first case, the theorist postulates a population each of whom has his own preferences as between a number of policies, and looks at how these preferences will be amalgamated into a 'collective choice' by various decision rules (such as majority voting). One well-known result of these investigations is Arrow's (1963) theorem, according to which *no* decision rule can simultaneously meet a number of reasonable-sounding conditions (such as that if each person prefers x to y, y should not be collectively chosen in preference to x). In the second case, the theorist again assumes a population with given policy preferences, and looks at how parties will behave under a democratic electoral system on the assumption that each party's aim is to win the election and each voter's aim is to secure policies that correspond as closely as possible to his preferences. This application was originally developed by Antony Downs (1957), and has since been considerably elaborated.

(3) *Normative political theory*. In this branch of the subject, the theorist is directly interested in the justification of political standpoints and policies. There is, however, disagreement about how strong a form of justification is possible. For some theorists, influenced by positivism, justification ultimately ends in a commitment to one or other basic political value. The theorist's

room for manœuvre is created by the fact that such values cannot be translated simply or immediately into policy. Thus someone may believe that his underlying commitment is to individual freedom, but this commitment does not, of itself, tell him whether he should be in favour (say) of a night-watchman state or an interventionist welfare state. The theorist's job, on this view, is to explore what the idea of freedom means, and then to apply it to practical issues, such as whether redistributive taxation reduces the freedom of the wealthy, or increases the freedom of the poor, or does both. The alternative view maintains that it is possible to go beyond this minimum programme and provide rational foundations for the basic values themselves. An important recent attempt in this direction can be found in the work of John Rawls (1972), who has tried to show that principles of distributive justice can be derived from the choices that rational individuals would make if they were ignorant of their personal characteristics and place in society. Although this attempt has not been judged a success on all sides, it has served as a landmark in the English-speaking world for those who believe that the more ambitious version of normative theory is feasible.

This distinction betwen types of political theory is useful as a labelling device, and it corresponds to a real division of labour in the academic community; but it is much more doubtful whether a rigid separation between the three enterprises can be sustained intellectually. Consider each pairing in turn:

(1) Normative theories necessarily rely on empirical research whenever they move from the most abstract kind of conceptual analysis to consider what various concepts and principles imply for the design of institutions and policies. It is impossible to say, for instance, whether democracy can be achieved through a scheme of parliamentary representation without having some understanding of how electoral systems operate. On the other hand, every empirical theory embodies normative assumptions. This is so because the concepts that are used to group phenomena together for explanatory purposes – concepts such as 'revolution', 'democracy' and 'social inequality' – embody assumptions about what is significant in human affairs, and which occurrences are relevantly similar and dissimilar. Thus

a theory that attempts to specify the social conditions under which revolutions are likely to occur presupposes that the term 'revolution' picks out a set of events which are interesting to the social scientist and have important features in common.

(2) Formal and empirical theory also feed off each other. Although those engaged in formal analysis frequently deny that their assumptions are meant to be empirically realistic, the undertaking itself would not be worth engaging in unless there was some connection between the assumptions made and behaviour in the real world. Thus Downs's theory of democracy would be little more than an intellectual conceit if political parties were not as a matter of fact sometimes prepared to alter their policies in order to attract voters. Conversely, the models developed in formal analysis are an important source of explanatory theory. A full theory of party competition will almost certainly need to incorporate Downsian mechanisms – that is, it will need to recognize that parties are driven by their interest in winning elections to adopt policies that correspond to voters' preferences – alongside other factors in explaining party behaviour.

(3) Finally, formal theory both borrows from and contributes to normative theory. This can be seen most easily in the case of the theory of collective choice. The conditions that a theorist will lay down for an acceptable decision procedure will reflect his normative commitments. One such condition might be political equality: each person's preference should have an equal chance of determining what the collective choice will be. Conversely, the results of formal analysis may have important normative implications. An upshot of Arrow's theorem, for instance, is that there is in general no simple 'best' procedure for making social choices; instead societies should be prepared to use different procedures in different areas of decision, depending on such factors as the likely configuration of individual preferences on a given issue.

All of this suggests that the older political theorists were right to see political explanation and political prescription as integrally related. It does not, however, mean that it is now easy to do political theory in the traditional way. Academic specialization has meant that most practitioners currently work in one small corner of the field; and those who try to present a synoptic view of political life are liable to be denounced as amateurs. But since political theory responds to a permanent intellectual need – the need to subject our everyday political attitudes and assumptions to critical questioning – one can safely predict that, in one form or another, the enterprise will continue.

David Miller
Nuffield College, Oxford

References

Arrow, K. (1963), *Social Choice and Individual Values*, New Haven.

Downs, A. (1957), *An Economic Theory of Democracy*, New York.

Rawls, J. (1972), *A Theory of Justice*, Oxford.

Further Reading

Barry, B. (1965), *Political Argument*, London.

Berlin, I. (1964), 'Does political theory still exist?', in P. Laslett and W. G. Runciman (eds), *Philosophy, Politics and Society*, Second Series, Oxford.

Connolly, W. (1974), *The Terms of Political Discourse*, Lexington, Mass.

Miller, D. and Siedentop, L. (eds) (1983), *The Nature of Political Theory*, Oxford.

Riker, W. H. and Ordeshook, P. C. (1973), *An Introduction to Positive Political Theory*, Englewood Cliffs, N.J.

Runciman, W. G. (1969), *Social Science and Political Theory*, Cambridge.

Weldon, T. D. (1953), *The Vocabulary of Politics*, Harmondsworth.

See also: *political science*.

Psychiatry

Psychiatry is a speciality of medicine concerned with the diagnosis, treatment and study of mental diseases or disorders. Its practitioners are psychiatrists (in the United States, physicians who complete four years of approved training following their graduation from medical school). A number of professionals from other disciplines treat patients with psychiatric disorders. The most important of these are clinical psychologists, psychiatric social workers and psychiatric nurses. They commonly refer to those who seek help as 'clients' rather than 'patients'. These professionals may work in various collaborative relationships with psychiatrists or as independent practitioners. They employ the same verbal therapies as psychiatrists. Psychiatry differs from these specialities in being a medical discipline whose practitioners are physicians. As such, psychiatrists are specifically trained to (1) make precise syndromal or aetiological diagnoses, whenever possible, and distinguish one syndrome from another; (2) diagnose (or know when to refer to other physicians) those organic conditions which mimic psychiatric disorders such as brain tumour, cancer of the pancreas, and hyperthyroidism (these conditions can present as anxiety or depressive disorders); (3) treat particular psychiatric disorders with psychotropic medications or other somatic treatments; (4) manage untoward psychological reactions to medical illness; and (5) integrate the biological with the psychological and social dimensions of mental disorders. In addition, the psychiatrist's training in medicine may encourage a research career in the biology of mental disorders. American psychiatrists as a whole have a high level of expertise in psychological treatments, particularly the psychodynamic approach. This is due to the impact of psychoanalytic theory on academic psychiatry especially since 1945, when many distinguished psychoanalysts assumed the chairs of academic departments.

Psychiatry relates closely to other medical specialities such as internal medicine, family medicine, neurology and pediatrics as well as to many scientific disciplines that contribute to the understanding of mental disorders. These include psychology, epidemiology, anthropology, sociology, genetics, and biochemistry.

The Range of Psychiatric Disorders

Although abnormal states of thinking, feeling, and behaving may be studied and treated in isolation, more often they are understood as part of specific syndromes, disorders, or diseases.

In the US the most widely accepted classification of psychiatric disorders is presented in the American Psychiatric Association's third edition of the Diagnostic and Statistical Manual of Mental Disorders (DSM-III). Although developed by psychiatrists in the United States, this classification is widely used by psychiatrists in other countries, and by other mental health professionals. The classification attempts to provide a comprehensive description of the manifestations of mental disorders while remaining atheoretical with regard to aetiology. A related classification of mental disorders with broad international acceptance is the ninth edition of the International Classification of Disease (ICD-9).

The following are the major categories of psychiatric disorders according to DSM-III:

– Disorders Usually First Evident in Infancy, Childhood, or Adolescence
– Organic Mental Disorders
– Substance Abuse Disorders
– Schizophrenic Disorders
– Paranoid Disorders
– Psychotic Disorders Not Elsewhere Classified
– Affective Disorders
– Anxiety Disorders
– Somatoform Disorders
– Dissociative Disorders
– Psychosexual Disorders
– Factitious Disorders
– Disorders of Impulse Control Not Elsewhere Classified
– Adjustment Disorders
– Psychological Factors Affecting Physical Condition
– Personality Disorders

The manual describes subcategories of the above major categories together with specific defining criteria for each disorder. There is a high degree of reliability for most of the disorders; that is, two observers of the same patient are likely to agree on the diagnosis. There is considerable variability in the established validity of these diagnostic categories.

Family and couple therapists criticize DSM-III on the

grounds that they regard the couple or the family, not the patient, as the pathologic unit. Behaviour therapists criticize DSM-III on grounds that it is the thought, feeling, or behaviour, not the syndrome or disease, that is the pathologic unit. Psychodynamic clinicians are apt to view psychopathology as part of a continuum based on the concept of 'developmental lines', rather than as discrete disease entities. In addition, they believe that each patient can be described only by a unique and complex formulation. Diagnostic categories are regarded therefore as both conceptually incorrect as well as oversimplifications of human problems. Despite these criticisms, there is a growing consensus amongst US psychiatrists that DSM-III will prevail and continue to grow in importance through future editions.

There are two extreme and opposing positions regarding psychiatric disease: (1) that psychopathology, both social and individual, is everywhere and that therapeutic intervention may be useful for all human conditions; (2) that mental illness is a myth, and therefore lies out of the purview of medicine.

Conceptual Models in Psychiatric Thinking
There are many conceptual frameworks by which psychiatrists attempt to organize their thinking about patients with mental disorders. The presence of multiple approaches, particularly when they are not made explicit, commonly leads to misunderstanding amongst psychiatrists and between psychiatrists and other medical professionals, mental health professionals, and patients. The four conceptual models most often used are (1) the biologic; (2) the psychodynamic; (3) the sociocultural and (4) the behavioural.

(1) According to the biologic model, psychiatric illness is a disease like any other. Its cause will be found to be related to disorders of genetics, biochemistry, and/or the functional anatomy of the brain. Abnormal behaviours are understood as partial manifestations of a syndrome or underlying disease process. In his relationship to the patient, the biologic psychiatrist behaves like any other physician: he elicits the history through careful questioning, establishes a diagnosis and recommends a treatment plan which the patient is expected

to accept. The biologic approach, after giving psychiatry its classification of mental illness in the late nineteenth century, was generally unproductive until the 1950s. From that time until the present its contributions to psychiatry have included the development of antipsychotic, antidepressant, and anti-mania medications; the increased understanding of the genetic transmission of some mental illness; and metabolic studies of depressive disorders. The biologic model has been least helpful in the study of the neuroses and personality disorders.

(2) According to the psychodynamic model, it is the develop-ment deficit, fixation, regressive response to current stress, and/or conflict within the mind that leads to psychiatric symp-toms. The symptom represents both an expression of an under-lying conflict as well as a partial attempt to resolve it. The concept of unconscious mental processes is all important. In the relationship to the patient, the therapist assumes a nondirective posture in order to elicit meaningful associations, as well as to develop a transference reaction in which the patient reacts to the therapist as he would to other important people in his life. The psychodynamic model had its origin with Sigmund Freud in the late nineteenth and early twentieth centuries. There have been significant theoretical developments since 1950 in ego psychology, object relations theory, and self psychology. Although the psychodynamic model is a general psychology of normal and abnormal behaviour, it is most helpful in the understanding and treatment of neuroses and personality disorders.

(3) The sociocultural model focuses on the way the indi-vidual functions within his social system. Symptoms are traced not to conflicts within the mind nor to manifestations of psychi-atric disease, but to disruptions or changes in the social support system. According to the sociocultural approach, symptoms, disorders, or the designation that someone is mentally ill may be seen as social phenomena: responses to breakdown or disor-ganization of social groupings, attempts at social communi-cation, a cultural or ethnic expression of distress, or a message by the social group that certain behaviours are no longer accept-able. Treatment consists in helping the patient deal better with the existing social system. The sociocultural approach was

reawakened in the 1950s. From that time until the present, the psychiatric ward was viewed as a social system, the relationship between social class and mental illness was established, and federal legislation was enacted to provide psychiatric care for catchment areas in the community.

(4) The behavioural model regards symptoms in their own right as the problem. Symptoms are manifestations neither of disease, intrapsychic conflict, nor social breakdown. In order to develop a treatment strategy, the behavioural formulation takes into account conditions antecedent to and reinforcing of the pathologic behaviours. The behavioural model, like the three models previously discussed, began its period of rapid growth in the late 1950s. Behavioural therapists are hopeful of offering several possible advantages to other forms of treatment including a shorter duration of treatment and applicability to a broad range of patients.

Which conceptual approach a psychiatrist uses depends on several factors including his own training and ideology, the diagnosis of the patient, and the availability of clinical services. The use of a single approach to explain all psychopathology (including the belief that all psychopathology will ultimately be explained by biochemistry) is reductionistic. In optimal clinical practice, the psychiatrist attempts to understand the patient simultaneously by means of several conceptual approaches or frames of references, with the understanding that even the four approaches described above may not exhaust the ways in which psychopathology of people can be understood. Various attempts to integrate several conceptual frameworks have been referred to as systems theory, biopsychosocial approach, multidimensional approach, or eclecticism.

Psychiatric Treatments

Psychiatric treatments can be divided into two major categories: the biologic approaches (somatotherapy) and the psychologic or verbal therapeutic approaches. The most commonly used somatic treatments are drugs followed by electroconclusive treatments. Other somatic treatments much less used include insulin treatment and neurosurgery. Drugs may be divided into four major groups: (1) the anti-anxiety agents; (2) antidepressant agents; (3) antimanic agents; and (4) antipsychotic agents. The anti-anxiety agents such as Librium and Valium are useful in the short-term treatment of some anxiety states. Their sedative-hypnotic effect makes them also useful for the short-term treatment of insomnia. This class of anti-anxiety agents (benzodiazepines), because of their relative safety, has rendered the barbiturates virtually obsolete. Antidepressant agents such as Tofranil and Elavil (tricyclics) and Nardil (MAO inhibiter) reverse depressive symptomatology, while the antimanic agents such as Lithium Carbonate reverse symptoms of mania or hypomania while sometimes functioning as an antidepressant. The antipsychotic agents such as Haldol and Thorazine are useful in managing the excitement, delusions, hallucinations, and disorientation of various psychotic states in schizophrenia, depressive psychoses, and organic psychoses. With prolonged use, the antipsychotic agents can cause tardive dyskinesia, a permanent involuntary movement disorder involving primarily the tongue, neck, and facial muscles. Electroconvulsive therapy, the passage of electrical current through the brain, is used primarily for depressed patients for whom drug therapy has failed, has or will produce serious side effects, or will take too long before exerting a therapeutic effect.

There are hundreds of psychologic treatments. They may be classified according to theoretical approach, structure of the treatment, and duration. In terms of ideology the psychodynamic approach, based on the principles of psychoanalytic theory, is the most widely used. Behaviour therapies which include the specific techniques of relaxation, cognitive restructuring, and flooding have made major inroads in clinical practice during the past twenty-five years. In addition, there are various interpersonal, existential, Jungian, Adlerian, and other therapies. To what degree specific dimensions of each ideological approach are uniquely therapeutic and to what degree there are common therapeutic dimensions of many approaches is a subject of considerable interest. As to structure, the therapist may treat the patient alone, with a spouse, as part of a family, together with a broader social network, or with a group of other patients. When therapy is provided to a couple or to a family, then the couple or family, not the individual, may be regarded as the patient. Most therapies take place once a week but may occasionally be as infrequent as once a month or as frequent as four or five times per week as in psychoanalysis. Depending on the goals of treatment, the sessions may range from one visit (evaluation), eight to twelve visits (brief or short-term therapy), one to four years (long-term therapy), or three to seven years (psychoanalysis). Treatment may take place in a private office, in a mental health centre, or in a psychiatric inpatient unit.

The therapeutic efficacy of the somatic treatments is well established. The efficacy of particular psychological treatments for designated symptoms or disorders has been receiving increasing confirmation during the past ten years. For certain depressive and schizophrenic disorders, it has been established that a combination of drug and psychological or social treatments is more effective than either used alone. Psychiatric treatment has also been shown to diminish patients' use of medical facilities.

Psychiatry – Past and Future

Psychiatric illness is not new to modern society. In the Hippocratic writings (400 B.C.) there are clear descriptions of the major psychiatric disorders. Throughout the centuries psychopathology was described, explained, and classified by the great physicians of the time. The degree of sophistication, or lack thereof, paralleled that for medicine in general. There was no autonomous discipline of psychiatry.

The historian George Mora divides modern scientific psychiatry into three overlapping periods: (1) From 1800 to 1860, the mental hospital, or asylum, was the centre of psychiatric activity. It was staffed by a new type of physician, the alienist, totally devoted to the care of the mentally ill. The major accomplishments of this period were the practice of 'moral therapy', the description and classification of mental disorders, and the study of brain anatomy. Famous names associated with this period are Esquirol, Morel, Kahlbaum, Tuke, Rush, and Ray. (2) From 1860 to 1920, the centre of psychiatry moved from the hospital to the university, which could simultaneously treat patients, teach, and do research.

The important names of this era include Griesinger, Meynert, Forel, Bleuler, Charcot, Jackson, Kraepelin, A. Meyer, and S. Freud. It was Kraepelin who provided a classification of mental disorders that is the intellectual precursor of DSM-III. Meyer developed the psychobiologic approach, trained a whole generation of leaders in American psychiatry and provided the fertile ground for the growth of psychoanalysis in this country. (3) The period from 1920 to the present has been referred to as the 'psychiatric explosion'. As described earlier, the greatest expansion of knowledge in psychodynamic, sociocultural, biologic, and behavioural approaches began in the 1950s.

It is anticipated that within the next one to two decades there will be important new developments in psychiatry. These will include: (1) greater sophistication in nosology with improved validity for certain diagnostic categories; at the same time there will be philosophical and empirical sophistication in understanding the limitations of the diagnostic or categorical approach to other mental disturbances; (2) significant advances in understanding the biology of mental processes in general and of the depressive and schizophrenic disorders in particular; (3) significant advances in the evaluation of psychologic therapies so that more effective matches can be made between disorder and treatment; (4) significant advances in the integration of biologic, psychodynamic, behavioural, and social approaches to the diagnosis and treatment of mental disorders; (5) advances in the integrative efforts between psychiatry and other medical disciplines such as neurology, medicine, and paediatrics.

The advances described above will further define psychiatry both as a mental health profession and as a medical speciality.

Aaron Lazare
Massachusetts General Hospital

Further Reading
American Psychiatric Association (1980), *Diagnostic and Statistical Manual of Mental Disorders (DSM-III)*, 3rd edn, New York.
Baldessarini, R. (1983), *Biomedical Aspects of Depression and its Treatment*, Washington, DC.

Brenner, C. (1982), *The Mind in Conflict*, New York.

Gedo, J. E. and Goldberg, A. (1973), *Models of the Mind: A Psychoanalytic Theory*, Chicago.

Greenhill, M. and Gralnick, A. (1983), *Psychopharmacology and Psychotherapy*, New York.

Lazare, A. (1973), 'Hidden conceptual models in clinical psychiatry', *New England Journal of Medicine*, 288.

Lazare, A. (1979), 'Hypothesis testing in the clinical interview', *in Outpatient Psychiatry: Diagnosis and Treatment*, Baltimore.

Lishman, W. (1978), *Organic Psychiatry: The Psychological Consequences of Cerebral Disorder*, Oxford.

Papajohn, I. (1982), *Intensive Behavior Therapy: The Behavioral Treatment of Complex Emotional Disorders*, New York.

Rutter, M. and Hersov, L. (eds) (1984), *Child Psychiatry – Modern Approaches*, 2nd edn, Oxford.

See also: *mental health; psychoanalysis*.

Psychoanalysis

Psychoanalysis is a procedure for the treatment of mental and emotional disturbances. Sigmund Freud originated and developed psychoanalysis as a result of his individual researches into the causes of hysteria, one of the common forms of mental illness in Europe in the latter part of the nineteenth century (see Jones, 1953).

The unique characteristic of psychoanalysis as a therapy derives from its theory of psychopathology. The central finding of psychoanalysis is that mental and emotional disturbances result from unconscious mental life. Treatment therefore depends upon the ability of the patient, with the help of the analyst, to reveal unconscious thoughts and feelings. The formula that propelled the psychoanalytic method from its inception ('what is unconscious shall be made conscious') remains vitally significant today. The changes that have occurred in the formula have resulted from a broadened and deepened understanding of the nature of unconscious mental life and how it functions developmentally in relation to consciousness and to the environment.

According to Freud's first conception of symptom formation,

morbid thought patterns occurred during a dissociated state and were prevented from normal discharge because of the altered states of consciousness. The undischarged tensions produced symptoms. The cure required some method of discharge – an abreaction or mental catharsis. By applying hypnosis, the noxious material could be brought to the surface and discharged through verbal association. This chain of inference, formulated first in collaboration with Joseph Breuer (1842–1925) who described his clinical experience in treating a female patient he named Anna O. (Freud, 1955, Vol. II) was dependent upon a quantitative hypothesis concerning unconscious mental life and its relation to conscious states. In this prepsychoanalytic period of research, excessive excitation and the blockage of discharge were thought to produce pathological effects.

A major shift occurred both in research and in the explanatory theory toward the turn of the century. Freud recognized, largely through his self-analysis but also through careful attention to what his patients told him, that a qualitative factor was as important as the quantitative in the pathological process. The unconscious thoughts and feelings contained sexual content and meaning which was linked to arousal, or in earlier language, the quantity of excitation.

The introduction of the qualitative factor altered the theory of neurosis and the therapeutic procedure and, indeed, the method of research. Instead of managing a procedure designed to discharge quantities of noxious excitation stored within the psyche, the problem shifted to uncovering the meaning of the symptoms, and, through association, their roots in the unconscious. Hypnosis no longer served the purpose, since it was imperative that the entire treatment procedure elicit the full participation of the patient. Freud asked his patients to recline on the couch and to say whatever came to mind. This method, called 'free association', created a contradiction in terms. Freud discovered that it was difficult for the patient to carry out his request. Difficulty in associating did not seem to be a random effect, but along with the symptoms could be understood as an inherent aspect of the patient's manner of thinking and feeling and the particular form and content of the presenting symptoms. Freud visualized the difficulties of free association as *resistance* and as part and parcel of the problem of unconscious content, attempting to break through the barriers that guarded conscious mental life.

The research and treatment method, called psychoanalysis, replicated the individual's intrapsychic struggle with the unconscious. Freud's model of neurotic suffering combined both the quantitative and qualitative ideas in the concept of intrapsychic conflict. Symptoms, those alien and debilitating conditions, appear as a result of conflict within the psyche.

According to this model, the terms of neurotic conflict begin with desire; the aim is gratification. The impulse to act, to seek direct gratification of desire, is inhibited by restrictive forces within the psyche. The most familiar type of restriction arises from the individual's moral standards, which render unacceptable the direct gratification of desire. This opposition of the forces of desire and morality produces the debilitating symptoms but in forms that will allow a measure of gratification of desire, however small and costly. Symptoms, resulting from intrapsychic conflict, are the individual's best effort at compromise.

However, as Freud discovered, symptom formation, since it utilizes compromises, follows principles of mental function which apply across a broad spectrum of activity. Therefore, the dynamics of intrapsychic conflict go beyond the pathological and enter into the realm of a general psychology. Normal mental activity such as dreaming, to cite one illustration, follows the same principle as the activity that leads to symptom formation (Freud, 1955, Vols IV and V). A dream is a symptom of mental conflict since it represents a compromise among forces in the unconscious that simultaneously push toward gratification of desire while inhibiting this tendency. The symbolic content of the dream disguises the conflict but also expresses all the terms of the conflict – both desire and prohibition.

This model of intrapsychic conflict underwent a variety of modifications throughout Freud's lifetime. For example, the idea of desire shifted from a dual instinct theory of sex and self-preservation to a dual instinct theory of sex and aggression. Closer attention to the object of desire (in contrast to the aim of discharge) revealed that while its normal pathway was outward toward objects and the environment, it could turn inward, particularly during stressful episodes in the individual's life. But even where desire turned inward, the object remained important in the psychoanalytic theory of conflict because of the observation that the individual retained an internalized image of the object, while seemingly relinquishing it in its real form. Even in the case of the most severe psychological disturbances – psychoses – the individual may appear uninterested in the object world, but the internal conflict evolves around the representations of these objects both in their beneficent and malevolent forms.

The formalization of the model of conflict led to the structural hypothesis which postulates three parts of the psychic structure: id, super-ego, and ego. The id is the part of the mind which generates desire, both sexual and aggressive impulses. The super-ego is the agency that involves the conscience (the imperatives of 'thou shalt not') and the ideals (the imperatives that one must achieve in order to feel loved and to experience self-esteem). The ego is the executive apparatus that consists of a variety of functions which together mediate the terms of the conflict between id, super-ego and, finally, reality.

Several problems arise in the application of the structural hypothesis, indeed, in working with all of these superordinate hypotheses in psychoanalytic theory. The hypothesis, called the metapsychology of psychoanalysis, poses a number of problems in application, both in strict scientific research as well as in clinical work. Some of these problems can be dismissed readily, such as the use of the structural hypothesis as though it referred to 'real' agencies of the mind. The id, super-ego, and ego are abstract concepts, an attempt to organize a theory of conflict. They are not anatomical entities, nor are they especially valuable as a guide to the phenomenology of conflict. But the structural hypothesis and the concepts of id, super-ego and ego serve a number of intellectual purposes in the theory of psychoanalysis. One example is the concept of resistance, or what prevents unconscious content from direct appearance in conscious images and thoughts. The work of psychoanalysis indicates that the derivatives of unconscious mental life are omnipresent in consciousness, but in such indirect and disguised forms (except in the case of delusional thinking and hallucinations) as to stretch credulity about the idea of unconscious derivatives affecting conscious thinking and activity. The structural hypothesis organizes Freud's observations and conclusions about resistance as a part of unconscious mental life: he posited the need to broaden the term of resistance (from barriers to consciousness) to defence as an unconscious function of the ego to limit the danger that occurs when the pressure to act on impulses becomes great (Freud, 1955, Vol. XX).

Another problem with the structural hypothesis of psychoanalysis derives from the logical consequences of using this hypothesis to distinguish among and explain the forms and functions of various pathologies. Psychological conflict implies that a psychic structure exists within the individual, so that, for example, moral imperatives no longer depend upon the parents for their force. The individual has a conscience which inflicts some measure of painful anxiety and guilt when unconscious desire seeks gratification.

The classical theory of psychoanalysis presumes that psychic conflict and structure become established during the last stages of infantile development, which is called the Oedipal stage (Freud, 1955, Vol. VII). In relinquishing incestuous desire, the child of approximately age five identifies with the objects and consequently emerges from infancy with a reasonably self-contained psychic structure. The pathologies linked to conflict in psychic structure, the transference neuroses, include hysteria, obsessional neuroses and related character neuroses. These pathologies are called transference neuroses because they do not impair the patient's ability, despite pain and suffering, to establish attachments to objects. However, the attachments are neurotically based in that the patient shifts the incestuous struggle from parents to other people. In the transference neuroses, the relationship to objects is not totally determined by the persistence of neurotic disturbance. For example, a person may be able to function reasonably well with other people except that he is incapable of sexual intimacy as a result of neurotic inhibition.

Psychoanalytic investigation, especially of the post-World War II period, has given rise to doubt about some of the formulations of the structural hypothesis and some of its derivatives in the explanation of pathologies. For example, can one clearly differentiate structural conflict from earlier developmental problems which derive from the deficits of infancy? The investigation of borderline conditions (a consequence of developmental deficits) or narcissistic disturbances (the conditions of impaired self-esteem and painful self-awareness), suggest that early internalizations of objects so colour the later identifications as to minimize the effects of psychological structure (see Segal, 1964). Critics argue that to treat such patients using classical techniques will prove futile. On the more theoretical plane, the critics also dispute the distinction between transference and narcissistic disturbances because of the importance of object attachments in the latter category of disturbance. Perhaps underlying the controversies within the psychoanalytic profession are more fundamental differences than the suggestion that one or more hypotheses are open to question. After all, any scientific endeavour attempts to disprove hypotheses and to modify the theory as a result of fresh observation and experimentation.

Almost from its inception, psychoanalysis has been the centre of debate in which the contenders, more than disputing particular hypotheses, are engaged in a test of contradictory world views. As indicated earlier, a tension inherent in psychoanalytic observation and explanation pervades the field. The dialectics of quantity and quality, of mechanics and meaning, colour the evaluation and practice in the field. The tension extends into more abstract polarities: humanity between science and humanism, tragic and utopian views of humanity, and conservative versus imperialistic visions of the place of psychoanalysis in improving human relations.

Freud cautioned against abandoning points of view implicit in the quantitative and qualitative position in psychoanalysis. While he was an artist in his observation of pathology and mental function (see, for example, Freud's exquisite narrative of an obsessional illness in his case 'The Rat Man' (Freud, 1955, Vol. X), Freud never abandoned the theory of instincts and its grounding in biology. From early on, the disputes in psychoanalysis have resulted from attempts to frame the theories of pathology and therapy along a single dimension, what Freud called the error of *pars pro toto*, or substituting the part for the whole. Thus, in contemporary psychoanalysis, the stress on developmental deficits over structural conflict arises in part from a humanistic perspective and leads to the use of the therapist not as an object in a transference drama that requires interpretation, but as a surrogate who will use his beneficent office to overcome the malevolence of the past, particularly of early infancy. These debates within psychoanalysis have strong intellectual, as well as cultural and philosophical, foundations. Some investigators place psychoanalysis squarely in the midst of interpretive disciplines rather than the natural sciences (Ricoeur, 1970). They link psychoanalysis to hermeneutics, linguistics and the humanities as against biology, medicine, psychiatry and the sciences. These debates also have economic and political ramifications concerning what constitutes the psychoanalytic profession and the qualifications of those who seek to enter its practice.

Psychoanalysis began as a medical discipline for the treatment of neurotic disturbances. It continues this therapeutic tradition of classical psychoanalysis in broadened application to the psychoses, borderline and narcissistic conditions through variants of psychoanalytic psychotherapy. As a result of its methods of investigation, its observations and theories, psychoanalysis has become a part of the general culture. The applications of psychoanalysis in literary criticism, history, political and social sciences, law and business are evidence of its infusion into the general culture. Writers, artists and critics, while debating the uses of psychoanalysis beyond the couch, understand the theory and experiment with its applications to the arts. Freud gave birth to a therapy and a theory and perhaps beyond his intent, to a view of the world and the human condition.

Abraham Zaleznik
Harvard University

References

Freud, S. (1953–66), *Standard Edition of the Complete Psychological Works of Sigmund Freud*, 24 vols, edited by J. Strachey, London.

Jones, E. (1953), *Sigmund Freud: Life and Work*, 3 vols, London.

Ricoeur, P. (1970), *Freud and Philosophy: An Essay on Interpretation*, New Haven.

Segal, H. (1964), *Introduction to the Work of Melanie Klein*, New York.

Psychology

Almost a hundred years ago, William James (1890) epitomized psychology as 'the science of mental life'. It is the discipline that gathers together all those who have a systematic interest in the mind and its workings, in people and the lives they lead. To say this, though, is to pose a puzzle, even a paradox. For what the visitor finds, when he enters a university department of psychology, opens a textbook of psychology, or dips into psychology's professional journals, seems both startling in its diversity, and, often, to have little to do either with the mind or with people. It is this puzzle that an account of psychology must explain.

Looking back to James and his contemporaries, the founding fathers of psychology, one sees scarcely a trace of the diversity to follow, or of the retreat, real or apparent, from their conception of the psychologist's subject-matter. These men wrote about the mind and about people, and did so without embarrassment. Francis Galton, for instance, allowed his curiosity to range from hereditary studies of genius, the invention of rudimentary statistics and the first attempts to test intelligence, to discussions of the mind that sit comfortably beside those of the early psychoanalysts. While Freud was still a young man, with his life's work ahead of him, Galton (1883) wrote: 'There seems to be a presence chamber in my mind where full consciousness holds court, and where two or three ideas are at the same time in audience, and an ante-chamber full of more or less allied ideas, which is situated just beyond the full ken of consciousness. Out of this ante-chamber the ideas most nearly allied to those in the presence-chamber appear to be summoned in a mechanically logical way, and to have their turn of audience.' Beyond or below this ante-chamber, Galton also discerned 'a darker basement, a storehouse from which older and remoter ideas can with greater difficulty be called up into consciousness.' Such language and assumptions were accessible not only to Galton's academic neighbours, but also to those outside psychology; Poincaré, for example, the great French mathematician, was intrigued by the source of his own mathematical insights, which seemed to arrive unbidden (Hadamard, 1945).

Without question, Galton's imagination was circumscribed by what we now see as ugly Victorian prejudices. 'It is in the most unqualified manner,' he said (1883) 'that I object to pretensions of natural equality.' He also observed that 'The mistakes the negroes made in their own matters were so childish, stupid, and simpleton-like, as frequently to make me ashamed of my own species.' Nowadays we would expect Galton to distinguish altogether more crisply between questions of diversity, essential to our evolution as a species, and questions of value. Nevertheless, he entertained the great problems of human self-awareness, and did so with unbridled energy. Thus, one morning, he decided that he would view the world around him as though being spied upon (Burt, 1961). By the time his walk was over 'every horse on every cabstand seemed to be watching me either openly or in disguise'. These 'persecutory delusions' lasted for the rest of the day, and could be revived at will three months later.

In the years after the First World War, the intellectual freedom of men like Galton was gradually abandoned. Psychology became the focus of a new enthusiasm: behaviourism. Under this influence, psychology, then establishing itself as an academic subject in universities, began to settle upon two of its abiding preoccupations: the first, with its status as a science, as opposed to a scholarly pursuit like history or a therapeutic one like medicine; the second, with the need to banish from the discipline all 'subjective' considerations, all mention of mental states, and to root psychology instead in the prediction of relationships between stimulus and response.

Gradually, throughout the 1930s and 1940s, the influence of

behaviourism strengthened, to the extent that, by the early 1950s, the subject-matter of psychology itself had been redefined. Instead of being taught that psychology was the science of mental life, students were taught that it was the 'science of behaviour' (Skinner, 1953). The behaviour in question, their professors made plain, was not just that of human beings, but of all animal species, from octopus to man – and these creatures, not in their wild state, but in the artificial environment of the laboratory.

Behaviourism was to remain the dominant orthodoxy in university departments of psychology until the late 1960s, when doubts were voiced (for example, Kagan, 1967; Hudson, 1972). The mood, since, has grown more pluralistic. While behaviourism produced neither the centrally placed bodies of knowledge nor the intellectual mastery that pioneers like Watson and Skinner promised, its legacy is all round us, in that the activities of professional psychologists make less than complete sense if this influence is ignored. The anxiety over psychology's status as a science remains, scarcely abated; and so too does the distrust of any argument that cannot be tethered to objective evidence about what people, animals or, more recently, computers can be seen to do.

Worries about the scientific respectability of psychology have led, in turn, to a sense of hierarchy within psychology. Precisely controlled experimental research, designed to test a theory that is itself carefully formulated, is highly regarded; field research or research which is geared to the practical needs of the world at large have a lower status. As in the scientific community as a whole, the pure is elevated over the applied. The subject-matter of academic psychology has organized itself, too, around a variety of abstract themes: learning, memory, attention, motivation, intelligence, personality, creativity, and so on. Pursuing these, psychologists have sometimes seemed to execute a wilful retreat from questions of practical relevance.

In the 1950s, when this retreat was at its most pronounced, it seemed at times that psychological research enjoyed higher prestige the further removed from ordinary human concerns it became. Experimental studies, of course, were not always narrowly conceived; Gregory's (1966) work on visual illusions,

for example, combined elegance with a wider sense of implication. But research on issues of pressing social concern was
usually treated, in comparison, as suspect. McClelland's (1961)
studies of the motives of the entrepreneur were accorded a
certain respect, as was the work, inspired by Nazi Germany,
on the authoritarian personality (Adorno, 1950), and the
research by social psychologists like Asch (1955) and Milgram
(1963) on social pressure and compliance. Even here, though,
the lure of theory, and of the apparent rigour of tests and
statistics, were sometimes to prove disruptively strong. Only
rather exceptionally did psychologists study a pertinent slice of
life without the protection of either, as Bronfenbrenner (1970)
was to do in his comparison of Russian and American experiences of childhood.

Another feature of psychology at this stage in its growth,
despite its optimism and energy, was its reliance on sources
outside itself for new initiatives. Obvious instances are the
impact on the discipline of the early information theorists and
of a linguist like Chomsky. Another instance, more subtle, is
that of Kelly (1955). His background was complex: first in
mathematics and physics, then in educational sociology and
psychology. He earned a living as an aeronautical engineer
before settling on a career in psychology. Perhaps because of
this grounding, half inside psychology, half out, his work on
the semantics of everyday life has remained fertile, even though
the area was one that more conventional psychologists like
Osgood (1957) had already begun to develop. In the hands of
the orthodox, the wider implications of a good idea were sometimes buried beneath technique that was rigorous but subtly
misplaced, evidence that was copious but inconclusive. Preoccupied with questions of rigour, psychologists also allowed
academic neighbours like the sociologist Goffman (1959) to pre-
empt important parts of their own subject-matter, placing upon
it constructions in which psychological notions played only an
insignificant part.

Whatever its excesses, behaviourism helped establish a
concern for rigour over questions of method. Less directly, it
pointed to a source of uncertainty – and, hence, of diversity –
that lies at the very heart of psychology, and which refuses to

go away. For the study of the mind is based upon an unresolved, and some would say unresolvable, tension: that between human consciousness and the brain in which that consciousness is housed. At the centre of psychology, there is the baffling relation of the mind to body; of the meanings in terms of which human beings order their lives, some crisply determinate, others ambiguous, vague or half-hidden, and the central nervous system without which such meanings could not exist.

In practice, psychologists leave the mind/body problem to philosophers. The shape that their discipline takes nevertheless reflects this point of strain. Psychologists have in the past tended to form two camps: on the one hand, the 'soft', those concerned with people, the relations between them, and the meanings with which their lives are imbued; on the other, the 'hard', who are committed to the study of the brain and how it works. The 'soft' have a natural affinity with social scientists, historians, therapists, while the 'hard' have close links with brain chemists, biologists, computer scientists.

This distinction between 'soft' and 'hard', although it still enjoys wide currency, is an unfortunate one. It provides a tempting line of fissure, and it is unrepresentative, too, of the variety that the inhabitants of many psychology departments nowadays display. If you walk into a psychology department, anywhere in the Western world, and listen to what is taught, or speak to the teachers about their research, you will probably find as many instances that violate this simple distinction between 'soft' and 'hard' as conform to it. In order to make sense of psychology as it now stands, another, more complex, model or metaphor is required.

Consider the members of staff in a particular department who have joined forces to teach an introductory course in psychology to first-year students (the instance is real rather than imagined). There are four of them. The first is a young woman who usually describes herself as a social psychologist. Her special concern is with stress, and her research has carried her into the clinical world, where she studies the anxieties experienced by surgical patients, especially those with breast cancer. She works in close collaboration with surgeons, and the aim of her research is in part the practical one of reducing the distress that serious illness and surgery induce.

Her teaching partner, in the first term of the course, is, superficially, of a different stamp. He was trained in a famous physiology department rather than a department of psychology, and his research is squarely scientific: it deals with the brain's ability to assimilate information reaching it from the eye, and he conducts it in a small, electrically-screened cubicle, with a high degree of experimental refinement and control. His interests in psychology range quite widely, but what he publishes is addressed to an audience that is very specialized indeed.

In the second term, another pair of lecturers take over. The first studies the relations of young mothers to their infants, the ways in which patterns of child-raising differ from one social class to another, and, more generally, the emergence of the individual's sense of identity – the ideas and commitments around which a sense of self is hung. Her partner started out in life as a mathematician. He is an expert in the study of memory and of mental imagery; and has carried out studies, for example, of the effects on memory of the kinds of head injury sustained in traffic accidents. More recently, he has become interested, too, in methods of teaching, and in the ways in which university students learn.

These four psychologists, members of a single department, plough four distinct furrows. Next year, their places on the introductory course could be taken by others. One, whose appointment is half in psychology, half in biology, specializes in animal behaviour, and is knowledgeable about the interaction of hereditary and environmental forces. He might speak to the students about the mating behaviour of red deer, or show them films of rats running in mazes. Another deals with psychoanalytic theory and feminism. Yet another does research on the chemistry of the brain, and hopes to shed light on the causes of senile dementia. A fourth is interested in the relation of Kelly's repertory grid analysis to information technology; a fifth pays systematic attention to the skill of reading.

The diversity that these academics represent is far greater than one would find in any other discipline on the university's campus. Yet they all see themselves and are seen by others as psychologists. They combine to teach the same students, and the students they teach see themselves, in turn, as becoming psychologists.

Despite their differences, a visitor might expect all these psychologists to share a belief in the same body of theories, in the sense that physicists share a belief in the theoretical edifice that Newton, Einstein, Hiesenberg and others have built. If so, he would be mistaken. There is no commonly accepted body of psychological theory. In practice, the best theorizing in psychology has been done at the local level, and attempts to create grand, overarching theories have met with little success.

This absence of a uniting theory may come as an uncomfortable surprise. Even more uncomfortable is the discovery that psychologists of different persuasions often have little to say to one another about research, and can differ with one another quite sharply about the kinds of psychology that students should be taught. They may disagree, for example, about whether a grounding in elementary statistics is essential, or whether students ahould be exposed to the ideas of Freud. Rather than exchanging views with one another, they often find it easier and more natural to talk to academic neighbours, outside psychology. The psychologist who specializes in animal behaviour may well find that he goes to conferences where he meets ethologists and geneticists, rather than psychologists whose special interests differ from his own. And his colleagues likewise.

Not only do many psychologists lack a driving interest in one another's research; it frequently happens that they cannot understand one another's publications. Thus a psychologist working on the computer simulation of short-term memory may find it hard, even impossible, to follow a paper written by a colleague who is excited by recent critiques of psychoanalytic theory, advanced by scholars on the Continent (see, for example, Bowie, 1979). And vice versa. At this point, the visitor may well protest that psychology is not a discipline at all; simply a cacophany, a muddle. To reach this conclusion is an error, however; and it is so because it rests on an excessively simple view of what a discipline is like.

The point is best made in terms of diagrams, as Campbell (1977) suggests. The usual assumption about a discipline like chemistry is that it consists of a common core of agreed theory, and a number of subsidiary specialities or applications. In diagrammatic terms, this might be represented as a pyramid, or as a nest of concentric circles, like the layers of an onion. Pyramids and concentric circles are not the only diagrams one can draw, though. Consider this:

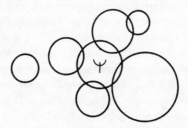

Figure 1

Psychology is represented by the centrally placed circle, marked 'Ψ'; other, related disciplines – social science, biology, computer science – by the adjacent circles. Some of the neighbouring circles overlap the 'psychological' circle, but none includes it. If the circle representing psychology is now abstracted from the rest, one sees this:

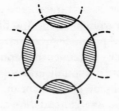

Figure 2

This diagram poses some interesting possibilities: for example, that it is in its areas of overlap with its neighbours – here, shaded – that the field of psychology is at its most exciting. It is in these zones of overlap that their interests bring the psychologist and his neighbours into contact – and, often, conflict. Thus both psychologist and computer scientist may have an interest in human memory, but very different presuppositions about how memory can best be explained. Likewise, psychologists and sociologists share an interest in crimes of violence but disagree sharply over their likely causes.

Analogous conflicts arise continually, and three or more disciplines sometimes stake a claim, as has happened in the field of sex and gender and the explanation of the psychological differences that men and women display. Those, like Kinsey, with a background in biology, have generated bodies of evidence about regularities in behaviour, although their researches, as it happened, were often informed by a libertarian, permissive system of moral values (Robinson, 1969). At the same time, evidence was drawn from anthropology, pioneers like Margaret Mead stressing the extent to which male and female patterns of behaviour were culturally rather than biologically determined (D'Andrade, 1967); and, then, from medicine and from within psychoanalytic tradition, there evolved a further body of work stressing the confusions of gender identity that can arise, and tracing these to the relation of the infant in question to the parent of the opposite sex (Stroller, 1968; Money and Ehrhardt, 1972). Into this area, there also moved endocrinologists, interested in the impact of sex hormones on behaviour; feminists, concerned with the extent to which evidence about sex differences becomes muddled with political prejudice; and those studying abnormalities of sexual behaviour – a perversion like fetishism, for instance, which seems a male preserve.

Such areas of overlap usually arise from contact between psychologists and their academic neighbours, but, from time to time, the contact is with specialists whose concerns are more immediately practical: the doctor concerned with the care of his patients, the police superintendent worried about relations between his junior officers and the Black community. Whether academic or practical, the moral pointed by the diagram is the same: intellectually, psychology is a discipline that thrives on exchange with the worlds of expertise that surround it.

Other morals flow too. If psychology is a field in which excitement characteristically arises around the edges, its heartland will consist not so much of specific theories or bodies of evidence, as of those broader concerns which have remained unchanged since psychology's beginnings as a branch of philosophy: the relation of mind to body, the origins of knowledge, the distinction between the real and the illusory. It is in their sensitivity to these centrally placed foci of conceptual unease that psychologists of quality mark themselves out from those whose contribution is more technical. It also follows that, in the shaded areas around the edge of the field, specialized languages and techniques will evolve in response to local needs. A consequence is that, considered as a whole, psychology will tend to be a polyglot, containing a number of languages rather than a single language. The risk, plainly, is that the task of translation will be skimped, and that psychology will tend to split apart as nations do. If this were to happen, professional life in the short run might be more tranquil, but the uniting commitment to the study of mental life would dissolve, and with it would be lost the chance to resolve the more complex problems that human beings pose.

Grant such a model of psychology, more complicated than the onion with its skins or the pyramid with its layers, but down-to-earth nonetheless, and what one finds inside a psychology department fits comfortably into place. The diversity and polygot nature of psychology represent not a lapse from some simple ideal, but the consequences that flow, quite properly, from the complexities of the psychologist's subject matter. This complexity, it is important to see, is not just a question of the styles that psychologists adopt, the schools of thought they form or the methods of inquiry they find it most comfortable to use. It is inherent in the problems themselves, as the work on sex and gender shows. The direction of an individual's sexual desires, his sense of his own maleness or femaleness, his presentation of himself in terms of his interests, habits and social style as typically male, typically female or more androgynous: all this will depend on physical questions – his chromosomes and sex hormones, his anatomy – but on these overlaid with the influence of parents and contemporaries and the values implicit in the wider culture. The confusions and perplexities that characterize this aspect of human experience demand patient scrutiny; and this, in its turn, may depend as much on clinical and on literary skills (see Brown, 1966; Gass, n.d.; Barthes, 1979) as it does on those of scientific research.

This point about the multifaceted nature of the psychologist's subject-matter can equally be made elsewhere. The question of mental illness, far from seeming depressing or sordid, is the focus of keen interest among laymen and psychologists alike. Insight into its causes or cure could come from a variety of quite different directions, and these could prove to be complementary. The attraction of mental illness as a research problem is precisely its many-sidedness.

The traditional view is that mental illness – or, more specifically, schizophrenia – is congenital. In support of this, there is the evidence of genetics. This shows that the closer the kinship between two people, the more likely both are to be schizophrenic, identical twins seeming to show the highest concordance of all (Kallmann, 1953). Adjacent, but separate, there is the work of the pharmacologists and brain chemists. They point to certain substances that can be recovered from the brains of schizophrenics that are not present in the same quantities in the brains of those who are not schizophrenic. Adjacent again, but again separate, there are arguments based on the analogy with the computer: the suggestion, for instance, that the schizophrenic brain is like a computer suffering from information overload.

Such theories and speculations can be categorized broadly as 'physical'. They have been subjected to vigorous attack over the last twenty years or so. One onslaught (for example, Laing and Esterson, 1964) advanced the claim that rather than going mad, people are driven mad – and driven mad, characteristically, by parents who exert 'double binds' upon them. More sweeping still has been the argument, often attractive to students of social science, that schizophrenia is what results when a society stigmatizes, isolates and humiliates its deviants, a process in which orthodox psychiatrists are seen as playing a malign role.

The key to the problem of schizophrenia, if there is one, could emerge from any of four or five separate areas of research, or from a combination of these. Along one path, a cure might arise from better parental practices; along another, from a revolutionary new drug therapy.

At meetings between opposed camps, an air of awkwardness

often reigns, and, frequently, there are displays of mutual incomprehension. More tellingly, though, rival camps also have the chance to probe the logical weaknesses in each other's positions. Thus it was quickly discovered that the genetic evidence about identical twins was less conclusive than it seemed, because identical twins share not only their genetic endowment but very similar environments too (Newman, 1937). In search of rigour, the debate was forced back from concordance in identical twins in general to concordance in those few pairs who had been separated from birth, and whose environments had of necessity been different (Shields, 1962). Inexorably logical, this step precipitated another, however. Gradually, research workers realized that, as they could not know in advance which aspects of an individual's environment might play a crucial part in causing schizophrenia, they had no means of demonstrating that the separated twins' environments were dissimilar in significant rather than trivial respects.

Step by step, in other words, the logical demands made upon the competing bodies of evidence were sharpened; and, one after another, bodies of evidence which at first sight had seemed clinching were revealed as helpful but inconclusive. More generally, it was also realized that the discussion of causes was logically separate from the discussion of cures. Many participants in the debate about the causes of schizophrenia assumed that evidence from genetics must be resisted because it was evidence that schizophrenia could not be cured. Only slowly did it dawn that schizophrenia might prove to be genetically transmitted, after all, and yet that, in one form or another, perfectly satisfactory clinical or social treatments might nonetheless be established.

While the debate about the causes of schizophrenia has recently seemed to lose a little of its intensity, another topic, eclipsed for several decades, is now moving back towards the limelight: the question of why we dream. Again, this is multifaceted. A popular view, derived from Freud (Sulloway, 1979), is that we dream in order to fulfil repressed sexual wishes. This line of reasoning, which sees dreams as pregnant with hidden meaning, did not recommend itself to behaviourists, however, many of whom professed to believe that dreams do not exist;

or, if they did, that they were purely random. The 1950s saw the establishment of laboratories for the study of sleep and dreaming. While important discoveries were made, the theorizing within these laboratories tended to be biological in inspiration. The dream, more often than not, was seen as a by-product of some physiological or chemical process in which a balance in the brain is restored (Oswald, 1980). More recently, analogies between brain and computer have led to the suggestion that the dreaming brain is akin to a computer in its 'off-line' state, during which its programmes are up-dated or 'cleaned'.

Such biological research nonetheless faced a difficulty: that of explaining the evolutionary function that sleep and dreaming must perform. The sleeping, dreaming animal is at the mercy of its predators; and any pattern of behaviour so blatantly dangerous must have a vital adaptive function if it is to survive. One task, then, is to state what this adaptive function is. Another is to explain (rather than explaining away) the widely held and carefully substantiated view that dreams, although in code, can sometimes serve as a complement to and comment upon waking thought (Rycroft, 1979); that, as Darwin (1871) observed, dreams are an involuntary kind of poetry.

Again, four or five bodies of evidence are relevant; there are four or five circles that can in principle overlap. Adopting an evolutionary frame of reference, and drawing heavily on the computer analogy, Crick and Mitchison (1983) have proposed that animals have the dreams associated with rapid eye movement sleep in order that their brains can clear themselves of 'parasitic' patterns of response; and that, without this capability, the brain would quickly become overloaded. A corollary of this argument, as the authors point out, is that we dream in order to forget; that dreams, on the whole, neither can nor should be recalled.

Such a theory is difficult if not impossible to test directly. One would have to show that the occurrence of a thought in an unrecalled dream reduces the likelihood of that thought recurring. On the other hand, it is an error to restrict psychology to the study of theories that can be directly verified or falsified; and an error, too, to assume that the issue of the dream's meaning is closed. Einstein was not alone among scientists in treating the dream as a useful source of insight, both in its own right and as part of a more general access to intuitive or imaginative modes of thought. There is no inherent reason why a theory like Crick and Mitchison's should not be modified to allow the brain to scan its own 'parasitic' products, and to glean from them ideas that it can set to good use. If this modification were adopted, dreams would be seen less as household rubbish, more as items jumbled together on a bric-á-brac stall, most virtually worthless, a few of genuine value and richly deserving rescue.

As with research on schizophrenia, there also exists the need to specify, with detachment and precision, what it is that dream theories are seeking to explain. In research on schizophrenia, there is still uncertainty about symptoms – whether 'thought disorder' is always present, and what 'thought disorders' consist of. Similarly with dreaming. The laboratory research on sleep and dreaming makes it clear that many dreams are more 'thought-like' than had previously seemed likely. This finding has implications that run in several directions. It brings to mind the possibility that this distinction between thought-like and dream-like dreams has its basis in the activities of the left and right cerebral hemispheres respectively. It raises once again the question of 'cognitive style' and the differences that individuals display in their access to the nonrational aspects of their own experience (Getzels and Jackson, 1962; Hudson, 1966); and it suggests that one might with profit look more closely at the dream-like states that occur while we are awake: not just reveries and fantasies, but at the dream-like states evoked in an altogether more disciplined and fastidious way in the verbal and visual arts (Hudson, 1982). As with schizophrenia, so with dreaming; a more scrupulous mapping of mental states could sharpen the pressures under which relatively simple-minded evolutionary and computer-based theories are at present placed.

Of course, not all debates in psychology appeal as directly to the layman as do those about schizophrenia or sleep and dreaming. Nor can all be contained relatively comfortably within frames of reference that are familiar. Sometimes, the

discipline faces a challenge from outside, and one with implications that cannot be foreseen. One such is the computer.

While early computers were 'stupid', their descendants are
showing signs of adaptability: the ability to learn from experience, and even to evolve their own instructions (Boden, 1977).
Arguably, students of artificial intelligence can now learn from
the adaptive systems that have evolved naturally: the brain
and also the genetic mechanisms whereby inherited patterns of
behaviour are passed from one generation to the next. It could
be of real value to designers of artificial brains, for example, to
know why natural brains dream. This new field – that of 'intelligent systems' – cuts across the established boundaries between
computer science, biology and psychology, and it will be of
interest to see how lively a part psychologists play in it.

The implications of the computer, though, are not tidily
circumscribed. It opens a door onto an immediate future in
which, to a wholly unprecedented degree, human beings will
live in intimate contact with machines: not only the computer
and word processor but the camera and television set – and
these instruments not just as useful servants, but as devices
that invade the individual's consciousness and alter it in both
profound and superficial ways.

The tendency of psychology over the last half century, a
period of massive professional growth and proliferation, has
been somewhat inward-looking. It has addressed certain themes
– ones that, over the years, have come to be seen as the
'classical' ones – and it has preserved from its formative stages
a deep preoccupation with objectivity in judgement, correctness
in method. Yet it seems unlikely that the human implications
of information technology can satisfactorily be met from such
a stance. Social change, both in this area and in others, will in
all probability be too rapid and too radical.

Whether the question at issue is the human implication of
the computer, or some other respect in which an advanced
industrial society is subject to change – the impact, for example,
of structural unemployment on the lives of those on whom
idleness is imposed – the challenge is in principle the same. In
order to make contributions of value, psychologists may have
to recover some of the intellectual freedom and vitality (though

not the ugly prejudices) that founding fathers like Galton and James enjoyed.

Liam Hudson
Brunel University, Uxbridge

References

Adorno, T. W. *et al.* (1950), *The Authoritarian Personality*, New York.

Asch, S. E. (1955), 'Opinions and social pressure', *Scientific American*.

Barthes, R. (1979), *A Lover's Discourse*, London.

Boden, M. (1977), *Artificial Intelligence and Natural Man*, Hassocks.

Bowie, M. (1979), 'Jacques Lacan', in J. Sturrock (ed.) *Structuralism and Since*, Oxford.

Bronfenbrenner, U. (1970), *Two Worlds of Childhood*, New York.

Brown, N. O. (1966), *Love's Body*, New York.

Burt, C. (1961), 'Galton's contribution to psychology', *Bulletin of the British Psychological Society*, 45.

Campbell, D. T. (1977), *Descriptive Epistemology*, preliminary draft of William James Lectures, Harvard University, unpublished.

Crick, F. and Mitchison, G. (1983), 'The function of dream sleep', *Nature*, 304.

D'Andrade, R. G. (1967), 'Sex differences and cultural institutions', in E. E. Maccoby (ed.), *The Development of Sex Differences*, London.

Darwin, C. (1871), *The Descent of Man*, London.

Galton, F. (1883), *Inquiries into Human Faculty*, London.

Gass, W. (no date), *On Being Blue*, Boston.

Getzels, J. W. and Jackson, P. W. (1962), *Creativity and Intelligence*, New York.

Goffman, E. (1959), *The Presentation of Self in Everyday Life*, New York.

Gregory, R. (1966), *Eye and Brain*, London.

Hadamard, J. (1945), *The Psychology of Invention in the Mathematical Field*, Princeton.

Hudson, L. (1966), *Contrary Imaginations*, London.

Hudson, L. (1972), *The Cult of the Fact*, London.

Hudson, L. (1982), *Bodies of Knowledge*, London.

James, W. (1890), *Principles of Psychology*, New York.

Kagan, J. (1967), 'On the need for relativism', *American Psychologist*, 22.

Kallmann, F. J. (1953), *Heredity in Health and Mental Disorder*, New York.

Kelly, G. A. (1955), *The Psychology of Personal Constructs*, New York.

Laing, R. D. and Esterson, A. (1964), *Sanity, Madness and the Family*, London.

McClelland, D. C. (1961), *The Achieving Society*, New York.

Milgram, S. (1963), 'Behavioral study of obedience', *Journal of Abnormal and Social Psychology*, 67.

Money, J. and Ehrhardt, A. A. (1972), *Man and Woman, Boy and Girl*, Baltimore.

Newman, H. H. *et al.* (1937), *Twins: A Study of Heredity and Environment*, Chicago.

Osgood, C. E. *et al.* (1957), *The Measurement of Meaning*, Urbana.

Oswald, I. (1980), *Sleep*, Harmondsworth.

Robinson, P. A. (1969), *The Sexual Radicals*, London.

Rycroft, C. (1979), *The Innocence of Dreams*, London.

Shields, J. (1962), *Monozygotic Twins Brought up Apart and Brought Up Together*, Oxford.

Skinner, B. F. (1953), *Science and Human Behavior*, New York.

Stoller, R. J. (1968), *Sex and Gender*, London.

Sulloway, F. J. (1979), *Freud, Biologist of the Mind*, London.

Race

Few concepts in modern times have been less understood and few more liable to misuse than the concept of race when applied to man.

Such powerful feelings has it aroused that its use is sharply declining among the writers of physical anthropology textbooks in the United States. Of twenty such textbooks published between 1932 and 1969, thirteen (65 per cent) accepted that races of man exist, three (15 per cent) claimed that they do not exist, while of the remaining four, two did not mention the subject while two stated that there was no consensus on the subject. On the other hand, of thirty-eight such textbooks that appeared between 1970 and 1979, only twelve, or 32 per cent, stated that races of man exist, whereas fourteen, or 37 per cent, claimed that races do not exist; of the remaining twelve texts, four were non-committal on the matter, three failed to mention race and five indicated that there was no consensus (Littlefield, Lieberman and Reynolds, 1982).

It is of course a moot point how much we may conclude from a study of the contents of textbooks, but it is, to say the least, striking that, during the 1970s, there was in the US so marked a swing away from the earlier widespread acceptance of the existence of human races. Critics of the study cited have raised the question of the degree to which that change reflects new concepts flowing from new data and novel approaches, and the extent to which the change might have been predicated upon extraneous factors, such as a swing of 'fashion', political considerations, or the composition of classes of students to which the texts were directed. Nor is it clear whether the tendency in the United States typifies other parts of the world of physical anthropology.

Certainly the change tells us that, even among experts, no less than in the public mind, the concept of race is being critically re-examined and that no consensus, let alone unanimity, among specialists on the validity or the usefulness of the race concept appears to exist at the present time. It is worthwhile therefore to examine the meaning of race. Since race is basically a concept of biology in general, we shall start by examining race as a biological notion.

Race as a Biological Concept

Many, perhaps most, species of living things comprise numbers of populations which may be dispersed geographically and among varying ecological niches. To impart order to the subdivisions within a species, biologists have used several terms such as subspecies, race and population to classify the various groupings of communities that make up a species. Thus, in a species within which two or more subspecies are recognized, a race comprises populations or aggregates of populations within each formally designated subspecies. Often the term race is qualified: biologists recognize 'geographic races' (which may be synonymous with subspecies); 'ecological races' where, within a species, there occur ecologically differentiated populations; and 'microgeographic races' which refers to local populations (Mayr, 1963).

Although students of any group of living things may differ from one another on the finer details of such intraspecific classifications, there has for some time been fairly general agreement that race is a valid biological concept. Classically, the differences among the races in a species have been identified by their morphology, that is, their observable physical structure.

In the last half-century, and especially since 1950, biologists, not content with studying the morphological make-up of populations within species, have been studying the genetic composition of the subdivisions within species. These studies have directed attention to a number of non-morphological traits such as the genes for blood-groups and for specific proteins. When these hereditary characters are analysed, they reveal that there are no hard and fast boundaries between races and populations within a species. For any such genetic marker, it is not uncommon to find that the frequency of the trait in question is distributed along a gradient (or *cline*) which cuts across the boundaries of races, as delimited by morphology. Such gene clines often do not parallel any detectable environmental gradient; they appear to be neutral in relation to natural selective agencies in the environment.

Different genetic markers within a species may vary along different gradients. Thus, if one were to base one's thinking about the subdivisions of a species on the distribution of any one genetic marker, one would be liable to reach a different conclusion from that which might flow from the use of another genetic marker.

Hence, newer methods of analysis combine the frequencies of many different genetic markers, in the hope that the resulting sorting of populations will more nearly reflect the objective genetic relationship of the subgroups within a species.

Character-gradients apply as well to some morphological features. That is, some structural features such as body size, ear size, or colouring, change gradually and continuously over large areas. Such gradients, unlike the genetic clines, appear to parallel gradients in environmental features and have probably resulted from the action of natural selection (Huxley, 1963). However, the frequencies of the genes governing morphological characters are less commonly used in the study of genetic inter-relationships within a species, for several good reasons: (1) such traits are often of complex, difficult and even uncertain genetic causation; (2) many of them and, particularly, measurable characters are determined not by a single gene-pair, but by numbers of different gene-pairs; (3) such characters are especially subject to environmental modification: for example, if animals live in a lush area and eat more food, they would be expected to grow bigger than those of the same species living in a more arid region. This 'eco-sensitivity' of the body's metrical traits renders them less useful in an analysis of genetic affinities.

In sum, race is a biological concept. Races are recognized by a combination of geographic, ecological and morphological factors and, increasingly, in the last third of the twentieth century, by analyses of the distribution of gene frequencies for numbers of essentially non-morphological, biochemical components. As long as one focused on morphological traits alone, it was sometimes not difficult to convince oneself that races were distinctly differentiated, one from another, with clear-cut boundaries between them; the progressive application of genetic insights and analyses to the problem revealed that recognizable gene variants (or *alleles*) are no respecters of such hypothetical boundaries. Often, indeed, one race merges with the next through intermediate forms, while members of one race can and do interbreed with members of other races. Hence, the importation of genetic appraisal into the discussions on race has led to a definite blurring of the outlines of each race, and so to an attenuation of the concept of race itself.

Race in Human Biology

The biological concept of race, as just sketched, has been applied to the living populations of the human species. At least since the time of the Swedish naturalist and systematist

Linnaeus (1707–78), all living human beings have been formally classified as members of a single species, *Homo sapiens*. The accumulation since the middle of the nineteenth century of fossil remains of the family of man has revealed that earlier forms of man lived which could validly be regarded as different species of the same genus, for example *Homo habilis* and *Homo erectus*. Our species, *Homo sapiens*, probably made its appearance between one-half and one-third of a million years before the present.

As *Homo sapiens* spread across first the Old World and, more latterly, the New World, the species diversified, in varied geographical zones and ecological niches, into numerous populations. At the present time we have a situation in which living humanity is divided into several major and many minor subdivisions among which the same kinds of variation are encountered as apply to other living things. Thus, the populations show morphological variation, including some gradients associated with environmental gradients, and varying gene frequencies with clines of distribution that, for individual genetic markers, breach the limits of morphologically defined groups of populations.

Physical anthropologists, relying on morphological traits, have for long divided living humankind into great geographical races (also called major races, subspecies and constellations of races). Most classifications recognized three such major subdivisions, the Negroid, Mongoloid and Caucasoid; some investigators designated other major races, such as the Amerind and the Oceanian. Within the major races, several dozen minor races (or, simply, races) were recognized, the number identified varying with the investigator. As with other living groups, historically the classification of living *Homo sapiens* was based on morphological traits, such as skin colour, hair form and body size. As genetic analysis came to be applied, in respect first of blood-groups and later of a variety of proteins, clines were found which cut across the boundaries of minor and even of major races. Moreover, it was found that the genic variation between the major races was small in comparison with the intraracial variation. Doubts began to be expressed as to whether there was any biological basis for the classification of human races (for example, Lewontin, 1972).

The problem is compounded by the fact that even when genetical analysis became based not just on a few traits such as the ABO, MN and Rh blood-groups, but on a number of traits, different results were obtained according to which combinations and numbers of traits were used. For example, Piazza *et al.* (1975) analysed frequency data for eighteen gene loci in fifteen representative human populations: they found that the Negroid populations were genetically closer to the Caucasoid populations than either group of populations was to those populations classified as Mongoloid. This, in turn, was interpreted as signifying an earlier phylogenetic split between Mongoloid, on the one hand, and Negroid-Caucasoid on the other, and a later (more recent) split between Negroid and Caucasoid.

However, Nei's (1978) analysis, based on eleven protein and eleven blood-group loci in twelve human populations, revealed a first splitting between Negroid and Caucasoid-Mongoloid. Subsequently, Nei (1982) and Nei and Roychoudhury (1982) used a still larger number of genetic traits, namely sixty-two protein loci and twenty-three blood-group loci, that is eighty-five gene loci in all, for which data were available for some eighteen world populations. Interestingly, while the protein data revealed a first splitting between Negroid and Caucasoid-Mongoloid, the blood-group data suggest a slightly closer affinity and therefore a slightly more recent splitting between Negroid and Caucasoid.

Clearly, at the time when this article is being written, the last word has not been said on the exact pattern of affinities among the living races. Nor is there a consensus as to whether the large size of intraracial genetic variation, compared with interracial, vitiates any biological basis for the classification of human races. As two representative recent studies, we may cite Lewontin (1972) who believes there is no basis; and Nei and Roychoudhury (1982) who disagree with Lewontin and assert that, while the interracial genic variation is small, the genetic differentiation is real and generally statistically highly significant. Furthermore, it is clear that, by the use of genetic distance estimates, Piazza *et al.* (1975), Nei and Roychoudhury (1982) and others have been enabled to study the genetic relationships among the mainly morphologically defined human races, to construct dendrograms and to impart some understanding of the pattern of recent human evolution. Thus, the latter investigators have found evidence from protein loci to suggest that the Negroid and the Caucasoid-Mongoloid groups diverged from each other about 110,000 $\pm$ 34,000 years before present, whereas the Caucasoid and Mongoloid groups diverged at about 41,000 $\pm$ 15,000 years before present. These estimates do depend on a number of assumptions and may be modified with the accretion of more data.

One further point may be mentioned here: the extent of genetic differentiation among the living races of man, as determined by the study of protein loci, is not always closely correlated with the degree of morphological differentiation. Indeed, evolutionary change in morphological characters appears to be governed by quite different factors from those governing genetic differentiation in protein-forming genes of the human races, on presently available evidence. Genetic differentiation at protein loci seems to occur largely by such biological processes as mutation, genetic drift and isolation, with migration playing an important role in the establishment of current genetic relationships among human races. On the other hand, morphological characters have apparently been subject to stronger natural selection than 'average protein loci' (Nei and Roychoudhury, 1972; 1982).

In short, the race concept can be applied to modern man, even when one uses the most modern analytical procedures of population geneticists, and such application has been found of heuristic value. Nevertheless, irrespective of sociopolitical considerations, a number of modern investigators of human intraspecific variation find it more useful and more valid to base such studies on populations, as the unit of analysis, and to discard the race concept in these attempts.

Abuses and Aberrations of the Race Concept
Among the various misconceptions that surround the concept of race, are ideas about 'race purity', the effects of racial hybrid-

ization, 'superior and inferior races', race and mental differences, race and culture. A full review of this vast subject is not possible here: it has been dealt with in a number of studies of recent decades such as those of Tobias (1970), Montagu (1972), Mead *et al.* (1968), Kagan (1968), Jensen (1969), Bodmer and Cavalli-Sforza (1970), Scarr-Salapatek (1971), Lochlin *et al.* (1975), Scarr (1980) and Gould (1981).

Although the foregoing selection of writers adopt widely differing standpoints, especially on the subject of race and intelligence (as supposedly reflected by IQ test results), it would not be unfair to claim that the following reflect the view of a great majority of physical anthropologists, human biologists and human geneticists at this time:

(1) Race is an idea borrowed from biology.

(2) At a stage when the study of human populations was primarily, if not exclusively, morphological and its objective classificatory, the race concept helped to classify the immense variety of living and earlier human beings of the species *Homo sapiens*. With the advent of genetic analysis and the discovery that clines of genetic differentiation transcend the supposed 'boundaries' of human races, the race concept has been appreciably weakened.

(3) While some population geneticists have found that race still serves a useful purpose in the study of the genetic affinities of living populations, in the determination of the causal factors that have operated to produce genetic differentiation and in the reconstruction of the phylogenetic history of modern human diversity, others have found the concept of such negligible value in these studies as to have led them to discard race entirely. Time will tell whether we are witnessing 'the potential demise of a concept in physical anthropology' (as Littlefield *et al.*, 1982 have been speculating), or whether the concept will survive the politico-social abuses to which it has been subject and which have been regarded by some as the primary cause of its decline from favour among many investigators and writers of textbooks.

(4) If, for purposes of this analysis, we accept the existence of

races of man (as of other living things), we must note that races differ not in absolutes, but in the frequency with which different morphological and genetic traits occur in different populations.

(5) The overwhelming majority of the genes of *Homo sapiens* are shared by all mankind; a relatively small percentage is believed to control those features which differentiate the races from one another.

(6) The formation of the modern races of man is a relatively recent process, extending back in time for probably not much more than 100,000 years. As against this period of recent diversification, at least forty times as long a period of its hominid ancestry has been spent by each race in common with all other races, as it has spent on its own pathway of differentiation. This statement is based on the evidence that fossilized members of the family of man (the *Hominidae*) are known from 4 million years before the present; molecular and some other evidence suggests that the appearance of the hominids may go back to 5 or more million years before the present.

(7) Racially discriminatory practices make certain assumptions about race, some overt, some tacit. These include the assumptions that:

    (i) races are pure and distinct entities;

    (ii) all members of a race look alike and think alike, which assumption, in turn, is based upon the idea that how one behaves depends entirely or mainly on one's genes;

    (iii) some races are better than others.

(8) The scientific study of human populations has provided no evidence to validate any one of these assumptions.

(9) Genetical and morphological analysis of human populations has failed to confirm that some races are superior and others inferior.

(10) Accidents of geography and history, difficulties of terrain, physical environment and communication, are sufficient to account for the contributions which different populations have made to the varying advancement of human culture and to civilization.

(11) Culture, language and outlook are not inseparably bound up with particular morphological or genetic racial features; for example, man's very culture is today altering the direction of his evolution, as the species spreads into every corner of the world, and as cultural and racial divergence gives way over large areas to cultural and racial convergence.

(12) The myth of the pure race has been thoroughly disproved. There are no pure (genetically or morphologically homogeneous) human races and, as far as the fossil record goes, there never have been.

(13) Not only is purity of race a non-existent fantasy, but there is no evidence to support the notion that purity of race is a desirable thing.

(14) Racial groups are highly variable entities; for many traits intraracial variability is greater than interracial variability. Intermediates exist between one race and the next.

(15) Members of all races are capable of interbreeding with members of all others, that is, all that have been put to the test.

(16) The supposed evils attendant upon race-crossing do not bear scientific scrutiny: neither sterility, diminished fertility, nor physical deterioration, has been proven to be a biological consequence of race-mixing. If there are unfortunate effects from such crossing, they are *social* (not biological) and they appear to result from the way in which other members of the populations in questions look at and treat the 'hybrids'.

(17) The study of the races of humankind has been based on physical (that is morphological, physiological and biochemical) and genetic traits; mental characteristics have not been used in the classification of the human races, nor have they been found useful for such a purpose.

(18) Scientific studies have not validly demonstrated any genetically determined variations in the kinds of nervous systems possessed by members of different human races, nor any genetically determined differences in the patterns of behaviour evinced by members of different races.

(19) The claim that genetic factors contribute as much as 75

or 80 per cent of the variance of IQ test-score results and are therefore largely responsible for Black-White differences in mean test-score results has been seriously questioned in a number of investigations. It has been shown that a heritability estimate of 0.75 does not apply to American Blacks, among whom a much smaller percentage of the variance of test-score results has been shown to be genetically determined, and a larger proportion environmentally determined. The immense literature that has accumulated since Jensen (1969) put forward his hypothesis that American Blacks are genetically inferior in intelligence to Whites has revealed many flaws that were implicit in the reasoning behind the hypothesis. The main conclusion that many of these studies have reached is that 'currently available data are inadequate to resolve this question in either direction' (Bodmer and Cavalli-Sforza, 1970). On the other hand, a number of investigations have led to the development of environmental hypotheses. For example, Scarr (1980) has found evidence in her studies to support a two-fold hypothesis: such differences as exist between comparable populations she attributes partly to environmental factors and partly to cultural factors. On this additional cultural hypothesis, her work has led her to stress a different relevance of extra-scholastic or home experience to scholastic aptitudes and achievement: 'The transfer of training from home to school performance is probably less direct for Black children than for White children' (Scarr-Salapatek, 1971). Clearly, at this stage of our ignorance, it is unjustified to include intelligence, however tested, among the validly demonstrated, genetically determined differences among the races of mankind.

Phillip V. Tobias
University of the Witwatersrand, Johannesburg

References
Bodmer, W. F. and Cavalli-Sforza, L. L. (1970), 'Intelligence and race', *Scientific American*, 223.
Gould, S. J. (1981), *The Mismeasure of Man*, New York.

Huxley, J. S. (1963), *Evolution: The Modern Synthesis*, 2nd edn, London.

Jensen, A. R. (1969), 'How much can we boost IQ and scholastic achievement?', *Harvard Educational Review*, 39.

Kagan, J. (1968), 'On cultural deprivation', in D. C. Glass (ed.), *Environmental Influences: Proceedings of the Conference*, New York.

Lewontin, R. C. (1972), 'The apportionment of human diversity', *Evolutionary Biology*, 6.

Littlefield, A., Lieberman, L. and Reynolds, L. T. (1982), 'Redefining race: the potential demise of a concept in physical anthropology', *Current Anthropology*, 23.

Lochlin, J. C., Lindzey, G. and Spuhler, J. N. (1975), *Race Differences in Intelligence*, San Francisco.

Mayr, E. (1963), *Animal Species and Evolution*, London.

Mead, M., Dobzhansky, T., Tobach, E. and Light, R. E. (1968), *Science and the Concept of Race*, New York.

Montagu, A. (1972), *Statement on Race*, 3rd edn, London.

Nei, M. (1978), 'The theory of genetic distance and evolution of human races', *Japanese Journal of Human Genetics*, 23.

Nei, M. (1982), 'Evolution of human races at the gene level', *Human Genetics, Part A: The Unfolding Genome*, New York.

Nei, M. and Roychoudhury, A. K. (1972), 'Gene differences between Caucasian, Negro and Japanese Populations', *Science*, 117.

Nei, M. and Roychoudhury, A. K. (1982), 'Genetic relationship and evolution of human races', in M. K. Hecht, B. Wallace and C. T. Prance (eds), *Evolutionary Biology*, 14.

Piazza, A., Sgaramella-Zonta, L. and Cavalli-Sforza, L. L. (1975), 'The fifth histocompatibility workshop: gene frequency data: a phylogenetic analysis', *Tissue Antigens*, 5.

Scarr, S. (1980), *Race, Social Class and Individual Differences*, Hillsdale, New Jersey.

Scarr-Salapatek, S. (1971), 'Race, social class and IQ', *Science*, 174.

Tobias, P. V. (1970), 'Brain size, grey matter and race – fact or fiction?', *American Journal of Physical Anthropology*, n.s. 32.

See also: *evolution*.

Social Problems

Until the early 1970s the sociology of social problems had, for over fifty years, looked for the underlying causes of a long list of human miseries and conditions considered destructive to society and offensive to conventional morality. This field overlapped with the study of social disorganization and deviant behaviour. Since then a new set of questions has emerged giving the study of social problems a fresh start and a more independent existence. These questions began with the observation that many troublesome behaviours have, at various times, been defined in different ways. People who drink alcohol to excess were thought to be sinners by the temperance movement in the early nineteenth century, regarded as criminals by the prohibition movement in the early twentieth century and as diseased addicts by the medical establishment after 1940. Homosexuality used to be both a crime and a mental disorder. Now it is a life style, thanks to the decriminalization movement and a particularly dramatic official vote by the American Psychiatric Association in December 1973. Child battering, wife abuse, and sexual harrassment all used to be unnamed, uncounted and invisible; now they are firmly-fixed constellations in the universe of social services, official statistics and problem populations.

The new sociology of social problems attempts to describe and explain how new definitions of social problems emerge, how troublesome persons or social arrangements are identified, how institutions are created to deal with them. The field has largely abandoned the attempt to explain deviant behaviour and social disorganization. Rather, it is attempting to explain how society, through an essentially political process, discovers and invents its problems. Attention to these processes of creating meanings concerning disturbing and troublesome behaviours and conditions distinguishes the new from the old approach to social problems.

Many contemporary problems that address the inequitable treatment of racial minorities, women, children, the elderly, prisoners, mental patients, the developmentally disabled and the unborn have been put on society's agenda by the vigorous actions of social movements. Social movements have also created awareness of problems concerning pollution, toxic wastes, the dangers of nuclear energy production and the threat of nuclear holocaust.

The helping professions promote solutions to social problems and are another important participant in the social problems process. The leading examples are the medical profession and its subalterns and the social welfare bureaucracies, which together have assembled what Kittrie (1972) has termed 'the therapeutic state'. A large number of troublesome behaviours previously punished as crimes have become subject to treatment and are now considered diseases. 'Treatments' for psychopaths and sociopaths, such as lobotomies or psychosurgery, aversive conditioning and behaviour modification, electric and chemical shock have replaced more primitive societal reactions, like punishment. The objective effectiveness of these treatments is of less importance than their political appeal and the prestige of the disciplines on which they rest.

A new tradition of research on the mass media, drawing on the insights of ethnomethodology, has enlarged the study of social problems, describing the 'creation' and production of news, and explaining how systems of classification and new vocabulary both reflect and take part in the struggle to name and control controversial issues.

Governments respond to claims that define conditions as social problems by: funding research on solutions to problems; establishing commissions of inquiry; passing new laws, and creating enforcement and treatment bureaucracies. But governments may also be the source of new definitions of social problems, especially embattled or ambitious agencies campaigning to increase their budgets and personnel. Research in the United States shows that the problem of marijuana use and more recently the concern about teenage alcoholism were created in this way.

Malcolm Spector
McGill University

Reference
Kittrie, N. (1972), *The Right to be Different*, Baltimore.

Further Reading
Conrad, P. and Schneider, J. (1980), *Deviance and Medicalization: From Badness to Sickness*, St Louis.
Spector, M. and Kitsuse, J. I. (1977), *Constructing Social Problems*, Menlo Park, Calif.
See also: *mental health*.

Social Work

It is perhaps not surprising that the term social work, combining the rich ambiguity of 'social' with the misleading and somewhat deterrent simplicity of 'work', has undergone considerable change in usage since it first appeared in England towards the end of the last century. It was then used to describe a perspective applicable from a number of different occupations rather than to announce the arrival of a particular new occupation. This perspective derived from the serious reconsideration of the role of citizen, and it can be illustrated from the dedication of a book entitled *The Spirit of Social Work* (Devine, 1911) to 'social workers, that is to say, to every man and woman, who, in any relation of life, professional, industrial, political, educational or domestic; whether on salary or as a volunteer; whether on his own individual account or as part of an organized movement, is working consciously, according to his light intelligently and according to his strength persistently, for the promotion of the common welfare'. (The fact that Devine was an American, indicates the speed with which 'social work' was exported to America and thence, eventually, to many other societies, developed and developing.)

This broadly brushed backcloth has been more or less evident in the present century as social workers have attempted to claim a role that is specialized and professional. It is perhaps one reason why an agreed and satisfactory definition of 'social work' is not yet forthcoming. Other features of social work activity have also contributed to this lack of agreement about the nature of social work. The broad purposes of social work have become more ambiguous as social workers have increasingly become state employees rather than volunteers or paid workers in non-statutory agencies. Sometimes public appreciation of social work has been blunted by the large claims made on behalf of social workers (for instance, that social work can cure a considerable range of private sorrows and public ills or simply that social workers represent the conscience of society). Changes in the dominant theories said to underpin social work – economics or sociology or psychoanalytic theories – and confusion between espoused theories and those actually informing practice have created at least the impression of significant ruptures as a tradition of practice struggles to assert itself. Finally, social work, like teaching, is both an 'attempting' and a 'succeeding' term: on occasions practitioners will deny the term to activity that was not particularly successful or that infringed one of the contested maxims that figure largely in professional talk.

A rough description of the contemporary social worker is of a person (traditionally a woman but increasingly in some societies a man) who as a representative of some statutory or non-statutory agency delivers a wide range of services, from income maintenance and welfare commodities, to directive and non-directive counselling. These services are directed or offered to individuals or to groups of different kinds, based on kinship, locality, interest or common condition. For the efficient and effective delivery of such services, social workers claim to use skills of various kinds, a range of theoretical and practical knowledge, and a set of values specific to social work.

Definition or general description take us some way towards grasping social work, but a more productive approach is to examine certain key questions concerning the form and the purposes of social work that have arisen at different times in the present century. In relation to form, two questions predominate: is social work to be treated as a profession (and if so, what kind of profession); is social work to be practised as an applied science, as an art, or as some kind of ministration? Flexner's (1915) consideration of the professional nature of social work raised questions that may still fruitfully be pursued. He concluded that social work met some of the criteria for professional status, but that social workers were mediators rather than full professional agents, that they pursued no distinctive ends, and that they were required to possess certain personal qualities rather than expertise in scientifically-derived technical skills. More recently, it has been suggested that social work can most easily be viewed as a semi-profession or as a bureau-profession. The characterization of social work as part of a humanistic as contrasted with a scientific movement is best studied through the work of Halmos (1965).

Controversy within social work is somewhat rare, but important questioning concerning the purpose of social work can be appreciated through three major debates (Timms, 1983). The first, between leaders of the influential Charity Organization Society and the Socialists at the turn of the century, concerned the emphasis to be given to the individual and to his social circumstances and to preventive as opposed to curative work. The second, between two American schools of social work, the Functionalists and the Diagnosticians in the middle of the century, raised questions concerning the independence of social work as a helping process contrasted with a process of psychological treatment. The third, most immediate, controversy revolves around the possibility of a social work that is politically radical or, specifically, Marxist.

Noel Timms
University of Leicester

References
Devine, E. (1911), *The Spirit of Social Work*, New York.
Flexner, A. (1915), 'Is social work a profession?', *Proceedings of the 42nd National Conference of Charities and Correction*.
Halmos, P. (1965), *The Faith of the Counsellors*, London.
Timms, N. (1983), *Social Work Values: An Enquiry*, London.

Further Reading.
Younghusband, E. (1978), *Social Work in Britain: 1950–1975*, 2 vols, London.
Timms, N. and Timms, R. (1982), *Dictionary of Social Welfare*, London.

Sociobiology

Although the term only gained wide currency after the 1975 publication of E. O. Wilson's *Sociobiology, The New Synthesis*, the theoretical roots of sociobiology go back to the mid-1960s, with publications by Hamilton (1964) and Maynard Smith (1964). Sociobiology is the study of animal behaviour, especially social behaviour, from the perspective of evolution by natural selection. As such, it is squarely in the mainstream of neo-Darwinian evolutionary theory.

The subject became intensely controversial and ideological in the late 1970s and, for that reason, many of its practitioners prefer to conduct their work under blander labels such as 'evolutionary ecology' or 'behavioural biology'. Some continue to use the older labels of 'ethology' or 'behaviourism', although sociobiology differs in emphasis from these two approaches. Behaviourism put the emphasis on the ontogeny rather than the phylogeny of behaviour, and stressed environmental conditioning to the neglect of the genetic basis of behaviour. Sociobiology insists on the equal importance of heredity *and* environment, since a phenotype is always the product of interaction between a genotype and a multiplicity of environmental variables. Ethology is more clearly an ancestral discipline of sociobiology in that it too is concerned with the evolution of animal behaviour. Until the 1960s, however, ethology tended to be heavily descriptive rather than explanatory and theoretical, and such theoretical basis as it had was rooted in group-selectionist thinking, holding that animals behaved for the survival of the group or the species.

More than any other development, it was the rejection of group selection as the main explanation for the apparent altruism of some forms of animal behaviour (such as alarm calls, the suicidal stinging of bees, or the mimicking of wing injuries by birds) which launched sociobiology as the dominant new approach to animal behaviour. Apparently altruistic behaviour was reduced to a simple model of maximization of reproductive success (or 'fitness') at the level of the individual organism, and ultimately of the gene (as popularized in Dawkins's 1976 book, *The Selfish Gene*). The central theorem of 'inclusive fitness', first presented in 1964 by W. D. Hamilton, is that an organism can be expected to favour the fitness of another, even at an apparent cost to its own fitness, if the following inequation holds:

$$k > \frac{1}{r}$$

where k is the ratio of benefits (for recipient) to costs (for 'altruist') of the interaction, and r is the proportion of genes shared by common descent between 'altruist' and recipient.

In sexually reproducing, diploid organisms, an individual shares one half of its genes with a parent, offspring, or full sibling; a quarter with a grandparent, grandchild, uncle-aunt, nephew-niece, and half-sibling; an eighth with a first cousin, great-grandparent, and so on. In an 'altruistic' transaction between parent and offspring, the benefit to offspring (in terms of fitness) has to be greater than 2, since the pair share one half of their genes; between first-cousins, the benefit-cost ratio would have to exceed 8, since they share an eighth of their genes, and so on. An individual's 'inclusive fitness' includes its own reproductive success plus the effect of its nepotism on the reproductive success of its relatives. Thus, through nepotism (favouring kin over non-kin, and close kin over distant kin), an individual can maximize its inclusive fitness better than by being ruthlessly selfish (for example, by cannibalizing its offspring when hungry).

In the last analysis, what looks like altruism is behaviour genetically programmed to maximize the replication of genes. Organisms are temporary assemblages of genes, programmed to maximize the reproduction of the very genes that do the programming. An organism is, evolutionarily speaking, a gene-carrying and gene-reproducing machine, as Dawkins (1976) so persuasively argues. Since apparent 'altruism' is reducible to ultimate genetic selfishness, the term 'nepotism' is a more accurate description of the preferential behaviour toward kin.

In species after species, ranging from social insects (bees, ants, wasps, termites), to warm-blooded vertebrates, and including human and nonhuman primates, nepotism has been shown to be an important basis of sociality, and predictor of beneficent behaviour. Given the ubiquity of nepotistic behaviour in humans, and the universal importance of kinship in human societies, there is no *a priori* reason to exclude humans from the purview of sociobiology. Indeed, application of the

sociobiological model to human systems of mating and reproduction have yielded promising results in such areas as incest
avoidance, the avunculate, matrilineal descent, adoption, infan-
ticide, polygyny and polyandry, sex roles and sexual behaviour
(Alexander, 1979; Chagnon and Irons, 1979; Symons, 1979;
van den Berghe, 1979).

One of the applications of the theorem of inclusive-fitness
maximization has been to strategies of parental investment and
mating. Females specialize in producing few, large, and therefore expensive, gametes (eggs), while males produce vast quantities of miniaturized, and therefore, inexpensive gametes
(sperms). Eggs are dear; sperms are cheap. Females go for
quality, males for quantity. Consequently, their reproductive
strategies differ: since the females of nearly all species invest
more in reproduction than the males, they maximize their
fitness by selecting the best possible mates, while males are
programmed for greater promiscuity.

Another consequence of this asymmetry of parental investment strategies is that nubile females are a scarce resource for
males, who therefore compete with one another for access to
females (sexual selection). Sexual dimorphism, in both anatomy
and behaviour, is clearly linked to the range of reproduction
systems in diploid animals. Monogamy, polygyny and polyandry, for example, are alternative strategies which vary both
between and within species. The theory of parental investment
permits a specification of the morphological correlates and
environmental conditions favouring the various options. The
application of this paradigm to human mating and reproductive
strategies has gone a long way, not only in explaining cross-
cultural uniformities in sex roles, family composition, double
standards of sexual behaviour, and so on, but also in accounting
for cultural variations in adaptation to different ecological
conditions. Male investment strategies in putative offspring
versus uterine nephews, for instance, have been linked to probability of paternity. Differential patterns of marriage (hyper-
gyny, polyandry, monogamy, polygyny, exogamy, and so on)
have been studied as situationally-variable adaptive responses
tending to maximize the inclusive fitness of the actors (Alexander, 1979; Chagnon and Irons, 1979; van den Berghe, 1979).

Reciprocity is another mechanism favouring fitness maximization and another basis of sociality, besides nepotism. Although social scientists have long recognized the importance of exchange and reciprocity in the maintenance of human sociality, it was Trivers (1971) who linked reciprocity to evolutionary theory and specified the conditions for its evolution. Human systems of reciprocity are extremely complex and vulnerable to free-loading, and the evolution of increasingly sophisticated forms of cheating, and of detecting cheaters, may have been one of the principal selective forces in the rapid increase in hominid intelligence. Reciprocity, however, is not a human monopoly. Indeed, sexual reproduction is probably the oldest and the most widespread template for reciprocity.

The role of coercion as a third important basis of sociality (besides nepotism and reciprocity) has hitherto been neglected in sociobiology. Coercion, that is the use of force or threat of force to garner resources at the expense of other individuals' fitness, is not a human monopoly, but human forms of coercion and intrasocietal parasitism are uniquely elaborate, and have become increasingly so with the evolution of state-level, class-stratified societies.

One of the central theoretical issues in human sociobiology at present is the relationship between genes and culture, a relationship mediated through the human mind, as Lumsden and Wilson (1981) clearly suggest. Among evolutionary theorists, there is general agreement that human culture has some emergent properties, and that the linkages between genes and behavioural phenotypes are seldom if ever direct. Clearly, there are no genes for specific cultural traits, like playing chess or riding bicycles. Rather, our genes give us flexible programmes to adapt by learning. These programmes range in flexibility but few of them are either completely closed and automatic, or completely open and malleable. We are predisposed to learn and to accept some cultural traits more readily than others. Thus, we learn painlessly certain very complex tasks (such as speech) that evolved sufficiently long ago to be wired into our brain, while we find it more difficult and stressful to learn much simpler tasks (such as control of excretory functions) for which probably no neural programmes exist because their selective advantage is too recent.

Human sociobiologists generally agree that culture is adaptive, and therefore interacts with genetic evolution by natural selection, since culture has fitness consequences for individual humans. Likewise, sociobiologists all agree that humans share a unique set of characteristics (as, indeed, do by definition all other species), some of which distinguish human evolution from that of infra-human species. However, the extent to which it is useful to regard genetic evolution and cultural evolution as two autonomous (though interrelated) processes, each responding to different mechanisms of selection and transmission, is hotly debated at present. Against those who argue for a co-evolutionary model of genes and culture as discrete but interacting processes, there are those who argue that culture is merely a species-specific set of proximate mechanisms of adapting fast through a high degree of ability to transmit learned behaviour socially by symbolic language.

As natural selection directly 'acts' on phenotypes, not genotypes, and as phenotypes always include an environmental component, it is, of course, fallacious to oppose genes and environment. Within this gene-environment interaction model, culture can be seen as the man-made part of the environment, preselected by the specifically human genome. The real issue is not whether culture is part of the natural world. It obviously is. Culture can have no empirical referent outside of the human organisms that invent and transmit it, and, therefore, its evolution is inevitably intertwined with the biological evolution of our species.

The issue is the degree of autonomy of the mechanisms of cultural evolution from those of genetic evolution. In the end, that question is not so much an empirical one, as one of level of analysis and of the type of question asked. Those who specialize in trying to understand human affairs attach greater importance to the unique characteristics of our species than those to whom we are but one species among millions. And, among students of human behaviour, those who delight in explaining cultural diversity and historical specificity are less concerned about our biological evolution than those who seek to understand the common nature of our humanity.

Sociobiology complements rather than threatens the traditional social sciences. It merely urges us to look at ourselves as part of a broader scheme of things which encompasses the whole of the natural world. In that sense, sociobiology is merely the latest phase of a process of scientific demystification which began with Copernicus, and successively reduced our claims to centrality and uniqueness. The price of lucidity about our place in the universe has always been a certain amount of existential discomfort. This may help explain the passion with which sociobiology is attacked.

Pierre L. van den Berghe
University of Washington

References

Alexander, R. D. (1979), *Darwinism and Human Affairs*, Seattle.

Chagnon, N. and Irons, W. (eds) (1979), *Evolutionary Biology and Human Social Behavior*, North Scituate, Mass.

Dawkins, R. (1976), *The Selfish Gene*, London.

Hamilton, W. D. (1964), 'The genetical evolution of social behaviour', *Journal of Theoretical Biology*, 7.

Lumsden, C. J. and Wilson, E. O. (1981), *Genes, Mind and Culture*, Cambridge, Mass.

Maynard Smith, J. (1964), 'Group selection and kin selection', *Nature*, 201.

Symons, D. (1979), *The Evolution of Human Sexuality*, New York.

Trivers, R. L. (1971), 'The evolution of reciprocal altruism', *Quarterly Review of Biology*, 46.

van den Berghe, P. L. (1979), *Human Family Systems*, New York.

Wilson, E. O. (1975), *Sociobiology, The New Synthesis*, Cambridge, Mass.

See also: *ethology; evolution.*

Sociology

Sociology is at present an unsystematic body of knowledge gained through the study of the whole and parts of society.

The knowledge contained in sociology covers a very wide and differentiated range of phenomena such as the conduct of individuals in institutions like families, churches and sects, workshops, armies, civic and political associations, territorial, ethnic and national communities; the patterns of relationship among individuals; the role of structure and authority in the working of institutions and communities; the stratification of societies; communities and institutions with respect to income and status or deference; the role of cognitive and normative beliefs in the actions of individuals and in the functioning of communities, institutions and societies.

The ordering of sociological knowledge is fragmentary and of many levels of particularity, from the most abstract and most generalized or theoretical to the most concrete and descriptive. Sociological knowledge varies in the degree of reliability and precision. Sociologists have invented or borrowed from other disciplines techniques of observation and analysis which are intended to improve the veracity of sociological knowledge.

Sociological knowledge is a knowledge of causal connections, or connections of interdependence among the phenomena studied. Sociologists seek to explain phenomena in terms of motives, states of mind, 'social' conditions.

The Legitimacy of Sociology

Ever since the name of sociology was coined by Auguste Comte, sociologists have sought to be more scientific in their methods and more systematic in their interpretation of their observations. They have not been content with the occasionally profound penetrating observations about human conduct and its motives or about the varieties of forms of government, their emergence and decline such as are to be found in Aristotle's *Politics* and the *Nichomachean Ethics*, or in the works of Thucydides and Tacitus, and of Machiavelli and Guicciardini and many others. Political and moral philosophy, great historical works, great and not so great works of literature contain many deep particular insights and generalizations which in substance could well be regarded as properly sociological as that term has come to be understood. But these have not been enough for sociologists. Long before sociology became as scientific as it is now – and that is not very scientific according to the standard of the natural and especially the physical sciences by which the intellectually more ambitious sociologists have measured themselves – there was a conviction that sociology was justified only if it became more systematic and more scientific in substance and method. The ambition to become scientific and to acquire a deeper and more coherent understanding of society has not been the only motive for the cultivation of sociology. Famous sociologists have thought that the justification for doing sociological work was the illumination of the minds of rulers and of the wide public about the practical 'social problems' which needed 'remedies' or solutions. Comte's dictum *Savoir pour prévoir pour pourvoir* is still given in one form or another by many sociologists as the justification for their discipline and their own work. Although the practical application of sociological knowledge raises serious ethical problems, the belief that sociological knowledge should be applied in practical action is perfectly consistent with the belief that it should be scientific in its methods and hence in its explanations, interpretations and theories. Indeed, many sociologists have believed that it could be effectively 'applied' in practical action only if it were scientific and systematic.

It was not merely an effort to make knowledge of society and its constituent parts more reliable, more precise and more systematic that drove the forerunners of contemporary sociology in the nineteenth century to try to improve the scientific quality of their subject. They also wished to render it acceptable to prevailing intellectual opinion and, in certain countries, to the academic world. Auguste Comte and Herbert Spencer, the first two eminent philosophers who also thought of themselves as sociologists, did not think of sociology as necessarily being a subject for teaching and study in universities. By the end of the nineteenth and in the first quarter of the present century, when universities ascended to pre-eminence among intellectual institutions, and when the amateur and vocational practice of science and scholarship had diminished, it behoved the proponents of sociology to prove their academic acceptability. This was an additional motive for making their subject scientific and persuading others that it was scientific. But even if it were proved to be scientific, there would be no convincing argument for it if its subject-matters were already being dealt with adequately by disciplines previously established in universities. It was necessary to show that it had its own subject-matter.

Sociology in the nineteenth century did indeed have its own subject-matter and one, moreover, the study of which was established for many decades before sociology was considered to be worthy of academic status: it had 'the poor', the outcasts, the humble, the insulted and injured, the criminals of modern societies. These were the objects of the most important pieces of empirical research of the nineteenth and early twentieth centuries. From the surveys of Louis René Villerme, Henry Mayhew, Eiler Sundt, Charles Booth and Seebohm Rowntree up to Thomas and Znaniecki's more self-conscious sociology in *The Polish Peasant in Europe and America* (1916), the peripheral sectors of society had become accepted as meriting careful study; that careful study fell to the lot of sociologists. In peasants, in *Lumpenproletarians*, wandering journeymen, and street vendors, in the unemployed, the half-employed, the poor and the immigrants, in the prostitutes, criminals and in deserted wives, in unmarried mothers and illegitimate children, sociology found a subject all of its own which was disregarded by other academically established disciplines. Political history, with its accounts of kings and wars and the fates of empires did not write about the poor. *Staatswissenschaft* and political science which dealt with laws and political institutions did not deal with them except as objects of criminal law. Neither did *Völkerkunde*, human geography, and ethnology, which dealt with remote places and primitive peoples. Economic theory, which proceeded as if men were rational, freely choosing actors seeking to maximize their incomes, had no place for those who lived under the constraints of tradition and ignorance and the constriction of poverty, who lived outside the law and who had no acknowledged impact on events except in revolutionary outbursts, short-lived riots and other outbursts of irrationality.

The argument for the legitimacy of sociology went more deeply than the practical value of knowledge of the 'dangerous debtor and dependent classes'. Sociologists contended that their 'discipline' could at least prospectively discover the laws of social life, not the laws enacted by legislatures or promulgated by rulers but the laws which were more fundamental than legislated laws. The condition of social order and conflict, of persistence and change from simplicity to complexity in the division of labour, from *Gemeinschaft* to *Gesellschaft*, from *solidarité mécanique* to *solidarité organique*, from rural to urban society, from primary groups to the larger, impersonal society became the theme of sociological interpretation. This was the profounder intellectual task which sociologists claimed for their discipline; it was one which no other discipline looked after and it performed the valuable intellectual service of laying bare and interpreting the nature of the modern age. Sociology participated in the *malaise* of the last part of the century, of the vague sense that somehow things were not right in the world, that modern society was developing in an unsatisfactory way. Sociologists claimed that it was legitimate for scholars to attempt to understand and explain what was going on in modern societies. Sociology was admitted into American and French universities at the time when it was beginning to be thought – for the first time – that universities should include the contemporary world among the subjects they taught about and investigated. Sociology seemed to meet that expectation.

The Foci of Sociology
Even though sociology is not a science in the sense of having a coherent, widely accepted body of general or theoretical propositions which rest on more particular propositions and which explain particular, reliably observed events, a vast amount of sociological knowledge does exist of varying degrees of precision, reliability and generality. Individuals who have been publicly designated as sociologists, as well as individuals who were not thought of as sociologists during their own lifetime but who have been declared retrospectively to have been sociologists, have in fact produced a very large heterogeneous and unarticulated mass of knowledge about various societies, parts of societies and kinds of actions. Despite their aspirations to be systematic, no sociologist has yet been able to systematize all this knowledge. The societies studied by sociologists have mainly been their own; they have given most of their attention

to their own contemporary societies and in the quite recent past. Although sociological theories, at least programmatically, ordinarily announce an intention of universal validity, sociological research at any given time has mostly been confined to the sociologists' own times and their own countries. 'Comparative sociology', which deals with other or several countries, and 'historical sociology', which deals with the remoter past, form only a very small part of the huge body of sociological literature. These two kinds of sociological literature have, however, increased in recent years.

There are various reasons for this temporal and territorial parochiality of sociology. The first reason derives from the long dominant, practical concern of sociology with 'social problems', in other words, with morally problematic conditions of the sociologists' own time and society. The second lies in the methods of sociology which require the use of deliberately acquired statistical data. The governmental acquisition of large quantities of information in statistical form is to a very large extent a phenomenon of the nineteenth and twentieth centuries, and sociologists wishing to have reliable evidence have perforce had to draw on such rather recently assembled information. The distrust of written, unpublished documents in archives and of printed books as evidence because of their questionable 'representativeness' has also, until recently, compelled sociologists to deal with contemporaneous situations. It is only in contemporaneous situations that sociologists could 'create' reliable data for their studies by direct observation and by interviews which by their nature can be conducted only on living persons, and by a combination of these two methods into 'participant-observation' which was for a time a much favoured procedure. This did not preclude the instigation of 'life-histories' which were also for a time among the sources used by some leading sociologists (for example, Dollard, 1935). These instigated 'life-histories' could only be produced by living persons, and this reinforced the temporal confinement of sociologists. Recently, sociologists have discovered statistical series describing aspects of life in the earlier centuries of modern times, and at least one sociologist who is also a classical scholar (Hopkins, 1978) has even done quantitative work on ancient

Roman society. An increasing number of sociologists have extended their territorial horizons and undertaken to study societies other than their own (Eisenstadt, 1963; Bendix, 1978). Still, the sociologists who study society remote from their own in time and space are a relatively small minority in the profession of sociology.

The majority of sociologists who carry out research are still mainly working, although in a more sophisticated manner, on the favoured topics of the empirical sociology as it took form up to the early twentieth century, namely, 'social problems'. They study the crises and dissolution of families, conflicts in the relations of spouses with one other and conflicts between parents and their children. They study criminality and delinquency in all their forms; they study the leisure-time pursuits of young persons; they study the aged, especially the isolated aged who cannot easily fend for themselves. They study processes of social selection, the advantages of birth in higher strata and the disadvantages of birth in lower strata. They study the impediments to democracy. The condition of 'the poor' and powerless, who had sunk somewhat from the horizon of sociologists in the period after the Second World War, has returned to its former prominence. Sociologists still continue to give much of their attention to this complex of phenomena, but as their numbers increased and they became better established, they have added numerous other fields to their stock-in-trade. To some extent, these new subjects are extensions of the study of 'the poor' and of other sore-spots of modern industrial societies.

Rural studies, in contrast, once a major subject of sociological interest, have become relatively less important in the schedule of sociological activities in Western countries (see Sorokin *et al.*, 1930–2). Migration from rural areas to large cities within any single country has diminished in prominence, while international migration and immigrants have reacquired, in the sociological research on the European continent, the prominence which they once had in American sociology in the first quarter of the present century. The study of urban communities has had an upsurge, after its decline in American sociology; more prominently even than in the past, urban studies have concerned themselves with derelict areas of the 'inner city' and with suburban communities.

The relationship among ethnic groups within a single society was an almost dominant subject in American sociology for the first half of the century (see Myrdal, 1944; Dollard, 1937; Warner, 1942); it then declined, but latterly it resumed its prominence after about two decades. It is a major topic nowadays in the United States. Studies of 'ethnic prejudice' were part of this run of activity; they too receded and have not recovered their ground. Ethnic relations, and particularly the study of 'nationalities', had been a topic of sociologists in Central Europe before the First World War and then almost disappeared. Within the past decade it has again become an important field for European and American sociologists.

The study of mobility between classes of occupation had been a major subject of empirical sociological studies in France, Germany and Great Britain in the decades preceding and following the turn of the century (Michels, 1934; Glass (ed.), 1954; Sorokin, 1927). It became a subject which drew increasing interest in the United States from the 1920s onward; it has remained a substantial interest of European and American sociology since that time. It has, with the study of the past, been the most active part of sociological research in Great Britain.

Industrial sociology – the study of social relations in workshops – ascended slowly to the point where it became a major field of research in the 1930s in the United States and then again briefly after the Second World War in the United States and Great Britain, but it has diminished since then (Roethlisberger and Dickson, 1939; Mayo, 1949). On the other side, the sociological study of the management and the careers of managers of business firms which had scarcely existed before the Second World War became more interesting to sociologists after the war in the United States and Great Britain. The study of the hierarchy of social status or deference was first undertaken in small communities in the United States in the 1930s and then flourished, after the war, on a national scale, following the development of sample surveys of attitudes. It has not been developed so much in other countries.

The study of the distribution of educational opportunity, that is, of the distribution of the amount of schooling of different occupational income and ethnic groups, became a very active field in Great Britain and the United States from the early 1930s; it has continued ever since then, with some fluctuations, to occupy the attention of sociologists in many countries (Floud, Halsey and Martin, 1956; Coleman (ed.), 1969). International comparison of educational attainment in relation to the level of industrialization, economic productivity and the rate of economic growth, although developed mainly by economists and educationists, has also been taken up by educational sociologists. Investigations of the teaching profession, of the 'social atmosphere' of classrooms, of the administration of schools and educational systems were taken up by sociologists. There is now a whole specialization called 'educational sociology'.

A quite new field of sociological study is that of military institutions. This appeared after the Second World War and a considerable body of literature has been produced on the cohesion and morale of armed forces, military discipline, the recruitment of soldiers of different ranks and the relations between armed forces and civil, especially political, institutions (Janowitz, 1960).

The sociological study of scientific institutions, of beliefs about science and its legitimacy, of the careers and reputation of scientists, the distribution of status and eminence among them and of the social constitution of the growth of scientific knowledge has emerged as a small but intensively cultivated object (Ziman, 1968; Polanyi, 1964; Merton, 1973; Ben-David, 1971). This subject existed to a very small degree before the Second World War. Some sociologists have even gone so far as to declare scientific knowledge itself to be a 'social phenomenon' in which truth and validity are no more than conventions like any other social convention. A closely related field called the 'sociology of knowledge', which came into the world first in Germany with great *éclat* in the 1920s and early 1930s and which attempted to explain beliefs in political, moral and social philosophy and in theology by reference to the 'class position' or 'social location' of different kinds of intellectuals, aroused great interest among German sociologists, but it did not go much beyond the programmatic phase (Mannheim, 1936; 1952;

1956; Shils, 1972). The study of 'intellectuals', their inter-relations and their social role has made some progress in a number of countries.

Political institutions, such as parliamentary bodies, parties, elections, political campaigns, had made a first appearance as sociological subjects in Germany, France and Italy before the First World War (Tingston, 1963; Lazarsfeld *et al.*, 1944; Berelson *et al.*, 1954; Lasswell, 1935, 1936). The voting behaviour and political attitudes of various occupational, religious and ethnic groups were studied in many countries in the 1920s and 1930s. It was also developing in the United States. This branch of sociological study received a tremendous impetus from the development in the United States, and then elsewhere, of the techniques of sample surveys, which first occurred outside of sociology but which was quickly incorporated into it. It has since flourished throughout the Western world in the inter-national collaboration of sociologists and political scientists.

The mechanisms of the exercise of political and bureaucratic power and the correlates of the acquisition of roles of authority began to interest American sociologists after the Second World War (Lipset, Trow and Coleman, 1956); it has been a topic which engaged the close attention of the most important German and Italian sociologists well before the First World War.

After the Second World War, some sociologists for the first time became interested in the formation and fortunes of new states (Geertz, 1967; Almond and Coleman (eds.), 1960). They studied the new states arising in former European colonies in Asia and Africa and related phenomena in Latin America; their interests were almost entirely contemporaneous. The study of 'political development' then engaged the interests of a small number of sociologists who worked closely with political scientists and anthropologists. Few of them placed this phenomenon in a historical context. Despite the pioneering work of Max Weber in this field, and the popularity among sociologists of Max Weber's writings, only one important book has been written in the comparative study of empires and the growth of states.

The sociological study of 'formal organization' was to some

extent an offshoot of the study of political power, private and public administration and of the study of industrial sociology by persons who were not academic sociologists (Simon, 1947; Barnard, 1948). This subject was scarcely studied by sociologists until after the Second World War, although one of its major inspirations, Max Weber's study of bureaucratic authority, was written either during the First World War or shortly before. Since that time, it has become a major interest of sociologists.

Almost since its beginning sociologists had been interested in the study of social movements, including in this the labour and socialist movements and the attendant phenomena of strikes, revolutions, demonstrations, crowds and mobs, rumours and political ideologies. These subjects were already taken in hand in several European countries, especially in France and Italy, in the late nineteenth century (Michels, 1934; Sombart, 1909; Geiger, 1926; Tilly, 1948). The interest then spread to Germany before the First World War and to the United States in the 1920s and 1930s. It has continued since then, although it has since ceased to be one of the more prominent concerns of sociologists.

The sociological study of religion, especially of the study of religious sects, has long been one of the major foci of sociological interest. The two greatest modern sociologists – Weber and Durkheim – placed religious phenomena firmly at the centre of their conception of society and it has continued in a very eminent position ever since then (Weber, 1930 [1922]; 1920; Durkheim, 1915 [1912]; Mauss, 1964, 1972; Le Bras, 1955). It is one of the most international of all the activities of sociologists. French, German, Dutch, British, Italian and American sociologists have all worked in this field in relatively large numbers.

The Methods of Sociology

Proto-sociological research began in the early nineteenth century in France and Great Britain with the use of governmentally gathered statistics; much of it was done by civil servants, civic spirited amateurs and social reformers. It aimed at the description of the magnitudes of particular phenomena such as consumption patterns, housing accommodations, crimes and other infringements on law and morality (see Bulmer, 1984; König, 1967–9; Hyman, 1963). Some early proto-sociologists collected information directly from the persons whom they were writing about through conversations, casual observations, and more immediately from the use of questionnaires and specially elicited written accounts of behaviour by the persons being studied or those who were thought to be familiar with them; the use of 'informants' and of specially qualified persons, such as magistrates and clergymen, continued for a long time to be one of the devices used in 'field work'. Although such research was not at that time called 'sociological', its procedures have greatly influenced contemporary sociological research and they still persist in modified form.

In the present century, the methods of sociological research have moved towards the creation of new data and away from exclusive reliance on already existing data, such as published official statistics. Even where official statistics are still used, there is a marked disposition to go beyond what has been published in census and other governmental reports and to re-analyse the 'raw' data contained in the original protocols in which they were recorded. Except for general demographic purposes, the categories and the units of official statistics were seldom quite what sociologists thought they needed to treat their intellectual problems realistically.

The next step forward was already indicated by the British social surveys of the late nineteenth and early twentieth centuries, which used interviews with either expert 'informants' or with the subjects themselves, or both. Robert Park, one of the formative sociologists of the early part of the present century, had been a newspaper reporter, and he saw the potentialities of the interview as a device for eliciting knowledge not otherwise available. The early development of the interview in American sociology as well as the collection of 'human documents' was concomitant with the practice of an extended period of residence or participation in the community or institution being studied. Thus interviews were combined with direct observation and casual conversations which supplied information about the person engaged in the conversation. This technique of 'participant-observation' also offered the possibility of direct observation of actions and conversations in which the observer did not himself participate but which he was enabled to observe by his quasi-membership in the community or institution.

Another technique for the 'creation' of data was the elicitation of 'personal' or 'human' documents of an autobiographical kind. This produced results similar to a prolonged interview or series of interviews reconstructing the course of life of the subject and centering on a series of significant experiences and situations in the life of the individual in question. The analysis of other sorts of personal documents such as unpublished diaries and published and unpublished letters was also used by sociologists in the period when the 'life-history' was in vogue. The 'open-ended' interview which proceeded by suggesting major topics to the person being interviewed and allowing him or her to respond freely has also been widely employed. The use of 'personal documents' has now diminished, yielding to 'open-ended' and especially to 'structured interviews' or questionnaires.

These techniques all produced a very rich kind of material, very suggestive to the analyst and often very valuable for purposes of illustration of a general theme, tendency, attitude or situation. What they did not offer was precision, reliability and comparability; they were insufficient for scientific purposes. A promising solution of this difficulty was offered by 'content analysis' which was a method of analysing documents which permitted references in texts to be classified systematically, that is, to be 'coded' and enumerated, so that impressions could be supported by the exact measurement of magnitudes. Content-analysis was cumbersome and expensive; its merits were also available through the use of standardized interviews made through the filling in of questionnaires; these asked the same question of all persons interviewed and they provided for precoded alternative responses. This new technique, in combination with the sample survey which was another protection against the deceptiveness of plausible but uncontrolled impressions and insights, won the day in the competition among the various methods of sociological investigation.

Experimentation has never obtained much suffrage among

the techniques of sociological research. Moral inhibitions and strictures on the manipulation of human beings, the unwillingness of human beings to submit to the manipulative designs of sociologists, and the difficulties of obtaining enough identical situations and persons sufficiently similar to provide 'experimental' and 'control groups' have had the result that the experimental procedure, which is the *sine qua non* of scientific work in the physical and biological sciences, made little progress as a technique of sociological research. The experimental method has as a result been used largely in situations in which artificially arranged small groups have been constituted, or where the 'experimental' or 'independent variable' has been trivial and entirely unlikely to have lasting or injurious consequences.

At the same time, the technique of 'controlled comparison' or what has been called the 'imaginary experiment' has been embraced as the best alternative to the impermissible and impossible experiment. With sufficient care and scale, enough instances of individuals, groups or situations can be located in which many features are identical and in which there were marked variations in the feature or features to which causal efficacy may be hypothetically imputed. Techniques of statistical correlation of varying degrees of complexity can then be applied to the data to discover whether there was in fact some degree of interdependence and hence presumably of causal relations between the 'independent' and the 'dependent variables'. This technique of correlation is equally applied to data created by the investigator through interviews (or observations), or in any other situation where sufficiently large numbers of cases or instances can be obtained.

The triumph of the sample survey, of 'created' data – in place of 'real' data observed as the events occur in the ordinary course of social life – and of the statistical correlation of variations, has not however culminated in the extinction of the techniques of 'participant-observation' and of more impressionistic analysis. The latter techniques continue to be used but they too have been affected by the increased sensitivity to statistical requirements. The great shifts in techniques of sociological research have also changed the patterns of organization of sociological research.

Well into the twentieth century, academic sociological research was primarily a 'one-man job'. The insistence, however, on the observation of many cases, and on the precoding, use, and the tabulation of a large body of data created approximately at the same time – a requirement imposed by the necessity of eliminating variations attributable to changes in variables which should be held constant if the research is to be scientific – and the complex statistical operations needed to order the data, have all contributed to turning sociological investigation from the activities of a single scholar, sometimes aided by one or several assistants, into collective hierarchical divisions of labour, acquiring and ordering data through the prescribed actions of a plurality of individuals. This change has necessitated the expenditure of large sums for the employment of staff whose remuneration is not provided for through regular salaries as university teachers and the small sums made available in regular university budgets. The change in the scale of individual investigations has been made possible by the availability of large sums of money for research from public and private patrons. Research has become a collective activity. It has become more 'institutionalized', that is, it has acquired an internal institutional structure of authority and co-ordinated division of labour and it has also become much more connected with some external institutions, which supply funds and control expenditures and others which 'use', in many different ways, the results of the investigation.

The Substance of Sociology
The multiplication in the number of sociologists creating huge quantities of data and publishing a great volume of papers, monographs and books has resulted in great increments of more or less reliable knowledge about many particular situations in many countries. The synthesis of this immense and heterogeneous amount of knowledge into a coherent body of generalized knowledge has not occurred. No one could possibly read all the sociological literature in the many languages containing the results of all this research. The task of synthesis is made even more difficult by the fact that even in studying quite similar but still different particular situations, sociologists use

categories for the classification of the data which do not allow unambiguous comparisons and syntheses.

This does not at all mean that sociological investigations are wholly disjunctive *vis-à-vis* those which have preceded them in the study of similar topics and problems. Sociological investigators do indeed study 'the literature' bearing on their topics and they aim to benefit from it. But in doing so and in trying to improve upon the deficiencies of the classifications of observations in the earlier work which become apparent in them by reflection, they change in varying degrees the classifications. When they try to improve definitions of the variables they are studying by making them more precise than they were in earlier enquiries, they thereby make more difficult the precise comparison and synthesis of their results with the results of other enquiries on the same topic.

These are not the only obstacles to synthesis. The phenomena studied by sociological research are conceived by the sociologists quite concretely, although not with the immediacy with which they are experienced by those persons who are the phenomena being studied. To move from concreteness to abstraction is always a difficult task. It is even more difficult to move into abstract categories which also summarize in abstract form the interdependence of the diverse phenomena which are reported by the sociologists investigating them. An inductive unification of the multifariousness of concrete sociological results into a coherent general theory is perhaps an impossibility. In any case it has never been done.

Nevertheless, the results of sociological research are not wholly random; they do fall into vaguely apprehended patterns in accordance with certain fundamental propositions. A sociologist brought up in the traditions of sociology as it has grown in the present century, has a number of postulates which he shares with the majority of other sociologists and which pervade most sociological research and the interpretation of its results.

The most fundamental of these postulates is that human actions are limited or determined by 'environment'. Human beings become what they are at any given moment not by their own free decisions, taken rationally and in full knowledge of the conditions but under the pressure of circumstances which delimit their range of choice and which also fix their objectives and the standards by which they make choices. The ends of their actions are determined by the influence of their previous 'environment', which limit their range of choice and to which they became habituated; their choices are determined also by their passions and their interests and they are also assimilated from the patterns presented by the 'culture' in which they have lived. The environment is also seen as consisting of the demands and resistances of the other human beings whose co-operation is necessary for the realization of any end of the acting subject. The resources of wealth, position and prestige are distributed in a determinate way in society, and the individual's shares of these goods facilitate or hamper his actions in pursuit of his own ends. The moral, cognitive and ratiocinative powers of the individual are as nothing alongside the imprinting and constrictive powers of the environment in shaping his beliefs and conduct. Thus the human being in society is both a product and victim of the society in which he lives.

When he frees himself to the extent that he can, and acts rationally, all he can do is to pursue his own 'interest'. His 'interest' lies in the maximization of his own advantages, the advantages being conceived of as wealth and power.

This complex idea is at the heart of sociological thought – if it is not inconsistent to speak of thought in a discipline which sometimes denies the reality and efficacy of rational thought. Sociology came into existence out of a variety of intentions. One of these intentions was to show the inadequacy of the conception of human beings as rational entities acting on the basis of knowledge formed by detached reflection on experience, or guided by rational deductions from ultimate or first principles. The forerunners of sociology wished to cast doubt on the dogmatic assertion and imposition of ideals by the dominant, particularly ecclesiastical, institutions of their time. They wished to weaken the argument that ideals are universally valid and that human beings act in accordance with them. The forerunners of sociology were concerned to show that there is no fixed eternal and universal human nature and that man's nature and his ideals change with circumstances. Sociology was intended as a corrective to the view that human conduct and morals are the same everywhere and that the principles of conduct pronounced by Christian moralists are natural to man.

They wished to free man from the superstitions which deformed his reason, but at the same time they were sceptical about his rational powers. The unifying theme of this dual postulate is that the human being is not a self-contained, self-determined, self-determining entity, uniform throughout the world and history, a child of God and reason.

This postulate, which long antedates sociology, is almost its touchstone. It makes sociology what it is. More refined, more differentiated, it still remains at the foundation of nearly all that is called sociology, both in theory and in research. When it leads to 'sociologism' it is a hindrance to the further development of sociology, but without it sociology would be without its task and without its hypotheses.

The naturalistic conception of man from which sociology proceeded perceived that human beings, like all other living organisms, are dependent on their environment. The geographical environment was accorded great causal importance by certain early sociologists. Others went more directly to seek the genesis and determinants of society in the biological nature of man. The coincidence of the Darwinian ideas about the origin and evolution of species seemed to some sociologists to provide adequate accounts of the rise and fall of societies and of the success and failure of human beings. The struggles among individual human beings and groups within societies, and of societies with other societies, were explained by the niggardliness of nature and the competition for survival. This theme became less prominent in sociological studies in the present century, and the significance of natural ecological and biological qualities have been denied by sociology in favour of a conception of the environment as preponderantly, if not exclusively, 'social'. 'Economic factors' have continued to have attributed to them a preponderant determinative power, but they have been separated from the realm of the natural order. One could say that the expulsion of the biological and natural ecological determinants of human existence has been one of striking features of sociological studies since the 1930s.

With all its ambiguities and limitations, the very idea of

the determinative influence of the social environment remains absolutely basic to sociology. It has, moreover, sharpened sensitivity to connections between spheres of social life which at first glance seem to be utterly unconnected. This capacity to discern connections between activities or institutional arrangements which appear to be unconnected derives from the postulate of the systemic character of society. Society, according to this postulate, is a whole of interdependent parts, each of which is the 'environment' for all of the others. Although sociologists have made little progress in the delineation of whole societies, either in theory or in particular investigations, the idea of a 'society' as a whole or as a system whose parts are interconnected in many ways, is a fundamental postulate of sociology.

The postulate regarding the 'environmental' determination of conduct or of the dependence of conduct on 'social forces' outside the individual has as a corollary a dual image of two types of societies. One is the small, territorially very restricted communities whose members know each other, dwell long together, and have biological links with each other through descent and kinship; in this to some degree self-sufficient local society, there are ties of solidarity and a unity which prevents the individual members from acting solely in accordance with their own individual interests or their 'class interest'. The contrasting image is that of a large society in which individuals live together in a far-flung differentiated division of labour, do not know each other through long association, biological and territorial ties, and have little sense of unity or solidarity with each other. They are bound to each other only by the belief that the individual interest of each is served by the collaboration of many other individuals in an elaborate division of labour. In this distinction the fundamental focus of sociologists on the outcasts of modern society, the 'uprooted', the 'disorganized', the 'anomic', the victims of an urban, commercial society, is extended on the one side to the self-contained solidary village or rural community (*Gemeinschaft*), and on the other to the modern urban market economy (*Gesellschaft*), the human costs of which formed the original subject-matter of sociology.

The attrition of the primordial determinants of conduct with the entry into the market-oriented, commercial industrial urban society, isolates individuals, makes them dependent on their own powers and resources, and compels them to organize themselves into associations aimed to realize particular, often very specific, ends as defined by their interests. Modern society, having renounced solidarity around primordial things, becomes, despite all the strictures expressed in sociology about the limited powers of reason, a scene of individuals and groups purposefully pursuing their own interests.

There is in fact at the heart of sociology a fundamental moral ambivalence. On the one side, it proceeds from an abhorrence of the disorders of life of the lower classes in modern urban industrial societies, and this in turn is connected with an appreciation of the small community centred around primordial things. On the other side it believes in the scientific rational 'solution of social problems'. It conceives of modern society as rational, bureaucratic with large concentrations of power. It tends to look on modern industrial societies as inhuman, amoral, held together only by coercion and interest. Both its intellectual traditions and its political bias dispose it to this view. At the same time, common sense, empirical observation and certain strands of theoretical traditions, show the untenability of this view.

The postulate of the determinative influence of environment implies or is at least compatible with the existence of a culture of symbolic constructions, of moral rules and models. These can be represented in a commonly shared set of rules which hold in check inclinations to pursue individual interests. These common rules fix ends and assert a proper relationship between individual ends and legitimately available and usable means. If such means of fulfilment are not available, or if they become excessive, 'anomie' results; it is the infringement on the expectation of 'normal', law-bound conduct. Although the conception of *anomie* fastens attention on the traditional subject-matter of empirical sociological investigations, namely, criminality, delinquency, suicide, and other irregularities of conduct, it also points to the existence of a moral order, in society.

This postulate of a moral order, although contradictory to the traditional emphasis on 'social disorganization', is entirely consistent with the postulate of the power of environment. It is indeed a differentiation and elaboration of that idea. According to it, individuals, when they are introduced, voluntarily or involuntarily, as infants, as children or later in life, into a small group or other collectivity, are gradually 'socialized' or 'assimilated' into the prevailing conception of 'normal' conduct, accepting its norms and beliefs. Whole categories of individuals, removed from their former collectivities and introduced into a new collectivity, undergo a process of 'disorganization', or in other words experience 'anomie', until they become 'reorganized' or 'resocialized' into a new collectivity in which their individual 'interests' are subordinated to 'collective' interests, as long as the means or resources are available for them to realize their newly defined 'interests'.

Another closely related postulate declares that when a collectivity becomes 'disorganized' or 'anomic', a strong counter-tendency emerges to seek solidarity through the affirmation of contact with 'sacred values' or 'norms'. There is a need for individuals to generate solidarity with other individuals, or in communities or already existing or new corporate bodies. There is, moreover, a tendency in human beings, when they are placed in market situations or in societies dominated by market or large corporate bodies with bureaucratic administration and a differentiated division of labour, to seek to establish more intimate affectional relations; these are variously called 'primary groups' or 'informal groups'. Human beings cannot survive in a social 'vacuum', that is, a structure without affection or without some tangible connection with sacred things which gives meaning to human existence.

Alongside the postulate of the ordering of the conduct of individuals through pursuing their interests under environmental constraints, there is another postulate which asserts that corporate bodies and whole societies are ordered by the coercive power of the legitimate authority of small minorities of the total population. According to this postulate, authority inevitably appears in large corporate groups and in all but the smallest societies because of the need for order and co-ordination, the restraint of internal conflict within the societies and groups for the conduct of relations with external groups and societies and for the gratification of desire for power, wealth and deference.

This postulate asserts that persons in positions of authority tend to seek their own individual, dynastic or class ends which may or may not be identical with the ends of the collectivity. Bureaucrats and immediate collaborators of those in the highest positions of authority tend to be impelled by considerations of maintenance of the corporate body and the consolidation of the power of those in positions of authority. There is a tendency among the subordinated strata of the collectivity to become 'alienated' or 'anomic' *vis-à-vis* the authorities who rule over them.

Alongside those postulates, which are widely shared among sociologists, there are some about which there is less consensus. Some of these postulates are to be found in the writings of the most esteemed sociologists but, for a variety of reasons, they have not been so completely accepted. The fundamental postulate of the variability of human conduct and belief in consequence of the variations in 'environment', and the refusal to admit any autonomy to the forces of reason and ideals, has made it hard for sociologists to attribute any validity to the outlook which asserted the partial autonomy of the 'higher' powers of the human mind such as intellectual curiosity, imagination, reason and religious sensibility. The first sociological enquiries sought out the physical and physiological miseries of the poor, housing conditions, health, drunkenness, diet, clothing. They studied the misfortunes of the human animal. Their humanitarian compassion was mingled with concern to avoid the catastrophes of violent revolution, bloodshed, and the destruction and confiscation of property in material goods. The idea that human beings are primarily biological organisms living in a physical environment was readily assimilable to the popularized Darwinian view of man which emerged after the appearance of sociology. Sociology has not always been able to free itself from that standpoint.

Nevertheless, certain major figures of sociology made some partially successful efforts to do so and in consequence the breadth of the postulates of sociology has been extended. This extension is apparent in the postulate that rulers seek legitimacy and that subjects or citizens demand legitimacy of those who exercise authority over them; the postulate of the sacredness of the social order is alien to the utilitarian view which gives primacy to interests and their pursuit.

The postulates regarding 'legitimacy' and the associated one regarding a 'normal' order of society both imply the existence in society of an order of symbolic configurations, both normative and cognitive. These configurations are transmitted in traditions and they are in an unceasing process of modification and revision while having great powers of persistence through many generations. Religious belief, scientific knowledge, artistic works, philosophical outlooks and moral codes belong to this order of symbolic configurations. Some of the foregoing postulates might be contradictory to some of the others but this does not mean that they are untenable. Their contradiction points rather to the diversity of the propensities of human beings and the opposing tendencies which enter into the conduct and into the patterns of their societies.

The postulates underlie the interpretation which sociologists make of their data; they guide the choice of variables as well as of interpretations. They are not equally shared by all sociologists and, when they are formulated in more exact terms, they usually alienate many sociologists who might accept them as long as they are left vague. Nevertheless, in the present state of sociology, these postulates serve as a general theoretical orientation. They function as a general theory. There is at present no systematically articulated general theory in sociology which finds general acceptance among sociologists. The most fully developed attempt to construct a general comprehensive theory of sociology in recent years has not been well received, although in fact many of the postulates of that general theory are adhered to by many sociologists.

Even though there is no general sociological theory about which there is consensus, and although the discrete results of the huge body of results of sociological research have not been ordered into a coherent descriptive account of any particular society, sociological study has contributed much that is interesting and illuminating to the understanding of contemporary societies and of societies in general. The sociological understanding of the ties that bind human beings together and of their conflicts, of the relations between superiors and subordinates, of the relations of rulers and citizens and subjects, of neighbours and of members of different ethnic groups with one another, of one religious community and another, has become much more intimate and more richly differentiated. There is cumulativeness of sociological knowledge but it is vague and general; successive investigations do deposit a residue of better understanding but the deposit defies precise formulations.

Nevertheless, it remains a genuine intellectual deficiency that the results of sociological investigations are not clearly and precisely cumulative and that they do not contribute in a definite manner to an explicit general theory which is open to corrections and revision as research goes on, and as it is undertaken in more societies and for longer and remoter historical periods. In this very crucial respect, sociology is not a science. But neither is it a congeries of arbitrary constructions. It exists in a middle zone, sometimes moving towards the zone of science, both in theory and in research, sometimes persisting in its tendency towards the arbitrary construction of notional artifacts, again both in theory and in research.

The Development of Sociology as an Intellectual Discipline and as a Profession

The name of 'sociology' is more than 150 years old. The antecedents of sociology are much older, and in the nineteenth century a great deal of valuable research and reflection which is now called sociological was not designated as such at the time. It has required a retrospective self-discovery to reclaim this knowledge and to incorporate it into subsequent sociological theory and research (see Eisenstadt and Curelau, 1976; Schelsky, 1959; Dahrendorf, 1963; Clark, 1973; Shils, 1980). Sociology has also drawn on the achievements of scientists and scholars who were not themselves sociologists in name or practice but whose knowledge has been drawn into sociology. The writings of geneticists, philosophers, statisticians, ecologists, ethnographers, political historians, lawyers and legal historians, psychometricians, economic historians, ecclesiastical historians, theologians, historians of ideas, and economic theorists have all been, and continue to be, drawn upon by sociologists. The early propounders of the claim of sociology to be accepted as an academic discipline tried to define the boundaries of sociology and to show that it was capable of being an autonomous discipline. It was in fact never this kind of subject and it is not so at present. The boundaries of sociology are very vague and this is wholly to the advantage of the understanding of society. Sociology, before it became an academic subject taught under that name, was the work of civil servants, clergymen, philanthropic businessmen, journalists, military officers, engineers, and professors of law, education and economics, all doing their sociological work avocationally or after retirement from their life-long professions. It began to be taught in American colleges and universities as early as the middle of the nineteenth century, but acquired a standing as a 'major' undergraduate and graduate subject, taught by a fully staffed department and with the proclamation of its intention to perform and promote research, only in 1892 at the University of Chicago.

Sociology became the object of professorial teaching, but without a surrounding department of sociology, at the University of Paris in 1906 where Durkheim became professor of education and, in 1913, professor of sociology. No further professorships of sociology were created in France until after the First World War when one was established at Strasbourg. In Great Britain a chair was created at the London School of Economics in 1907, and after that date and until after the Second World War, one additional chair in 'social science' was created at the University of Liverpool. In Germany, there was no chair of sociology in any university until after the First World War. Thereafter, there was one chair of sociology at the University of Frankfurt am Main, and several chairs in which sociology was joined with philosophy or other subjects. Sociology as a subject of teaching and research was suspended or abolished in German universities during the period of National Socialism. In Italy sociology was taught, but without specially designated professorships, since early in the present century; in the Scandinavian countries there was no professorship for sociology until after the Second World War. Since 1945 sociology has flourished in the sense of the great multiplication of appointments at professorial level and at the middle and lower ranks of the academic hierarchy in nearly all countries. This has occurred in nearly all universities; new universities have had departments of sociology in their original establishment; older universities which were resistant to sociology have also accepted it.

With its institutional establishment within universities, sociology has spilled over its departmental boundaries. In university departments of political science and anthropology, even of economics, more attention and more respect are paid to sociology. Departments of literature and language, of history ancient and modern, of Chinese and Indian studies, Biblical studies and of comparative religion and the history of science draw on sociology. Indeed, there is scarcely a branch of learning in the 'human sciences' which does not turn to sociology occasionally and which does not here and there attempt to incorporate 'the sociological approach' into its work. Law and medical faculties often find places for sociologists on their staff or sponsor research which is sociological in method and substance.

While sociology has become practically universally adopted as a subject of academic study and specialization, and has entered into many other academic fields, sociological research, which once had to be done avocationally by persons who were not university teachers of the subject, has, to an increasing degree since the Second World War, become a non-academic subject once more. It is by no means that the universities are doing less sociological research; on the contrary, they do more than ever. But much more is being done by survey-research organizations, some attached to universities and some without any formal connection with universities. More of it is being done for 'customers', governmental and private, who pay to have the research done on problems which they specify in anticipation of some practical use for the results.

Sociology and the World
Sociologists, almost since the beginning, have had a distrustful attitude to the world as they saw it. They saw it as a realm of encrusted and hardened prejudices and superstitions, of irrationality of conduct, of injustice in the distribution of

burdens and rewards, of the erosion of community and the uprooting of 'the people', of egotism and self-seeking, of injurious conflict and disorder. From both conservative and progressive points of view, sociologists have found fault with their own contemporary societies. The beginnings of empirical sociological research were largely aimed at disclosing to the educated public the dark sides of their society, the misery, vice and squalor of the condition of the impoverished, unemployed, dangerous, debtor and dependent 'classes' (see Lazarsfeld *et al.*, 1967). The foundation of modern theoretical sociology had as its main theme the replacement of the small community of solidarity and mutual support by the individualistic, competitive, impersonal, even inhuman society, without a common faith. Sociologists, at least many of them, sought to cure these deficiencies by making them better known to those who were thought to be in a position to ameliorate them. The greatest sociologist, Max Weber, thought that one of the functions of sociological study and research was to enable individuals to 'face the hard facts'; he meant 'hard', not in the sense used by contemporary sociologists who use the term to describe data obtained by scientific techniques of investigation, but rather in the sense of being disagreeable because they showed the hardness of life itself.

Sociology has not deviated far from this original path. Sociologists have constantly aimed at showing where things have gone wrong. Many of the leading sociologists have had reforming intentions. They have, however, also believed that by making their methods as scientific as possible, they could be objective and dispassionate in their analysis. They have incessantly tried to see things in their society as they really are, and to hold in check while doing their research their desires, passions and ideals of a society which would be better according to their lights.

Despite this traditional critical attitude towards the existing social order in Western countries, towards the capitalistic economic system, and towards politicians, sociologists have been drawn into the service of the reigning authorities. Sociological research is now thought to be capable of producing sound knowledge which can be of practical utility. The extent to which much of this knowledge is used in the practical activities of governmental officials, politicians and businessmen may be questioned, but there cannot be any doubt that many of those persons in positions of power believe that it is potentially useful. In this respect, the earliest and enduring ambitions of sociologists have been realized to a noteworthy degree.

Sociology, partly because it has been a subject studied by undergraduates, has entered the public consciousness. The educated public generally regards sociological knowledge as offering insight about the world as it is. Although sociologists have not been accredited by governments in the way that economists have been, they stand very well with the educated public and the media of mass communication.

Sociologists have been more successful than their intellectual achievements probably merit. They have come into an age and culture which believes in the desirability of knowledge and they have been given the benefit of the doubt. They are well established in higher education and they receive much financial support from governments and private philanthropic foundations and, to a lesser extent, from private business firms. They are allowed much freedom to pursue their intellectual interests. A large part of the original programme of sociology has been achieved. The intellectual part of that programme – the discovery of the fundamental laws of social life – still remains.

Edward Shils
University of Chicago
Peterhouse College, Cambridge

References

Almond, G. and Coleman, J. S. (eds) (1960), *The Politics of the Developing Areas*, Princeton, N.J.

Barnard, C. (1948), *The Function of the Executive*, Cambridge, Mass.

Ben-David, J. (1971), *The Scientist's Role in Society: A Comparative Study*, Englewood Cliffs. N.J.

Bendix, R. (1978), *Kings or People*, Berkeley and Los Angeles.

Berelson, B., Lazarsfeld, P. and McPhee, W. (1954), *Voting*, Chicago.

Bulmer, M. (1984), *The Chicago School of Sociology*, Chicago.

Clark, T. N. (1973), *Prophets and Patrons: The French University and the Emergence of the Social Sciences*, Cambridge, Mass.

Coleman, J. (ed.) (1969), *Equality of Educational Opportunity*, Cambridge, Mass.

Dahrendorf, R. (1963), *Die angewandte Aufklaerung*, Munich.

Dollard, J. (1935), *Criteria for the Life History*, New Haven.

Dollard, J. (1937), *Caste and Class in a Southern Town*, New Haven.

Durkheim, E. (1915 [1912]), *The Elementary Forms of Religious Life*, London. (Original French edn, *Les formes élémentaires de la vie religieuse: le système totémique en Australie*, Paris.)

Eisenstadt, S. (1963), *The Political Systems of Empires*, New York.

Eisenstadt, S. and Curelau, M. (1976), *The Form of Sociology: Paradigms and Crisis*, New York.

Floud, J., Halsey, A. and Martin, F. (1956), *Social Class and Educational Mobility*, London.

Geertz, C. (1967), *Old Society and New States*, New York.

Geiger, T. (1926), *Die Masse und ihre Aktion, ein Beitrag zur Soziologie der Revolution*, Stuttgart.

Glass, D. (ed.) (1954), *Social Mobility in Britain*, London.

Hopkins, K. (1978), *Conquerors and Slaves*, Cambridge.

Hyman, H. (1963), *Survey Design and Analysis*, Glencoe, Ill.

Janowitz, M. (1960), *The Professional Soldier*, Glencoe, Ill.

König, R. (ed.) (1967–9), *Handbuch der empirischen Sozialforschung*, Stuttgart.

Lasswell, H. (1935), *World Politics and Personal Insecurity*, New York.

Lasswell, H. (1936), *Who Gets What, When, How?*, New York.

Lazarsfeld, P., Berelson, B. and Gaudet, H. (1944), *The People's Choice*, New York.

Lazarsfeld, P., Sewell, W. H. and Wilensky, H. L. (eds) (1967), *The Uses of Sociology*, New York.

Le Bras, G. (1955), *Études de sociologie religieuse*, Paris.

Lipset, S., Trow, M. and Coleman, J. (1956), *Trade Union Democracy*, Garden City, N.J.

Mannheim, K. (1936 [1929]), *Ideology and Utopia*, London. (Original German edn, *Ideologie und Utopie*, Bonn.)

Mannheim, K. (1952), *Essays on the Sociology of Knowledge*, London.

Mannheim, K. (1956), *Essays on the Sociology of Culture*, London.

Mauss, M. and Hubert, H. (1964 [1899]), *Sacrifice: Its Nature and Function*, London. (Original French edn, *Essai sur la nature et la fonction de sacrifice*, Paris.)

Mauss, M. (1972 [1904]), *A General Theory of Magic*, London. (Original French edn, 'Equisse d'un théorie générale de la magie', Paris.)

Mayo, E. (1949), *The Social Problem of an Industrial Civilization*, London.

Merton, R. K. (1973), *Science, Faith and Society*, Chicago.

Michels, R. (1934), *Umschichtengen in den herrschender Klassen nach dem Kriege*, Stuttgart.

Myrdal, G. (1944), *An American Dilemma: The Negro Problem and Modern Democracy*, New York.

Polanyi, M. (1964), *Science, Faith and Society*, Chicago.

Roethlisberger, F. J. and Dickson, W. J. (1939), *Management and the Worker*, Cambridge, Mass.

Schelsky, H. (1959), *Ortsbestimmung der deutschen Soziologie*, Dusseldorf.

Shils, E. (1972), *The Intellectuals and the Power*, Chicago.

Shils, E. (1980), *The Calling of Sociology*, Chicago.

Simon, H. A. (1947), *Administrative Behavior*, New York.

Sombart, W. (1909 [1896]), *Socialism and the Social Movement*, London. (Original German edn, *Sozialismus und soziale Bewegung im 19 Jahrhundert*.)

Sorokin, P. (1927), *Social Mobility*, New York.

Sorokin, P., Zimmerman, C. and Galpin, C. J. (1930–2), *Systematic Source Book in Rural Sociology*, 3 vols, Minneapolis.

Tilly, C. (1948), *The Vendée*, Cambridge, Mass.

Tingston, H. (1963), *Political Behavior*, Totowa, N.J.

Warner, W. L. (1942), *The Status System of an American Community*, New Haven.

Weber, M. (1930 [1922]), *The Protestant Ethic and the Spirit of Capitalism*, London. (Original German edn, *Die protestantische Ethik und der 'Geist' des Kapitalismus*, Tübingen.)

Weber, M. (1951), *The Religion of China*, Glencoe, Ill.

Weber, M. (1952), *Ancient Judaism*, Glencoe, Ill.

Weber, M. (1958), *The Religion of India*, Glencoe, Ill.

Ziman, J. (1968), *Public Knowledge: The Social Dimension of Science*, Cambridge.

Further Reading.

Durkheim, E. (1933 [1893]), *The Division of Labor in Society*, New York. (Original French edn, *De la division du travail social: étude sur l'organization des sociétés supérieures*, Paris.)

Durkheim, E. (1951 [1897]), *Suicide, A Sociological Study*, London. (Original French edn, *Le suicide; étude sociologique*, Paris.)

Durkheim, E. (1953 [1924]), *Sociology and Philosophy*, London. (Original French edn, *Sociologie et philosophie*, Paris.)

Durkheim, E. and Mauss, M. (1963 [1901]), *Primitive Classification*, London. (Original French edn, 'De quelques formes primitives de la classification', *Année Sociologique*, I.)

Lipset, S. M. and Bendix, R. (1964), *Social Mobility in Industrial Society*, Berkeley and Los Angeles.

Mauss, M. (1954 [1925]), *The Gift*, London. (Original French edn, 'Essai sur la don', *Année Sociologique*, I.)

Merton, R. (1949), *Social Theory and Social Structure*, New York.

Michels, R. (1915), *Political Parties*, Glencoe, Ill.

Park, R. *et al.* (1967), *The City*, Chicago.

Park, R. and Burgess, E. (1921), *Introduction to the Study of Society*, Chicago.

Parsons, T. (1937), *The Structure of Social Action*, Glencoe, Ill.

Parsons, T. (1951), *The Social System*, Glencoe, Ill.

Shils, E. (1975), *Centre and Periphery*, London.

Shils, E. (1981), *Tradition*, Chicago.

Simmel, G. (1955 [1908]), *Conflict and the Web of Social Relationships*, Glencoe, Ill. (Original German edn, *Soziologie: Untersuchungen über die Formen der Vergesellschaftung*, Berlin.)

Tönnies, F. (1957 [1887]), *Community and Society*, Ann Arbor. (Original German edn, *Gemeinschaft und Gesellschaft*.)

Weber, M. (1949), *Methodology of the Social Science*, A selection of and translation of his essays by E. Shils, London.

Weber, M. (1968 [1922]), *Economy and Society*, New York.
(Original German edn, *Wirtschaft und Gesellschaft*, 2 Vols,
Tübingen.)

Women's Studies

Women's studies as an identifiable area of teaching and
research emerged in the late 1960s, although the intellectual
antecedents go back further, most notably in the work of Simone
de Beauvoir and Virginia Woolf. Courses on women were not
unknown prior to the 1960s but they were few and far between.
One of the earliest known courses in America on the status of
women in the United States was offered by the Department of
Sociology at the University of Kansas in 1892. There were also
some early twentieth-century examples of economics courses
devoted to women's labour in an industrial society. One of
these, given at the University of Washington at Seattle in 1912
by Professor Theresa McMahon, was on the subject of 'Women
and Economic Evolution, or the Effects of Industrial Changes
on the Status of Women'. A recent review of McMahon's
teaching and writing described her work as something of an
anomaly for its time, and it is noted that 'academic studies of
the relationship between economics and the status of women
are essentially a phenomenon of the 1960s and 1970s – there is
little to bridge the gap between McMahon's essays and current
attempts to analyse the subject' (Page, 1976).

The contemporary women's movement provided the impetus
for the establishment and growth of women's studies across the
disciplines. In 1969, feminists at Cornell University organized
a conference on women which reflected the concerns of the
movement and which led to a faculty seminar to examine the
portrayal of women in the curriculum of the social and behavioural sciences. As a result of the seminar, an interdisciplinary
course was established on 'The Evolution of Female Personality', followed in 1970 by a female studies programme that co-
ordinated six courses from different departments of the university. At about the same time, across the continent, a women's
studies programme started at San Diego College in California,
providing such courses as 'Women in Comparative Cultures',
'Women in Literature', and 'Contemporary Issues in the Liber-

ation of Women'. By the end of the year there were 110 courses on various US campuses. The number has continued to grow and there are now estimated to be some 30,000 courses in US colleges and universities (Boxer, 1982). The number of women's studies programmes, i.e., interdisciplinary degree programmes, is nearly 500.

The women's studies movement, for that is what it has become, is by no means limited to the United States. Similar programmes were established in other countries during the seventies in Europe and, more recently, in Asia and Latin America. Canada and the UK are well advanced in the number and scope of courses available. The UK, for example, has an MA course in Women's Studies at the University of Kent at Canterbury and also an MA in Human Rights with a specialization in Women's Rights at the University of London. However, the greatest expansion in women's studies in the UK has occurred in adult education and in non-degree granting areas of education (Klein, 1983). In Italy women's studies is taught by academic women primarily in courses sponsored by trade unions and organizations which grew out of the Italian women's movement (Balbo and Ergas, 1982).

Women's studies spread to the developing world slowly at first and then more rapidly following the U.N. Mid-Decade Conference for Women in Copenhagen in 1980. At that time, as part of the Forum of Non-Governmental Organizations, a series of women's studies seminars and workshops was conducted under the joint sponsorship of The Feminist Press and the National Women's Studies Association of the US, The Simone de Beauvoir Institute of Canada, and SNDT Women's University of India. About 500 people from 55 countries attended, most of whom formed the membership of an international network of scholars and practitioners. Women's studies is now flourishing in India and a Women's Studies Association has been formed. A Latin-American Women's Studies Association came into being in 1981. Other parts of the world are active to various degrees except for Eastern Europe, which has thus far largely ignored the subject. In some areas, as in Africa, efforts are concentrated on research rather than teaching.

An important factor in the growth of women's studies during

the seventies was the formation of women's caucuses or committees within professional associations to press for more recognition of women scholars and their concerns. Although the
primary purpose of these committees was to advance the
professional status and career opportunities of women, they also
directed attention to women as a subject of teaching and
research in the disciplines. Some were more active than others,
depending in part on the nature of the discipline and the
number of women in it. Those at the forefront of the movement
were in the fields of literature, history, sociology, and
psychology. As early as 1970, the Commission on the Status of
Women of the Modern Languages Association was instrumental
in the publication of course syllabuses and reading lists in a
'Female Studies' series, which served as a resource for teachers
in the humanities and social sciences. Similarly, the Committee
on Women Historians of the American Historical Association
provided the impetus for the preparation and publication of a
monograph on *Teaching Women's History*, by Gerda Lerner.

Later, as the field progressed, a National Women's Studies
Association (NWSA) was founded in 1977. Its stated purpose
was 'to further the social, political, and professional development of women's studies throughout the country, at every
educational setting'. From the beginning, NWSA drew a large
and enthusiastic membership that consisted not only of scholars
but also teachers in elementary and secondary schools and in
community-based programmes, as well as librarians and others
interested in feminist education. NWSA thus provided a mechanism for mutual support among women's studies constitu-
encies and for the dissemination of knowledge about women's
studies. It also served as a model for similar organizations in
other countries or regions of the world.

Women's studies scholarship was not at first accepted as a
legitimate area of academic endeavour, and was largely ignored
except by the feminists who were its adherents. Most attention
was negative: it was viewed as polemic or faddish and not to
be taken seriously. But women's studies has continued to grow
and flourish to the present day with no abatement in sight.
Foundations and other funding agencies offered critical support.
When the Ford Foundation initiated a fellowship programme

for research on women in 1972, it served not only to support the efforts of individual scholars – men as well as women – but also to give visibility and legitimacy to the field. Foundation support also made possible the establishment of organized research centres which provided institutional resources for women's studies scholarship.

There are at the present time some forty women's studies research centres throughout the United States, nearly all of them established in the last ten years. Most are campus-based, but some are free-standing including several in Washington, DC that focus on issues of public policy concerning women. These centres supplement the efforts of individual scholars and make possible the development of large-scale and interdisciplinary research programmes. Among the best known are the Bunting Institute at Radcliffe College, the Center for Research on Women at Wellesley College, and the Center for Research on Women at Stanford University. In Washington, the Women's Research and Education Institute (WREI) functions as the research arm of the Congressional Caucus on Women's Issues. In that capacity, WREI acts as a bridge between researchers and policy makers on issues of particular concern to women. It maintains regular contact with the network of women's research and policy centres, working on the one hand to stimulate researchers to consider the broader implications of their work, especially as it affects public policy, and on the other to examine policies from the perspective of their effect on women.

In 1981, the research and policy centres joined to form a National Council for Research on Women to share resources and to promote collaborative programmes of research, curriculum development, and public information. Council programmes include a Data Base Project to co-ordinate efforts to improve the storage and retrieval of information on research about women. The project involves the construction of a comprehensive indexing system and computerized data base containing bibliographic references to published, unpublished, and non-print material about women. Through its member centres the Council links over 2,000 scholars and practitioners. The Council also works to strengthen ties with centres of scholarship in other countries, of which there are a small but growing number.

The growth of women's studies teaching and research during the seventies and since then has been accompanied by a parallel expansion in the volume of books and journals for the dissemination of the new knowledge. Academic presses now commonly have a section on women's studies along with other disciplines. Articles relating to women's roles and experience regularly appear in professional journals. In addition, a number of new journals are devoted entirely to women's studies. The most widely-known of the new journals is *Signs: Journal of Women in Culture and Society*, established in 1975 and published by the University of Chicago Press. Two other notable journals in the field are the London based *Women's Studies International Forum* and *Feminist Studies*, published in association with the Women's Studies Program at the University of Maryland.

In the current stage of the evolution of the new scholarship about women, the issue is no longer its legitimacy and further growth, but rather its place in the curriculum. A variety of programmes in recent years have attempted to integrate the new knowledge into the so-called 'mainstream' curriculum, with the purpose of enlightening all students, men and women, not only those taking women's studies courses. This is not simply a matter of adding new material to the curriculum; what is involved is the introduction of new perspectives that may challenge the assumptions and methods of the disciplines. It is now well known, for example, that periodization in history and labels such as 'The Dark Ages' and 'The Renaissance' have their conceptual basis in a distinctly male vantage point. The female experience in those eras was sharply different: 'The Dark Ages' were a period of ascendancy for women and 'The Renaissance' a period of contraction in women's roles. Similarly, in the field of economics, feminist scholars have looked at the differential labour force participation of men and women and found that the response to wage changes is considerably more complex than the textbooks had assumed. Women's studies scholars have not only influenced the content of the disciplines but also the methodologies used.

Mainstreaming projects currently under way in the United

States include faculty development projects, summer institutes, and organized efforts to restructure curricula. A mark of the maturity of the field was a conference in 1981 sponsored by the Association of American Colleges, bringing together college and university administrators and women's studies scholars to consider the implications of the new scholarship on the traditional goals and assumptions of liberal education and the resulting possibilities and imperatives for curricula and institutional change.

Mariam Chamberlain
Russell Sage Foundation, New York

References

Balbo, L. and Ergas, Y. (1982), *Women's Studies in Italy*, London.

Boxer, M. J. (1982), 'For and about women: the theory and practice of women's studies in the United States', *Signs, Journal of Women in Culture and Society*, 7.

Klein, R. D. (1983), 'A brief overview of women's studies in the U.K.', *Women's Studies International Forum*, 5.

Page, A. N. (1976), 'Theresa McMahon's "Women and economic evolution", a retrospective view', *Journal of Economic Literature.*

Further Reading

Langland, E. and Gove, W. (eds) (1983), *A Feminist Perspective in the Academy: The Difference it Makes*, Chicago.

Sherman, J. A. and Beck, E. T. (1977), *The Prism of Sex*, Madison.

Spender, D. (1981), *Men's Studies Modified*, London.